Extending the Eclectic Paradigm in International Business

Extending the Eclectic Paradigm in International Business

Essays in Honor of John Dunning

Edited by

H. Peter Gray

Rutgers University

Edward Elgar
Cheltenham, UK • Northampton, MA, USA

Published by
Edward Elgar Publishing Limited
Glensanda House
Montpellier Parade
Cheltenham
Glos GL50 1UA
UK

Edward Elgar Publishing, Inc.
136 West Street
Suite 202
Northampton
Massachusetts 01060
USA

A catalogue record for this book
is available from the British Library

Library of Congress Cataloguing in Publication Data
Extending the eclectic paradigm in international business : essays in honor of
John Dunning / edited by H. Peter Gray.
    p. cm.
  Includes bibliographical references.
    1. International business enterprises. 2. Industrial location. 3. Investments,
Foreign. 4. Globalization. I. Dunning, John H. II. Gray, H. Peter.
HD2755.5 .E95 2003
338.8′8—dc21

2002190736

ISBN 1 84064 888 0

Printed and bound in Great Britain by MPG Books Ltd, Bodmin, Cornwall

Contents

Contents

List of figures

List of tables

List of contributors

Sam Beldona, Center for International Business Advancement, Barton School of Business, Wichita State University, Wichita, KS

John R. Dilyard, Department of Management, St. Francis College, Brooklyn, NY

Lorraine Eden, Professor of Management, Texas A&M University, College Station, TX

Robert Grosse, American Graduate School of International Management, World Business Department, Glendale

Timo J. Hämäläinen, Finnish National Fund for Research and Development, Helsinki, Finland

Changsu Kim, Department of Marketing and International Business, Nanyang Technical University, Singapore

Zu Kweon Kim, Department of Management, Texas A&M University, Corpus Christi, TX

Sarianna M. Lundan, Associate Professor of International Business, University of Maastricht, The Netherlands

Ann Markusen, The Humphrey Institute of Public Affairs, University of Minnesota, Minneapolis, MN

Rajneesh Narula, Professor of International Economics and Management, Copenhagen Business School, University of Copenhagen, Denmark and the Centre for Technology, Innovation and Culture, University of Oslo

Kingsley O. Olibe, Department of Accounting, Middle Tennessee State University, Murfreesboro, TN

Terutomo Ozawa, Professor of Economics, Colorado State University, Fort Collins, CO

Yong Suhk Pak, Yonsei University, Seoul, Korea

Michael A. Santoro, Department of Management, Graduate School of Business, Rutgers University, Newark, NJ

Marguerite Schneider, New Jersey Institute of Technology, Newark, NJ

J.-C. Spender, Dean, School of Business and Technology, Fashion Institute of Technology, State University of New York, NY

Douglas E. Thomas, Anderson School of Management, University of New Mexico, Albuquerque

Bindu Vyas, Assistant Professor, School of Management, King's College, Wilkes-Barre, PA

Katharine Wakelin, Leverhulme Centre for Globalisation and Economic Policy, School of Economics, University of Nottingham, England

Lorna H. Wallace, Global Growth, PO Box 4773, Palos Verdes, California

Cliff Wymbs, Zicklin School of Business, Baruch College, CUNY, New York, NY

1. Dunning's Rutgers Years

H. Peter Gray

John Dunning has always had an element of the scholar gypsy in him. It was this wanderlust that allowed him to accept a Seth Boyden visiting professorship of international business (IB) at Rutgers – the State University of New Jersey for eighteen months beginning in 1987. While he was a visiting member of the faculty of the Business School, Governor Thomas Kean of New Jersey decided to fund the creation, at Rutgers, of six 'State of New Jersey professorships' to be awarded to world-class scholars in six different fields. Serendipity had begun to exert its influence and the then dean, David Blake, succeeded in 1989 in bringing Dunning to the School of Business of Rutgers as one of the six. This was to be a long-term relationship as distinct from the avowedly temporary visiting Seth Boyden professorship. The appointment was a complex arrangement because of the need for John to continue as a member of the faculty of the University of Reading until the end of 1992 when he would reach mandatory retirement age in the United Kingdom. John was a regular member of the Rutgers Business faculty for alternate calendar years. However, he always visited Newark once or twice in the 'off years' in order to meet with his graduate students and to goad those who were not giving the writing of their dissertations the wholehearted commitment which was both deserved and needed.

This book is a tribute to the contributions made by Dunning to the Graduate School of Business between 1989 and 2001 by many of the people who were associated with him in the IB program. In fact, Dunning's full-time appointment with the University ended in 2000 but he continued to supervise dissertation-writing graduate students until those students who had begun their doctoral programs during his tenure had successfully defended their dissertations. During his twelve-year affiliation with Rutgers, sixteen students have received doctorates.[1] Many of these students hold professorial rank in universities and others are working in governments and research organizations. The contributing authors to this volume include ex-students and colleagues of John Dunning in the Rutgers Graduate School of Business in Newark as well as some IB professors who served as external members of doctoral dissertation committees. Some potential contributors had to withdraw because of the pressure of other commitments. The chapters have been arranged alphabetically by the surname of the lead author of each contribution.

Dunning's bibliography, from 1988 to 2002, presented in Appendix A,[2] can be seen as representing the major scholarly product of his Rutgers years (albeit including some four years when he was alternating between Reading and Newark). The bibliography lists seven authored books, twelve edited books, over fifty chapters in books and over fifty refereed articles. He came to Rutgers as an established scholar, indeed he was the elected president of the Academy of International Business in 1987–8, and this reputation meant that Dunning had many demands upon his time. This is apparent in the nearly one-to-one ratio of 'chapters in books' to 'refereed articles'. In addition to his scholarly writings, there has been a major commitment to what may be termed 'public service'. Probably the most demanding task was serving as the senior economic advisor to the research director of UNCTAD and the related tasks of serving as chairman of the editorial board of *Transnational Corporations* and as general editor of a 20-volume library series commissioned by the UN Centre on Transnational Corporations. In addition, Dunning served as president of the International Trade and Finance Association in 1995. During the 'Rutgers years' John Dunning was awarded honorary doctorates by the University of Madrid (1990) and the University of Antwerp (1997) as well as being awarded an honorary professorship of the University of International Business and Economics in Beijing. He presented the Geary Lecture in Dublin at the Economic and Social Research Institute (1993), the Inaugural Lecture at the initiation of the new international business department at the University of Maastricht (1994); the 6th Prebisch lecture at UNCTAD in Geneva (1994); and the 6th Tore Browaldh lecture at Göteborg University (1994).

Dunning's Rutgers years and, indeed, his career, mark him as a true internationalist both in his writings and in his willingness to make himself available to institutions in Europe, Asia and Africa. Much of his contribution to showing how developing nations could attract multinational enterprise as a developmental impetus derived from his appointment as the British representative in a United Nations Group of Eminent Persons. The report of this Group, of which he was one of three main authors, was, in turn, responsible for the creation, within the United Nations, of a Centre on Transnational Corporations. The Centre was ultimately transferred to UNCTAD in 1989, thereby cementing its concern with economic development. This Centre had two responsibilities. The first was to collect and interpret data on transnational corporations, thereby undertaking research on various economic and social aspects of TNCs – particularly as they affected developing countries. The second was to advise governments of developing countries on how to negotiate advantageously with large multinational corporations based in the industrialized world. Dunning has retained his connection with this organization throughout its lifetime and in this way, he has served as an adviser on all twelve of the *World Investment Reports*, the first of which was published in 1991.

In the preface to her dissertation, a doctoral program student wrote: 'I have nothing but awe-inspired admiration for Professor Dunning, who, as far as I can tell, must be the hardest working man in academe'. Dunning also worked and works outside academe, as Sarianna Lundan has since become much more aware!

During Dunning's Rutgers years, the major thrust of his writing added two new dimensions to the well-respected eclectic paradigm for which he is best known. Beginning with the December 1992 article in *Transnational Corporations*, Dunning focused in depth on the interface between the problems that faced policymakers in an open, even globalized economy. Macroeconomic performance and growth often hinged, particularly in developing countries, on the ability of governments to attract new inward direct investment (or not to lose existing investment). This analysis soon recognized the need to incorporate the managerial and strategic problems which faced MNE executives. The second new dimension was, in fact, a return to an early interest: Dunning integrated (sub-national) location theory into his three-tined paradigm.[3] Here, the presence at Rutgers of Professor Ann Markusen, a leading economic geographer, was important. It was she who emphasized the apparent contradiction between the ability of MNEs to move knowledge capital and related resources among nations and their inability to move the agglomeration advantages that derived from the existence of a set of [research] institutions in a particular area. Local presence was inevitable for any MNE which wished to have access to the interactive conferences of local firms and universities. These two innovations plus the introduction of dynamic ownership advantages to the eclectic paradigm in 1998, extended the range of analytic concern of the field of international business.

Several developments contributed to the globalization of the world economy. Among these are the integration of erstwhile national financial markets by liberalization of those markets incorporating free capital convertibility; the great strides in information technology which facilitated international portfolio investments as well as managing foreign affiliates from a central headquarters; and the huge reduction in impediments to the international exchange of goods and services (in both artificial barriers and transportation costs). Foreign direct investment and international production may have been the first among equals and this is the particular focus of IB scholars in general and John Dunning in particular. These phenomena are all interdependent and it is this combination of developments that has created the existing globalized economy in which heretofore national economies have suddenly found themselves to have lost the clarity of the definition of their nationhood.

When Dunning started his scholarly career in the early 1950s, only the idea of international trade without artificial impediments at national boundaries would have been visualized as desirable and most visions of lower impediments to international trade were defined in reductions to impediments rather than their virtual elimination. National governments have not yet come to grips with the full implications of globalization in any of its dimensions.[4] Given that democratic governments are still elected by national electorates, there is an obvious potential clash between the perceived desirability of economic and other dimensions of globalization and the much more directly perceived costs of globalization when external shocks impinge on the macroeconomic efficiency of national economies. Solutions for these problems will not be easy but, without a full understanding of the implications of foreign direct investment by multinationals, they would be impossible.

The Rutgers years show one thing more. In the United Kingdom, John Dunning was required to retire in 1991 at age 65. In the United States, a university cannot discriminate by age and require its professors to retire at some specified age. This elimination of age discrimination could be controversial. John Dunning's work at Rutgers from 1992 on (after his retirement from the University of Reading) shows very clearly that any law or regulation that professors be required to retire at 65 years of age could waste a tremendous amount of talent.

To have this volume published by Edward Elgar (USA) Ltd. is eminently suitable. John's first *Festschrift* honoring his contributions to the University of Reading (Buckley and Casson, 1992) was published in England by Edward Elgar Publishing Limited. The Rutgers *Festschrift* is to be published by the foreign affiliate of that company.

NOTES

1. A list of the students who earned the PhD degree in Management with a concentration in international business, is given in the Appendix. An asterisk indicates the students for whom Dunning was chairman of the dissertation committee.
2. The bibliography includes some overlap with publications listed in Peter J. Buckley and Mark Casson's *Reading Festschrift* (1992). This bibliography has been limited to four categories of publication: authored and co-authored books; edited books; chapters in books; and refereed articles.
3. Dunning has particularly emphasized location at the sub-national level. His interest in this

problem began very early in his career with a study of the concentration of US-owned factories in mid-Scotland and was further enhanced by a couple of consulting projects in the 1960s.
4. Richard Langhorne came to Rutgers University in 1999 and his book, *The Coming of Globalisation* (Basingstoke: Palgrave, 2000) recognizes the importance of MNEs and international production in the impairment of nationhood. It is an interesting coincidence that two books were published almost simultaneously: Langhorne's *The Coming* and Alan M. Rugman's *The End of Globalization* (2000).

BIBLIOGRAPHY 1988–2002*

Books Authored (Co-authored if Applicable)

Explaining International Production, London: Unwin Hyman, 1988.
Multinationals, Technology and Competitiveness, London: Unwin Hyman, 1988.
Multinational Enterprises and the Global Economy, Reading, MA, and Wokingham, England: Addison Wesley, 1993.
The Globalization of Business: The Challenge of the 1990s, London and New York: Routledge, 1993.
Alliance Capitalism and Global Business, London and New York: Routledge, 1997.
American Investment in British Manufacturing Industry, Revised and updated edition, London and New York: Routledge, 1998.
Global Capitalism at Bay? London and New York: Routledge, 2001.

Books Edited (Co-edited, if Applicable)

(With Peter Robson) *Multinationals and the European Community*, Oxford: Basil Blackwell, 1988.
(With A. Webster and Paul Kegan) *Structural Change in the World Economy*, London: Routledge, 1989.
The Theory of Transnational Corporations, UNCTC Library on Transnational Corporations, London: Routledge, 1992.
(With R. Narula) *Foreign Direct Investment and Governments: Catalyst for Economic Restructuring*, London and New York: Routledge, 1996. (Paperback edition published in 1998)
Governments, Globalization and International Business, Oxford: Clarendon Press, 1997. (Paperback edition published in 1999)
(With K. Hamdani) *Globalization and Developing Countries*, New York: United Nations, 1997.
Globalization, Trade and Foreign Direct Investment, London: Elsevier, 1998.
New Jersey in a Globalizing Economy (ed.), Newark, NJ: Rutgers University, CIBER, 1999.
Globalization: A Two Edged Sword (ed.), Newark, NJ: Rutgers University, CIBER, 1999.
(With G. Boyd) *Structural Change and Co-operation in the Global Economy* (eds) Cheltenham, UK and Northampton, MA: Edward Elgar, 1999.

Regions, Globalization and the Knowledge Based Economy, Oxford, Oxford
  University Press, 2000. (Paperback edition to be published in 2002)
(With J. Muchielli) *Multinational Firms: The Global–Local Dilemma*, London and
  New York: Routledge, 2002.

NB. In each of the above Dunning contributed one or two (usually two) chapters.

Chapters in Books

(With R.D. Pearce) 'The nature and growth of MNEs' in C.W. Nobes and R.H.
  Parker (eds), *Issues in Multinational Accounting*, London: Philip Allan, St.
  Martins Press, 1988, 1–26.
'Transnational corporations in a changing world environment: are new theoretical
  explanations required?' in Weiza Teng and N.T. Wang (eds), *Transnational
  Corporations and China's Open Door Policy*, Lexington, MA: D.C. Heath, 1988,
  3–32.
(With J.A. Cantwell) 'Le nouve forme di coinvolgimento delle imprese britanniche
  nel Terzo Mondo' in R. Burlando (ed.), *Transferimenti di Tecnologie
  Finanziamenti ai Paesi in Via di Sviluppo*, Milano: Franco Angeli, 1989, 127–66.
'Trade and foreign-owned production in services: some conceptual and theoretical
  issues' in H. Giersch (ed.), *Services in World Economic Growth*, Tubingen: Mohr,
  1989, 108–51.
'The theory of international production' in K. Fatemi (ed.), *International Trade:
  Existing Problems and Prospective Solutions*, New York: Taylor and Francis
  International Publishers, 1989, 45–84.
(With J. A. Cantwell) 'Japanese direct investment in Europe' in B. Burgenmeier and
  J.L. Mucchielli (eds), *Multinationals and Europe 1992*, London and New York:
  Routledge, 1990, 155–84.
'The eclectic paradigm of international production: a personal perspective' in C.N.
  Pitelis and R. Sugden (eds), *The Nature of the Transnational Firm*, London and
  New York: Routledge, 1991, 117–36. (A revised and updated version of this chapter
  is to be published late in 1999 in a new edition of the Pitelis and Sugden volume)
'European integration and transatlantic foreign direct investment: the record
  assessed' in G. Yannopoulos (ed.), *Europe and America 1992: US–EC Economic
  Relations in the Single European Market*, Manchester: Manchester University
  Press, 1991.
(With J.A. Cantwell) 'The changing role of MNEs' in F. Arcangeli, P.A. David and
  G. Dosi (eds), *The Diffusion of Innovation*, Oxford: Oxford University Press,
  1991.
'Governments, economic organization and international competitiveness' in L.G.
  Mattson and B. Stymne (eds), *Corporate Industry Strategies for Europe*, Elsevier
  Science Publishers, 1991, 41–74.
'Some concluding remarks' in P.J. Buckley, and J. Clegg (eds), *Multinational
  Enterprises in Less Developed Countries*, Basingstoke and London: Macmillan,
  1991, 313–21.
(With J.A. Cantwell) 'MNEs, technology and the competitiveness of European
  industries' in G.R. Faulhaber and G. Tamburini (eds), *European Economic
  Integration: The Role of Technology*, Boston and London: Kluwer Academic
  Press, 1991, 117–48.
'The political economy of international production' in P.J. Buckley (ed.), *New*

Directions of International Business, London: Edward Elgar, Aldershot, UK and Brookfield, US, 1992.

'Multinational enterprises and the globalization of innovatory capacity' in O. Grandstrand, L. Hakanson and S. Sjolander (eds), *Technology, Management and International Business: Internationalization of R&D and Technology*, Chichester and New York: Wiley, 1992.

'The governance of Japanese and US manufacturing affiliates in the UK: some country specific differences' in B. Kogut (ed.), *Country Competitiveness, Technology and the Organization of Work*, Oxford: Oxford University Press, 1993, 203–24.

'Governments and multinational enterprises: from confrontation to cooperation?' in Lorraine Eden and Evan Potter (eds), *Multinationals in the Global Political Economy*, Basingstoke and London: Macmillan Press, 1993, 59–83.

(With Philippe Gugler) 'Technology based cross-border alliances' in R.A. Culpan (ed.), *Multinational Strategic Alliances*, Hummelstown, PA: International Business Press, August 1993, 123–65.

'MNE activity: comparing the NAFTA and the European Community' in Lorraine Eden (ed.), *Multinationals in North America*, Calgary: University of Calgary Press, 1994, 277–308.

'The strategy of Japanese and US manufacturing investment in Europe' in Mark Mason and Dennis J. Encarnation (eds), *Does Ownership Matter?*, Oxford: Clarendon Press, 1994, 59–86.

'Explaining foreign direct investment in Japan: some theoretical insights' in M. Yoshitomi and E. Graham (eds), *Foreign Direct Investment in Japan*, Cheltenham, UK and Brookfield, US: Edward Elgar, 1996, 8–63.

'The role of FDI in a globalizing economy' in C. J. Green and T. L. Brewer (eds), *Investment Issues in Asia and the Pacific Rim*, New York: Oceania, 1996, 43–64.

'Reconfiguring the boundaries of international business activity' in G. Boyd and A.M. Rugman (eds), *Euro-Pacific Investment and Trade*, Aldershot, UK and Brookfield, US: Edward Elgar, 1996, 1–18.

(With R. Narula) 'The investment path revisited: some emerging issues,' in J.H. Dunning and R. Narula (eds), *Foreign Direct Investment and Governments: Catalysts for Economic Restructuring*, London and New York: Routledge, 1996, 1–41.

'The economic theory of the firm as the basis of a "core" theory of international production' in I. Islam and W. Shepherd (eds), *Current Issues in International Business*, Aldershot, UK and Brookfield, US: Edward Elgar, 1996, 63–72.

'Governments and the macro-organization of economic activity: an historical and spatial perspective' and 'A business-analytic approach to governments and globalization' in J.H. Dunning (ed.), *Governments, Globalization and International Business*, Oxford: Oxford University Press, 1997, 31–72, 114–31.

'Micro and macro organizational aspects of MNEs and MNE activity' in B. Toyne and D. Nigh (eds), *International Business: An Emerging Vision*, Columbia, South Carolina: University of South Carolina Press, 1997, 194–204, 660–1.

'Technology and the changing boundaries of firms and governments' in OECD (ed.), *Industrial Competitiveness in the Knowledge Based Economy*, Paris: OECD, 1997, 53–68.

'Some concluding remarks,' in P.J. Buckley, and J.-L. Mucchielli (eds), *Multinational Firms and International Relocation*, Cheltenham, UK and Brookfield, US: Edward Elgar, July 1997, 238–46.

'Talouden globalisoituminen talonspolit ii kan muukoshaastreetja yerkarsallinen hallinto' in T. Hämäläinen (ed.), *Murroksen Acka*, Helsinki Werner Söderström Osakeyhitioö, 1997, 35–52.

'Pour une nouvelle vitalité de la filière Atlantique' in A. Lapointe (ed.), *Commerce Atlantique, Integration Économique et Alliances Stratégiques*, Montreal: HEC, 1997, 11–25.

'Re-energizing the transatlantic connection' in G. Boyd (ed.), *The Struggle for World Markets*, Cheltenham, UK and Northampton, MA: 1998, 1–11.

'Regional integration and foreign direct investment: a comment in US International Trade Commission' (ed.) *The Economic Implications of Liberalizing APEC Tariff and Non-Tariff Barriers to Trade*, Washington, D.C. Publication 3101, April 1998, 1–52.

(With E. Bannerman and S. Lundan) 'Competition and industrial policy in Northern Ireland' *Belfast, Northern Ireland Economic Development Office Research Monograph*, No. 5, March 1998, 78.

'The changing geography of foreign direct investment' in K. Kumar (ed.), *Globalization, Foreign Direct Investment and Technology Transfer: Impacts on Prospects for Developing Countries*, London and Boston: Routledge, 1998, 43–89.

'The global economy, national governments and supranational regimes' in P.K.M. Tharakan and D. Van Den Bulke (eds), *International Trade, Foreign Direct Investment and the Economic Environment*, Basingstoke: Macmillan, 1998, 77–100.

'Globalization, technological change and the spatial organization of economic activity' in Alfred Chandler Jr., Peter Hagström and Örjan Sölvell (eds), *The Dynamic Firm*, Oxford: Oxford University Press, 1998, 289–314.

'Does ownership really matter in a globalizing economy?' in D. Woodward and D. Nigh (eds), *Foreign Ownership and the Consequences of Direct Investment in the United States*, Westport, CT: Quorum Books, 1998, 27–42.

'The global economy, domestic governance, strategies and transnational corporations: interactions and policy implications' in N. Kobayashi (ed.), *Management: A Global Perspective*, Tokyo: The Japan Times, 1998, 3–39.

'US owned manufacturing affiliates and the transfer of managerial techniques: the British case' in M. Kipping and O. Bjarnar (eds), *The Americanization of European Business*, London and New York: Routledge, 1998, 74–90.

'Reconfiguring the boundaries of international business activity' in Z.J. Acs and B. Yeung (eds), *Small and Medium Sized Enterprises in the Global Economy*, Ann Arbor: University of Michigan Press, 1999, 24–44.

(With R. Narula) 'Technocratic-corporate partnering, extending alliance capitalism' in G. Boyd and J.H. Dunning (eds), *Structural Change and Cooperation in the Global Economy*, Cheltenham, UK and Northampton, MA: Edward Elgar, 1999, 137–59.

(With R. Narula) 'Developing countries versus multinationals in a globalizing world: the dangers of falling behind' in P.J. Buckley and P. Ghauri (eds), *The Global Challenge for MNEs*, London: Elsevier, 1999, 467–88.

'The changing nature of firms and governments in a knowledge-based globalizing economy' in J. Engelhard and W.A. Oehsler (eds), *International Management: Effects of Global Changes on Competition, Corporate Strategies and Markets*, Wiesbaden: Sonderdruck, 1999.

'Some paradoxes of the emerging global economy: the multinational solution' in F. Burton, M. Chapman and A. Cross (eds), *International Business Organization*, Basingstoke: Macmillan, 1999, 5–214.

(With Lorna Wallace) 'New Jersey in a Globalizing Economy' in N.A. Phelps and J. Alden (eds), *Foreign Direct Investment and the Global Economy*, London: The Stationery Office, 1999, 253–68.

'The eclectic paradigm of international production: a personal perspective' in C. Pitelis and R. Sugden (eds), *The Nature of the Transnational Firm* (second edition), London and New York: Routledge, 1999, 119–39.

'Globalization and the theory of MNE activity' in N. Hood and S. Young (eds), *The Globalization of Multinational Enterprise Activity and Economic Development*, Basingstoke: Macmillan, 2000, 21–52.

'Globalization and FDI in Asian Developing Countries,' in C.W.M. Naastepad and S.T.H. Storm (eds), *Essays in Honor of George Waardenburg*, New Delhi: Oxford University Press, 2000 (forthcoming).

(With C. Wymbs) 'The geographical sourcing of technology based assets by multi-national enterprises' in D. Archibugi, J. Howells and J. Michie (eds), *Innovation Policy in a Global Economy*, Cambridge: CUP, 1999, 185–224.

'Assessing the costs and benefits of foreign direct investment: some theoretical con-siderations' in P. Artisien-Maksimenko (ed.), *Multinationals in Eastern Europe*, Basingstoke: Macmillan Press, 2000, 10–57.

'Some paradoxes of the emerging global economy: the small country solution' in D. Van den Bulcke and A. Berbeke (eds), *Globalization and the Small Open Economy*, Cheltenham, UK and Northampton, MA: Edward Elgar, 2001, 13–35.

'Revisiting UK FDI in US manufacturing and extractive industries in 1960' in G. Jones and L. Galvez-Muñoz (eds), *Foreign Multinationals in the United States*, London and New York: Routledge, 2001, 50–69.

Articles (Refereed)

'The eclectic paradigm of international production: a restatement and some pos-sible extensions', *Journal of International Business Studies*, **19**, Spring 1988, 1–31.

'The theory of international production', *International Trade Journal*, **111**, 1988, 21–66.

'Multinationals and the growth of services: some conceptual and theoretical issues', *Services Industries Journal*, **9**, 1989, 5–39.

'The study of international business: a plea for an interdisciplinary approach', *Journal of International Business Studies*, **20**, Summer 1989, 411–36.

(With J.A. Cantwell) 'Multinational enterprises, technology and the competitive-ness of European industries', *Aussenwirtschaft*, **46**, April 1991, 45–67.

'The prospects for foreign direct investment in Eastern Europe', *Development and International Cooperation*, **VII**, June 1991, 21–40.

'Governments and multinational enterprises: from confrontation to cooperation?', *Millennium*, **20**, 1991, 225–44.

'Transatlantic foreign direct investment and the European Economic Community', *International Economic Journal*, **6**, 1992, 1–23.

'The competitive advantages of countries and TNC activity', *Transnational Corporations*, **1**, February 1992, 135–68.

'The global economy, domestic governance, strategies and transnational corpora-tions: interactions and policy implications', *Transnational Corporations*, **1** (3), December 1992, 7–46. (With David D. Levy) 'International production and sourcing (1993): trends and issues', *STI Review* (OECD), **13**, December 1993, 13–60.

'Towards a new partnership', *International Economic Insights*, July/August 1993, 23–5.

'Internationalizing Porter's diamond', *Management International Review*, **33**, Special Issue no. 2, 1993, 7–15.

'Re-evaluating the benefits of foreign direct investment', *Research Policy*, **23**, 1994, 9–22.

'The global economy and regimes of national and supranational governance', *Business and the Contemporary World*, **VII** (1), 13 February 1995, 124–36.

(With Sumit Kundu) 'The internationalization of the hotel industry: some new findings from a field study', *Management International Review*, **2**, 1995, 101–33.

'Re-evaluating multinational enterprises and the globalisation of innovatory capacity', *Research Policy*, **23**, 67–88.

(With Rajneesh Narula) 'The R&D activities of foreign firms in the US', *International Studies of Management and Organization*, **25**, 1995, 39–73.

(With D. Lecraw) 'The UNCTC curricula on TNCs: a contribution to international business in developing countries', *Journal of Teaching in International Business*, **6** (3), 15 May 1995, 1–15.

'What's wrong – and right – with trade theory?', *International Trade Journal*, **IX**, Spring 1995, 163–202.

'The role of FDI in a globalizing economy', *Banco Nazionale de Lavoro Quarterly Review*, **193**, June 1995, 1–20.

'Think again Professor Krugman: competitiveness does matter', *International Executive*, **37** (4), July/August 1995, 315–24.

'Reappraising the eclectic paradigm in the age of alliance capitalism', *Journal of International Business Studies*, **26** (3), 1995, 461–91.

'Globalization: new challenges for the teaching of international business', *International Management Development Association News*, **1** (2), Winter 1995, 4–8.

'Globalization, foreign direct investment and economic development', *Economics and Business Education*, Part 2, **14**, 1996, 46–51.

'The geographical sources of competitiveness of firms: some results of a new survey', *Transnational Corporations*, **5** (3), December 1996, 1–30.

Commentary: 'How should national governments respond to globalization?', *The International Executive*, **39** (1), Jan/Feb, 1997, 55–6.

'The European internal market program and inbound foreign direct investment Part 1', *Journal of Common Market Studies*, **35** (1), March 1997, 1–30.

'The European internal market program and inbound foreign direct investment Part 2', *Journal of Common Market Studies*, **35** (2), June 1997, 189–220.

'Governments and the macro-organization of economic activity: an historical and spatial perspective', *Review of International Political Economy*, **1** (1), Spring 1997, 42–86.

(With Sangeeta Bansal) 'The cultural sensitivity of the eclectic paradigm', *Multinational Business Review*, Winter 1997, 1–16.

(With Sarianna Lundan) 'Foreign direct investment in Japan and the United States: a comparative analysis', *International Trade Journal*, **XI** (2), 1997, 187–220.

(With R. Van Hoesel and R. Narula) 'Explaining the new wave of outward FDI from developing countries', *International Business Review, Special Issue*, 1998.

'Globalization and the new geography of foreign direct investment', *Oxford Development Studies*, **26** (1), 1998, 47–69.

(With S. Lundan) 'The geographical sources of competitiveness of multinational enterprises: an econometric analysis', *International Business Review*, **7** (2), 1998, 115–33.

'MNEs: an overview of relations with national governments', *New Political Economy*, **IV** (1), 1998, 280–84.

'Location and the multinational enterprise: a neglected factor', *Journal of International Business Studies*, **29** (1), First Quarter 1998, 45–66.

(With R. Narula) 'Explaining international R&D alliances and the role of governments', *International Business Review*, **7** (4), October 1998, 377–97.

(With J. Dilyard) 'Towards a general paradigm of foreign direct and portfolio investment', *Transnational Corporations*, **8** (1), 1999, 1–52.

(With R. Narula) 'Developing countries versus multinational enterprises in a globalizing world: the dangers of falling behind', *Forum for Developing Studies*, **2**, 1999, 261–87.

'The eclectic paradigm as an envelope for economic and business theories of international business activity', *International Business Review*, **9**, 2000 163–90.

'Whither global capitalism?' *Global Economy Quarterly*, **1** (1), 2000 3–48.

(With R. Narula) 'Industrial development, globalization and multinational enterprises: new realities for developing countries', *Oxford Development Studies*, **28** (2), 2000, 141–67.

(With L. Nachum and G. Jones) 'UK FDI and the comparative advantage of the UK', *The World Economy*, **5**, 2000, 701–20.

'The future of the WTO: a socio-relational challenge', *Review of International Political Economy*, Autumn 2000, 474–82.

'Regaining competitiveness for Asian enterprises', *Journal of International Business and Economy*, **1** (1), 2000, 1–16.

(With C. Kim and J.D. Lin) 'Incorporating trade into the investment development path: a case study of Korea and Taiwan', *Oxford Development Studies*, **29** (2), 2001, 145–54.

'The eclectic (OLI) paradigm of international production: past, present and future', *International Journal of the Economics of Business*, **8** (2), 2001, 173–90.

(With C. Wymbs) 'The challenge of electronic markets for international business theory', *International Journal of the Economics of Business*, **8** (2), 2001, 273–302.

(With L. Nachum and G. Jones) 'The international competitiveness of the UK and its multinational enterprises', *Structural Change and Economic Dynamics*, **12**, 2001, 277–94.

(With J.A. Cantwell and O.E.M. Janne) 'Evolution of multinational corporate technological systems in the UK and the US', *Journal of Interdisciplinary Economics*, **13** (1–2) 2002 (forthcoming).

(With S. Lundan) 'The geographical sources of competitiveness and the performance of multinational enterprises', *Global Economy Quarterly*, **2** (1), 2002 (forthcoming).

(With A. McKaig-Berliner) 'The geographical sources of competitiveness: a survey of professional service firms', *Transnational Corporations*, **10** (1) 2002 (forthcoming).

NOTE

* As noted in Chapter 1, this is an incomplete bibliography limited to four categories of publications between 1988 and 2002.

APPENDIX: IB DOCTORATES AWARDED 1993–2002

Name	Graduation date
Rajneesh Narula	October, 1993
Sumit Kundu	May, 1994
Sarianna Lundan	May, 1996
Saad Laraqui	May 1998
Lorna Wallace	October, 1998
Clifford Wymbs	May, 1999
John R. Dilyard	October, 1999
Timo J. Hämäläinen	October, 1999
Jyh-Der Lin	January, 2000
Yong S. Pak	May, 2000
Zu Kweon Kim	October, 2000
Bindu Vyas	October, 2000
Alison McKaig-Berliner	May, 2001
Dermod Wood	May, 2001
Changsu Kim	January, 2002
Gladys Torres Baumgarten	June, 2002

2. A variant of the eclectic paradigm linking direct and portfolio investment

John R. Dilyard

INTRODUCTION

Among all the forces that have shaped the fortunes of multinational corporations and the history of globalization since the latter half of the 20th century, none has surpassed foreign direct investment (FDI) in its influence and scope. Likewise, no other force has been as scrutinized as FDI; it has been the focal point of international business literature for much of the last forty years. A leading voice in the creation of that literature has been John H. Dunning, whose contributions to current understanding of all aspects of FDI are voluminous. Indeed, it would be difficult to imagine a work on FDI today that did not include at least one reference to Dunning.

Dunning's most significant contributions have come in helping us understand why FDI takes place, where it is made, how it is strategically used by MNCs to improve their global competitiveness, how it affects country competitiveness, how (and why) governments treat it and how it is used by industries in response to changing competitive conditions (Dunning, 1970; 1981a; 1986; 1988b; 1993a). Thanks to Dunning, we have come to know FDI as a mode of entry into a foreign market, the exercise of an advantage held by a MNC over its rivals, and as a transfer mechanism for efficiency, technology and skills across national and firm borders. It is also a means by which economic development can be enhanced through the creation of jobs and the dissemination of skills and a new level of competitiveness across the economy.

While the bulk of FDI continues to take place among the industrialized countries (FDI in high income OECD countries in 2000 was $809.8 billion as opposed to $178.0 billion in all developing countries), its rate of growth in developing countries has been remarkable. The level of net flows of FDI to all developing countries in 2000 was over 77 times the level in 1971. During the 1990s, net[1] flows of FDI increased at a rate of over 22% per year

(World Bank, 2001). Some of that growth can be explained by the traditional reasons for FDI – the search for new markets by MNCs, their desire
to secure their position through direct ownership, and the desire of firms in
developing countries to gain access to new technology or skills. Another
possible force behind the growth of FDI in developing countries could be
the desire by governments to attract it because it not only provides new
technology and skills but also a much-needed commodity that is in scarce
supply in developing countries – capital.

FDI AS A TRANSFER OF CAPITAL

FDI is not traditionally seen as a transfer of capital. Rather, it is normally
viewed as a mode of entry to a foreign market, a means to pursue global
strategic objectives, a transfer of technology and/or skills (or a means to
access technology and skills), or a response to market opportunities (such
as differences in exchange rate values, competitive environment, etc.) that
arise in different locations. True, it is an investment that ultimately may
require the use of capital, but, as in many investment decisions, the benefit
of FDI is first assured before the means of financing it are discussed.
Essentially, those who engage in FDI are not doing it because they are primarily interested in moving capital around.

   From the perspective of a developing country with limited ability to raise
private capital on its own, or a firm that does not have the kind of access
to capital markets that would allow it to raise capital in a cost-effective
manner, however, FDI can act as a transfer of capital. Over the past few
years international development agencies such as the International
Monetary Fund and the World Bank have encouraged developing countries to increase their level of private capital investment. Growing a domestic private capital market takes time, as does establishing a socioeconomic
infrastructure favoring private institutions (see Dilyard and Gray, 2000),
and domestic sources of capital (the banking system and citizens). Few
developing countries have all three, some have two of the three, and most
fall short in at least one of the requirements. FDI provides an alternative
source of capital for these countries, and it does not hurt that FDI can
bring in fringe benefits such as new technology and skills. Nor does it hurt
that FDI opens up the country to foreign financial markets through the
equity and debt financing activities of the investing entity.[2] Because impediments to foreign capital flows increase their cost, thereby reducing their
attractiveness, there is a built-in incentive for a developing country government to improve the efficiency of its internal financial markets to make it
easier for outside capital to enter the country and be distributed. This

improved efficiency then increases the ability of domestic firms to also access foreign financial markets. As a result, flows of private capital from outside investors into a developing country should increase.[3]

Foreign Portfolio Investment

Those private capital flows will take two forms, direct and portfolio. The volume of the former will be limited by the opportunities for FDI and the degree to which the host country desires its domestic businesses to be controlled by outside owners. The potential for foreign portfolio investment (FPI), however, is much larger. Not only can those firms covered by FDI continue to attract outside financing, but, presumably, so can domestic firms. As firms and the country's economy grow, so would the level of private portfolio investment. A distinction is being made here between portfolio investment in general and private portfolio investment. Portfolio investment includes government bonds and bonds that are guaranteed by a third party. Private portfolio investment consists of equity and long-term debt in which the full risk is borne by the investor. Focusing on private portfolio investment allows for a better comparison between the reasons behind FPI and the reasons for FDI.

Studies of the determinants of FPI have tended to focus on endogenous factors that pull FPI toward countries or exogenous factors that push FPI into countries. Schadler *et al.* (1993) and Hernandez and Rudolph (1995) cite improving economic conditions and progressive macroeconomic policies as endogenous factors that attract outside investment. Calvo, Leiderman and Reinhart (1992), Fernandez-Arias (1994), and Fernandez-Arias and Montiel (1995 and 1996) point to slow economic growth and low interest rates in developed countries which have caused investors to seek opportunities elsewhere, particularly in developing countries. Taylor and Sarno (1997), however, found evidence that both endogenous and exogenous factors are involved.

Virtually all of the studies use statistical analysis to back their findings, and virtually all of them use combinations of the same sets of exogenous and endogenous factors. Exogenous factors, for instance, include interest rates for US treasury bills, or returns on the New York Stock Exchange. Endogenous factors, on the other hand, include macroeconomic variables that can be quantified, such as GNP growth, and some that cannot be quantified, such as the presence of exchange controls or the initiation of the privatization of previously state-owned enterprises. Portfolio investment in these studies, however, includes public and guaranteed debt, and there is no differentiation made between the effect the factors may have on the decision of an investor to acquire public or guaranteed debt and the decision to acquire private debt or equity. As a result, those explanations of the size and direction of FPI are incomplete.

The Eclectic Paradigm and Portfolio Investment[4]

Clearly, portfolio investors, like direct investors, weigh a variety of factors when considering an investment. Included in those factors are an investment's expected return, its risk, and how it correlates with existing investments. When a portfolio investment includes a global element, either because the investment is in a firm located in another country or a firm that does business in one or more other countries, factors affecting risk and return are joined. Not only does the particular nature of the future cash flows to be generated as a result of the investment (and their variability) play a role in determining risk and return, so does the particular nature of the location in which the investment is being made. Microeconomic forces primarily influence the former, and macroeconomic forces primarily influence the latter.

There is thus a confluence of factors that become involved in the decision to engage in portfolio investment that are not easily separated, just as there is a confluence of factors affecting FDI that also are difficult to separate. Rather than focus on specific kinds of push or pull factors as a framework to explain FPI, it may be more worthwhile to use a framework that instead encompasses a variety of factors. One such framework is Dunning's eclectic paradigm of international production that described the act of FDI as a way to mobilize a firm's ownership and location advantages in an internal as opposed to arm's length transaction (Dunning, 1993a). If it is recognized that the decision to engage in FPI involves firm-specific (ownership) factors and country-specific (location) factors that are separate but interrelated, then it is possible to look at the act of using international financial markets as an external mechanism (as opposed to internalizing the transaction within the firm) as a way to mobilize those ownership and/or location factors through FPI.

Portfolio investors can be considered to fall into two broad categories, financial firms and non-financial firms. Financial firms are defined as those entities that primarily invest for others, and include mutual funds, insurance companies, pension funds, investment banks, brokerage houses, and commercial banks.[5] Non-financial firms are those that own small amounts of other firms but have no intention of exerting any management control over them. The issue of control is significant because the World Bank uses control as the determining factor in classifying FDI. Because the actual intent of an investment is impossible to determine without inside knowledge, the World Bank uses an ownership level of 10% as the threshold at which control can be exercised.

It is possible, however, that this threshold can be reached with the investors having no intention of exerting management control. For example, a consortium of investors pool their resources to purchase stock in a company that is being privatized and collectively acquire 25% of the company, while another consortium also acquires 25%; the remaining 50% is retained by domestic investors who manage the company. Neither consortium controls the company, however the investment qualifies as FDI under the World Bank definition. The matter is further complicated if members of the consortium see their share of the investment as either a way to gain knowledge of the country or market, to get experience with privatization, or to speculate that the value of the privatized firm will increase and they could sell their share for a gain. The first two have similarities to reasons behind FDI, but the last one is more purely speculative in nature and more like a portfolio investment. Thus, while the appearance of the investment is direct, the intent is portfolio.

Portfolio investors can be said to have two primary objectives when making a portfolio investment – gain (measured in interest yield and/or capital gain) and risk diversification. Different measures of gain and different measures of risk diversification might be involved, however. Each investor individually decides on the desired mix of risk and return, and each investor individually will determine how long the investment will be kept. In addition, each investor has a particular purpose for that investment, whether it is diversification, speculation, or knowledge seeking (getting involved in a newly opened or different market to see how it works and whether or not further involvement in it is justified). While it is impossible to know why all portfolio investors make the investments they choose, it is possible to categorize the reasons in terms of four major objectives that can be applied to financial and non-financial firms:

- Yield – The return on the investment, measured as a percent.
- Capital gain – The monetary or percent appreciation of the market value of the investment during the term in which the investment is held.
- Diversification – Creating a portfolio that reduces risk (through low correlations with other investments in the portfolio) while maintaining or enhancing yield.
- Speculation[6] – Targeting investments that have the potential for high yields and/or capital gains, but in which the risk is such that they are not included in a diversified portfolio.
- Market knowledge/access – Making investments in selected sectors to learn more about the markets/industries or to gain access to a new market.

Even though each type of investor has identical objectives, the way those objectives are pursued can differ. For instance, how an investor chooses to diversify a portfolio or portfolios will depend on the type and mix of assets in the fund, their correlation coefficients with each other and with potential new investments, and the degree of risk reduction through diversification desired. Investors participating even in the same markets can have widely diverging attitudes toward and interest in investing in those markets (Helliar *et al.*, 1998).

The pursuit of investment objectives in different ways implies that each investing entity brings to the investment decision a set of criteria, constraints or attributes that causes it to select the investment strategies it does. In other words, the investing firms possess certain advantages that they mobilize in unique ways when constructing their investment portfolios, just like a multinational company would use its configuration of advantages in choosing the method with which it would expand across borders.

Can portfolio investment then be described within the ownership, location and internalization variables of the eclectic paradigm? To answer this question it is necessary first to recast ownership, location and internalization variables in the context of a portfolio investor.

For FPI, ownership refers to the origin of investment, or the investing entity. The advantages consist of the knowledge and skills of the entity that make it able to operate effectively and efficiently in global financial markets. These attributes include research, risk management techniques, and fast, safe transfer of funds. The size of portfolios and their diversity (countries, industries, sectors, etc.) also provide ownership advantages.

Location advantages in FPI revolve around the direction of investment, or the places (countries) in which investments are made. These advantages relate to the socioeconomic infrastructure of the country, and involve a commitment to establishing a market-based economy, the existence of a legal and regulatory framework conducive to private investment, and the sophistication of the financial system that provides the conduit for investment flows. Time (how long a country has been the recipient of FPI) and history (the pattern of returns as well as the attitude toward private investment) also play a role in providing location advantages.

FPI by its nature, however, is not an internalized transaction. Those engaging in FPI combine the ownership and location factors to make an external transaction within a market; they are not internalizing the transaction through a direct investment. The decision to go through an externalized transaction could have many reasons, including risk reduction through diversification, the mobility of capital, and information asymmetries in which one investor, perhaps by virtue of its ownership advantages, knows more about a particular market or markets than other investors.

Ownership, location and externalization variables are summarized in Table 2.1. A summary of investor activities according to these variables appears in Table 2.2. An investor's ownership advantages, such as the size of investable funds, the diversity of its product mix and the capabilities of its human and technology-based resources, influence the size, kind, characteristics, and location (geographic and sector) of investments it makes. The location advantages provided by where those investments are made

Table 2.1   A description of ownership, location and externalization variables for portfolio investment

---

Ownership (origin of investment)

Size of investable funds
Number of different of funds, such as geography- or sector-based
Access to new/additional investable funds
Ease of transfer of investments among funds
Research capabilities and access to information about other markets/countries
Experience and capabilities of fund managers
Client preference for and attitude about risk
Tax status in home country
Risk management capabilities, including use of derivative products
Electronic funds transfer and communication capabilities

Location (direction of investment)

Political stability of countries in which investments are made
Commitment to a market economy
Degree of market openness and integration with global or regional markets
Level of market sophistication or maturity
Level of government support for portfolio investment
Ease with which returns/gains can be repatriated
Ease of capital repatriation and/or dividend remission
Condition of financial market infrastructure (e.g. banking system)
History of or prospects for economic growth

Externalization (reason for foreign investment)

Correlation of returns with other markets, especially home market
Lower transaction costs
Mobility of finance capital
Possession of proprietary or non-public information

Table 2.2   The execution of OLE advantages in private portfolio investment

Advantage	How executed
Ownership	Choice of investment (e.g. debt or equity), including amount, term, yield, location (geographic and sector), and covariance with other similar investments in other locations
Location	Investment made to pursue firm and client diversification objectives, as well as to meet client preferences for country and/or sector exposure
	Knowledge-gathering investment Taking advantage of favorable tax or repatriation policies
Externalization	Selective participation in countries, geographic regions or sectors to pursue portfolio structure objectives, as well as the movement among and between countries, regions and sectors

influence the mix of investments (by geography and sector) and their purpose, such as to achieve diversification or to expand into new markets in which the investor will use its ownership advantages. Finally, how the investor chooses to mix its ownership and location advantages in the geographic and sector choice of investments to meet its diversification or risk management objectives is determined by its externalization advantages.

Considering private portfolio investment within this framework has some distinct advantages over trying to explain it solely in terms of responses to push and pull factors. The biggest advantage is that it allows for the possibility that each investor or type of investor will have a different underlying purpose or strategy for engaging in portfolio investment, not only from a geographic sense but also in terms of sector and type. It also includes the possibility that, from a strategic use sense, investments that appear to be portfolio (particularly by non-financial firms) are in fact direct, and those that appear to be direct are in fact portfolio.

Linking Direct and Portfolio Investment

Putting portfolio investment under its own eclectic paradigm therefore provides a more robust framework to explain the pattern and direction of FPI in developing countries over the last twenty-five years. Looking at FDI from the perspective of a developing country needing capital allows FDI to be seen as a source of capital. As a result, in the context of developing countries, FDI and FPI become linked, not so much from the sense of cause and effect but more in the sense that the existence of one aids the existence of the other. In effect, this is saying that FDI and FPI could be complementary if they are seen mostly as sources of capital.

Demonstrating how FDI and FPI could be complementary, however, is difficult. One of the main reasons is the nature of the data. It is possible to collect flow data for each type of investment and define variables that affect each (see, for example, Calvo, Leiderman and Reinhart, 1992; Chuhan, Claessens and Mamingi, 1993; Claessens, Dooley and Warner, 1995; Dooley, Fernandez-Arias and Kletzer, 1996; and Taylor and Sarno, 1997). Usually the data are aggregated. This hides industry-specific or geographic-specific phenomena that may influence the patterns of investment. It also includes public portfolio investment, which obscures any dynamic that may be occurring between the types of private flows, particularly equity and debt.

The variables used also tend to be macroeconomic, which cannot capture some of the internal dynamics involved in private direct and portfolio investment.[7] The timeliness of data can be an issue as well. For example, Taylor and Sarno's 1997 work covered the period January 1988 to September 1992. While this period experienced increases in direct and portfolio investment in developing countries, even greater increases, especially in private portfolio investment, took place after 1992. Studies that examined flows through 1997, on the other hand, missed the effects of the East Asian debt crisis.

A difficulty encountered when trying to look at direct and portfolio investment together is that the decisions to make a direct or portfolio investment involve non-quantifiable variables. Direct investment, for example, is the result of a series of strategic, operational, logistic and financial decisions. Portfolio investment, while arguably more responsive to the more strictly quantitative criterion of the expected return on the investment, is also influenced by investor perceptions of the tradeoff between the risk and reward the investment offers.

Common financial analysis techniques (standard deviation, net present value and total return, for example) are used to quantify the risks and returns facing portfolio investors. Common parameters for risk, such as company (and country) credit ratings, degree of variability in return from 'risk-free' investments, and covariance of returns, also exist. What is not common, however, is how an investor puts all the variables and measures together to form an opinion or to make an investment. Different types of portfolio investment carry different risks. It follows that different investors view and respond to the different risks in different ways and put their own value on the investment even after all quantifiable issues have been addressed. In other words, portfolio investment involves contextual variables as well.

While using the eclectic paradigm as a framework to examine the contextual nature of portfolio investment provides robustness, there is still the matter of proof that FDI and FPI are linked. Dilyard (1999) found evidence suggesting that FDI and FPI flows to three East Asian countries (Indonesia, Malaysia and Thailand) and three Latin American countries (Argentina, Brazil and Chile) over the years 1975 to 1995 could be explained by similar sets of variables. An update of the analysis using data through 1997 (Dilyard, 2001) found that common explanatory variables for FDI and FPI continued to be present, but that the mix of variables changed, due largely to the beginning effects of the East Asian debt crisis. While it would be possible to use data from all developing countries in a similar analysis, it is doubtful any meaningful conclusions could be reached, mostly because the variables are a combination of macroeconomic and financial indicators whose uniqueness would become obscured by using all developing countries.[8]

Empirical Analysis of Links Between Direct and Portfolio Investment

Realistically speaking, it is probably not possible to prove definitively that FDI and FPI are linked in a causal or complementary way. Because it is not possible to get into the minds of investors (either direct or portfolio), all that can be observed is the result; cause and effect get subsumed in the data. The data, however, can be examined to see if the patterns of flows of FDI and FPI exhibit any correlation with each other. Table 2.1 charts net flows of FDI and FPI, as well as gross flows of new long-term debt, in all developing countries from 1971 to 2000. Table 2.3 presents three-year averages (for presentation purposes) of these flows of FDI, FPI, and gross long-term debt (GLTD) to all developing countries from 1971 to 2000. Gross flows (new debt actually paid out) of new long-term debt are included because these indicate investor willingness to provide capital.[9] Net flows include the normal payments on existing debt, but can also reflect retirement or cancellation of debt. As a result, net flows of debt can be negative (as they were during the Latin American debt crisis of the 1980s). It does not mean, however, that investors are fleeing; while net flows of long-term debt to all developing countries were negative from 1980 to 1988, gross flows of new long-term debt averaged over $8 billion per year (World Bank, 2001). Tables 2.4 through 2.6 present this information by decade for the six geographic regions used by the World Bank.[10] Table 2.7 presents the information by income classification (low or middle).[11] Table 2.8 presents the correlation between FDI and FPI and FDI and GLTD for all developing countries, regions and income classification.

Table 2.3   FDI, FPI and GLTD in all developing countries: three-year
averages from 1971–2000 ($ billions)

Years	FDI	FPI	GLTD
1971–1973	2.5	2.5	5.8
1974–1976	3.3	5.0	10.4
1977–1979	6.6	6.5	15.3
1980–1982	9.1	11.8	24.0
1983–1985	9.2	0.0	9.4
1986–1988	14.1	−1.7	8.5
1989–1991	27.6	11.2	17.1
1992–1994	67.9	58.7	48.8
1995–1997	137.0	90.6	97.7
1998–2000	180.1	50.3	108.7

Source: World Bank (2001).

Table 2.4   FDI in geographic regions* by decade ($ billions)

Years	EAP	ECA	LAC	MENA	SA	SSA
1970s	0.9	0.1	3.0	−0.5	0.1	0.7
1980s	4.9	0.2	5.9	1.4	0.3	1.1
1990s	47.9	13.0	44.7	3.3	2.5	4.9

Notes: * Geographic regions are identified by their abbreviations. The key for the
abbreviations, which is applicable for Tables 2.4 to 2.6 is as follows: EAP = East Asia and the
Pacific; ECA = East Europe and Central Asia; LAC = Latin America and the Caribbean;
MENA = the Middle East and North Africa; SA = South Asia; SSA = Sub-Saharan Africa.

Source: World Bank (2001).

Table 2.5   FPI in geographic regions by decade ($ billions)

Years	EAP	ECA	LAC	MENA	SA	SSA
1970s	0.9	0.9	3.0	–	–	0.2
1980s	2.5	0.2	0.7	0.1	0.1	0.1
1990s	21.0	7.3	27.3	1.1	2.9	1.2

Source: World Bank (2001).

Table 2.6   GLTD in geographic regions by decade ($ billions)

Years	EAP	ECA	LAC	MENA	SA	SSA
1970s	2.0	1.7	7.0	0.1	0.1	0.4
1980s	5.6	1.3	5.5	0.3	0.4	0.7
1990s	22.7	9.5	41.6	1.1	1.3	1.0

Source: World Bank (2001).

Table 2.7   FDI, FPI and GLTD in low and middle income countries by decade* ($ billions)

Years	Low income countries		
	FDI	FPI	GLTD
1970s	0.9	0.5	1.2
1980s	1.6	1.0	2.6
1990s	11.1	6.3	8.1
Years	Middle income countries		
	FDI	FPI	GLTD
1970s	3.3	4.6	10.4
1980s	12.4	2.5	11.0
1990s	101.4	55.9	68.1

Note: *Data by income categories do not include figures for the year 2000.

Source: World Bank (2001).

Table 2.8   Correlation between FDI and FPI, and FDI and GLTD, 1971–2000

Country grouping	FDI to FPI	FDI to GLTD
All developing	0.83	0.98
East Asia	0.73	0.85
East Europe/Central Asia	0.88	0.91
Latin America	0.67	0.95
Middle East/N. Africa	0.53	0.59
South Asia	0.69	0.86
Sub-Saharan Africa	0.58	0.64
Low income*	0.68	0.90
Middle income*	0.84	0.98

Note: * Correlations for low income and middle income categories cover 1971–1999.

It is worth noting that the correlation between FDI and FPI detailed in Table 2.8 probably would have been higher had it not been for the East Asian crisis that began in 1997. From 1971 to 1996, the correlation between FDI and FPI in each of the regions or income categories was as follows: all developing countries, 0.96; East Asia, 0.99; East Europe/Central Asia, 0.89; Latin America, 0.80; Middle East/N. Africa, 0.11; South Asia, 0.86; Sub-Saharan Africa, 0.63; low income, 0.94; middle income, 0.94.

For all developing countries, the correlation between net flows of FDI and FPI from 1971 to 2000 was 0.83, and the correlation between FDI and GLTD of long-term debt was 0.98. The correlation between net flows of FDI and FPI would have been higher had it not been for the East Asian crisis. Table 2.3 shows a sharp downturn in FPI beginning in 1998. From a peak of $106.3 billion in 1996, FPI fell precipitously to $33.1 billion in 1999 before rising again in 2000 to $54.8 billion.[12] At the same time, net flows of FDI increased from $131.5 billion in 1996 to $185.4 billion in 1999 before dipping slightly to $178.0 billion in 2000. These divergent flows resulted in a correlation of -0.97 from 1997 to 2000. Using just the years 1971 to 1996 to calculate the correlation between FDI and FPI results in a correlation of 0.96.

Increasing levels of FDI flows accompanied by decreasing levels of FPI flows might appear contrary to the assertion that FDI and FPI are linked. Yet, one of the features of the East Asian crisis was a reallocation of investments within countries and regions. In Thailand, the origin of the crisis, while FPI recorded net outflows of $1.1 billion, $2.0 billion and $2.5 billion in 1997, 1998 and 1999, respectively, FDI registered net inflows of $3.9 billion, $7.3 billion and $6.2 billion as direct investors took advantage of depressed values to acquire assets (World Bank, 2001). As a region, East Asia saw a slight increase in average FDI flows from the 1994 to1996 period to the 1997 to 1999 period ($53.5 billion versus $61.6 billion) and a large decrease in average FPI (from $36.9 billion to $9.1 billion). In Latin America, flows of FDI averaged $75.8 billion during 1997 to 1999 (as opposed to $33.8 billion during the preceding three-year period), and FPI averaged $34.1 billion during 1997 to 1999 (as opposed to $16.8 billion during 1994 to 1996). What this represents is a continued demand for both FDI and FPI, and a search for a suitable source of supply.

The regional feature of FDI and FPI flows requires further discussion. It is commonly acknowledged that the distribution of FDI and FPI is skewed to a relatively few number of countries. Two regions, East Asia and Latin America, historically have accounted for a large proportion of all the FDI and FPI flows to developing countries. During the 1990s, these two regions accounted for $92.6 billion of the $116.3 billion average net flows of FDI, and $48.3 billion of the $60.8 billion average net flows of FPI (see

Tables 2.4 and 2.5). Similarly, the flows are skewed by income categories as well. Those countries classified as middle income have averaged over nine times the amount of average flows of FDI in the 1990s as low income countries, and around nine times the amount of FPI (see Table 2.7).

It therefore is interesting to note the correlation observed between FDI and FPI in these two regions. Excluding the period of the East Asian crisis results in a correlation of 0.99 between FDI and FPI for East Asian countries, as opposed to 0.73 when the crisis years are included. In contrast, the correlation between FDI and FPI for Latin America for 1971 to 1996 is only 0.80. One reason for this is that Latin America went through a crisis of its own in the 1980s that resulted in net outflows of long-term debt. The correlation between FDI and FPI for the period of time prior to that crisis (1971–81) is 0.92, and after the crisis, but prior to the East Asian crisis, (1990–96) it is 0.88. As the net outflows of long-term debt reveal, the crisis period in Latin America was characterized by much restructuring. It is therefore perhaps more important to look at the correlation between FDI and GLTD, as that represents the willingness to extend financing. The correlation between FDI and GLTD for the 1971 to 1981 period is 0.92, while it is 0.87 for 1990 to 1996.

It also is worth noting that the other region, that is, East Europe and Central Asia, which, after East Asia and Latin America, has received the largest amount of FDI and FPI, particularly in the 1990s, also has a high correlation between FDI and FPI. East Europe is also fairly unaffected by the East Asian crisis. The two regions in which the correlation between FDI and FPI is lowest (Middle East and North Africa, and Sub-Saharan Africa) also receive the smallest amount of FPI relative to FDI. These regions also do not receive much in the way of financing, as evidenced by a low level of gross long-term debt flows (see Table 2.6). The link between FDI and FPI, therefore, appears to be more complicated than can be explained by examining the correlation between the two by regions.

Many of the world's poorest countries can be found in those two regions that receive the least absolute amounts of FDI and FPI. It may be useful, then, to look at the correlation between FDI and FPI by income levels. As Table 2.7 shows, low income countries, which include most of those in the Middle East and North African and Sub-Saharan regions, have a low overall correlation between FDI and FPI. It is possible, however, to further categorize countries according to a level of indebtedness, two for low income countries and two for middle income countries.[13] Table 2.9 presents the correlation between FDI and FPI and between FDI and GLTD for these additional categories.

The correlation between FDI and FPI through 1996 is fairly high for all four indebtedness categories. It is interesting to note, however, that the

Table 2.9   *Correlation between FDI and FPI, and FDI and GLTD,*
1971–1999

Country grouping	FDI to FPI	FDI to GLTD
Severely indebted low income	0.73	0.92
Moderately indebted low income	0.35	0.38
Severely indebted middle income	0.42	0.89
Moderately indebted middle income	0.84	0.96

largest differentials in the correlation between FDI and FPI for the periods including and excluding the East Asian debt crisis occur in the moderately indebted low income and severely indebted middle income categories. A possible reason for this (and the relatively low correlation between FDI and FPI prior to the East Asian debt crisis) in the severely indebted middle income category is that Argentina and Brazil are part of this group. Although these two countries were not severely affected by the East Asian crisis, each went through two other crises related to Latin American debt problems. The first was in the mid-1980s, when Latin America as a whole experienced a net outflow of FPI and flat levels of FDI, and the second was the result of contagion from Mexico's debt problems in the early 1990s.

The correlation between FDI and FPI in this grouping also probably would have been higher had the East Asian crisis not intervened. The correlation between these two flows from 1971 to 1996 by the various indebtedness categories is as follows: severely indebted low income, 0.92; moderately indebted low income, 0.84; severely indebted middle income, 0.78; moderately indebted middle income, 0.92.

The reasons behind the correlation observed for moderately indebted low income countries, on the other hand, are more complicated. Most of the countries in this group are those Sub-Saharan African countries that do not fall into the severely indebted low income range, and a few South Asian countries such as Bangladesh. It is possible that these countries find themselves in something of a 'no-man's land', doing well enough to not need public or guaranteed long-term debt (hence the low correlation between FDI and GLTD), but not so well that they can attract private long-term debt or FDI.[14] A possible reason why the correlation between FDI and FPI for the entire 1971 to 1999 timeframe is much smaller than the correlation for the pre-East Asian crisis period is that the countries in this group are more prone to be adversely affected by contagion. Having little to offer investors in the first place, they are thus less likely to be an alternative location for FPI when problems arise in another sector. Indeed, during the period 1997 through 1999 FPI in moderately indebted low income countries saw a net outflow of $312 million. At the same time, FDI was averaging $3.5 billion each year, the highest level of flows ever experienced in this group.

Observations and Conclusions

Because it is not possible to look at aggregate data and understand precisely what is in the minds of investors, there is no way to ascribe specific reasons behind specific decisions. All that can be observed is the consequence of many sets of decisions. That these decisions could be influenced by many sets of unique factors complicates the issue further. For FDI, having a framework such as the eclectic paradigm to understand how, why and where it is made allows for the capture of these unique factors. FPI is also influenced by many unique factors, and it therefore makes sense to consider looking at it within a framework that captures the disparate influences, an eclectic paradigm, if you will, that is a variant on Dunning's eclectic paradigm.

Once explanations for FDI and FPI are viewed in the same kind of framework, then it is possible to consider that in some cases the two are possibly complementary, and even could be interchangeable. This possibility is heightened when the recipient is looking primarily for capital rather than tangential, intangible benefits that may come from investment. Aggregate data again hide the motivations behind individual FDI and FPI decisions, but persistent trends can be revealing. Perhaps the best that can be done is to see if FDI and FPI move together and exhibit signs of being correlated with each other.

In developing countries, those that most likely view FDI and FPI in terms of their ability to provide capital, there is such a correlation. That the correlation is stronger in those regions, income categories or indebtedness levels in which FDI also is strong suggests that it is reasonable to consider that a link between the two begins with FDI. The ultimate proof that FDI and FPI are linked, however, will require an analysis of FPI that addresses the complexity and diversity of the decisions behind it, and the recognition that it is the result of a confluence of factors. Having an eclectic paradigm that is adapted for portfolio investment will make that analysis easier.

NOTES

1. Flows of FDI and FPI in this essay, unless otherwise stated, are inflows net of any out-flows.
2. This is not to say that developing countries do not have access to outside financial markets without FDI. Governments of developing countries can (and do) access outside markets for their financing (this would continue even after FDI), and in some cases firms

can also. The former has potentially damaging inflation and exchange rate consequences, and the latter is done at high cost.

3. To distinguish these flows of capital from FDI, they will be termed portfolio investment.
4. This section is based largely on Dilyard (1999) and Dunning and Dilyard (1999).
5. Each of these entities does have the ability to make investments for themselves, but the largest volume of their business is done for clients.
6. The amount of speculation a financial firm is able to do is limited by its fiduciary responsibility to its clients. Most, if not all, the speculative investments are made for the firms' own accounts or in special funds in which the participants fully understand the speculative nature of the fund.
7. See Taylor and Sarno (1997) for a good example of how available data are gathered and what variables are used to model capital flows from developed to developing countries.
8. The macroeconomic variables included GDP, and the financial indicators included such items as the proportion of short-term debt to total debt, the size of interest payments, and the difference between domestic and foreign interest rates.
9. All forms of long-term debt, including public or guaranteed, are included in these gross flows. While obviously this does not represent private flows of capital, it still represents a willingness to provide capital that can be seen favorably by those entities considering FDI.
10. The World Bank separates developing countries into six major regions: East Asia and the Pacific; East Europe and Central Asia; Latin America and the Caribbean; Middle East and North Africa; South Asia; and, Sub-Saharan Africa.
11. Low income countries are those in which per capita GNP is $755 or less. Middle income countries have per capita GNP levels from $756 to $9,265.
12. See Kaminsky, Lyons and Schmukler (2001) for a discussion of mutual fund investment in emerging markets and their volatile response to times of crisis.
13. Indebtedness is defined in terms of two ratios – total debt service to average exports, and the present value of debt service to average GNP – calculated for 1997, 1998 and 1999. Severely indebted countries are those in which the debt service to exports ratio is 220% or higher, or the debt service to GNP ratio is 80% or higher. Moderately indebted countries are those in which the ratios are between 132% and 180%, and 48% and 80%, respectively.
14. Sub-Saharan Africa and South Asia as regions have attracted little FDI over the last twenty years. Only 2% of all FDI going to developing countries went to South Asia, and only 6% has gone to Sub-Saharan Africa. Both have attracted even less FPI (World Bank, 2001).

3. Why multinationality matters: exploring the 'L' in the OLI paradigm

Lorraine Eden, Douglas E. Thomas and Kingsley O. Olibe

INTRODUCTION

Asking whether the degree of multinationality of a firm affects its performance is an old question in the international business literature. However, being an old topic does not imply the debate is settled. Sullivan (1994) reviews 17 studies; seven report a positive relationship, five negative and six indeterminate. Our own literature review found more than two dozen performance–multinationality studies using a wide variety of proxy variables. The studies show a generally positive relationship, but the results are not always significant nor of the expected sign.

Hitt, Hoskisson and Ireland (1994) and Gomes and Ramaswamy (1999) argue that, while methodological problems are partly responsible for these inconsistent results, the real problem is the lack of theory building. Both papers address this lacuna by hypothesizing that multinationality has benefits and costs. Initially, benefits dominate costs because the multinational enterprise (MNE) chooses familiar locations and simple organizational structures, but eventually costs rise as locations become more culturally distant and the firm adopts a more complex structure. As a result, the multinationality–performance relationship should be inverse U-shaped, rising and then falling.

We extend this research by nesting the theoretical foundations for the multinationality–performance relationship in the OLI paradigm (Dunning, 1993a), which argues that MNEs create value by using their ownership (O) advantages in conjunction with location (L) advantages of foreign countries. In the original OLI paradigm, L refers to *country specific* advantages; we reconceptualize L as *firm specific* advantages of having a multinational network.[1] We hypothesize that multinationality has three facets: two measuring depth (foreign market penetration and foreign production presence) and a third, breadth (country scope). Increasing breadth and/or depth has both advantages and disadvantages for the MNE that affect performance. We hypothesize that both O and L advantages positively and interactively affect performance, but that the net benefits from multinationality taper off as L increases.

The chapter is organized as follows. First, we provide a brief literature review and next develop our theoretical framework and hypotheses. We test the hypotheses on a sample of US manufacturing MNEs over the 1990–4 period using moderated multiple regression analysis. Our empirical analysis, discussion and conclusions follow.

LITERATURE REVIEW

Because there are already good reviews available of the extensive literature on the multinationality–performance relationship (see Sullivan, 1994; Gomes and Ramaswamy, 1999), we focus on papers published in the past five years. Two themes dominate this research.

The first theme is related to the measurement of multinationality. Nguyen and Cosset (1995) argue that multinationality has three facets: structural, performance related and behavioral. They find that different proxies can lead to different results and argue that scholars should be cautious in drawing comparisons across studies using different measures of multinationality. Sullivan (1994, p. 338) finds nine different multinationality proxies in the literature and develops a five-component index that he concludes 'reduc[es] the error that results from sample, systematic, and random bias'.[2] Ramaswamy, Kroeck and Renforth (1996) criticize the use of factor analysis to select the variables and constant weights to form the index. They argue that, given the lack of theory for selecting the index's components, an overall index may be theoretically suspect and premature.[3] Sullivan responds that a composite scale is 'a useful method to enhance the goodness of the sample, clarify the extent of random and systematic error, fortify the reliability and content validity of results, and contribute to estimating construct validity' (1996, p.190).

The second focus has been on building theory to explain the multinationality–performance relationship. Allen and Pantzalis (1996) propose operating flexibility as a theoretical framework, and breadth and depth as the two key components of multinationality. They hypothesize that multinationality positively affects performance by increasing the MNE's ability to shift resources and factors across borders and within a transnational network. Using proxies for breadth and depth of multinationality, they find the high breadth, low depth multinationals achieve superior performance.[4] Others have argued that multinationality has both costs and benefits (Hitt, Hoskisson and Ireland, 1994; Gomes and Ramaswamy, 1999). The multinationality–performance relationship is curvilinear (inverted U) because greater geographic dispersion increases the costs of coordinating, integrating and managing the MNE's overall operations. The benefits of multinationality arise from the ability to leverage scale economies; utilize home-based skills, competencies and resources; and arbitrage differences in factor costs across countries. However, as multinationality increases, the MNE must adopt more complex and costly organizational structures and move to less familiar settings where higher cultural diversity raises transactions costs. Recent empirical work supports the inverted-U multinationality–performance relationship (see, for example, Hitt, Hoskisson and Kim, 1997; Riahi-Belkaoui, 1998; Gomes and Ramaswamy, 1999).

The past few years have seen an explosion of research on the multinationality–performance relationship. The beginnings of a theoretical framework are emerging but there is still broad disagreement on the measurement and definition of multinationality. We argue below that the OLI paradigm can provide a solid theoretical underpinning for this relationship.

THEORETICAL FRAMEWORK

The OLI or eclectic paradigm (Dunning, 1993a) asserts that MNEs are successful because of their ownership (O), location (L) and internalization (I) advantages. If a firm is to be profitable abroad, it must have some ownership advantages, not shared by its competitors, which are internal and specific to the enterprise but readily transferable across borders within the MNE network. There are three basic types of O advantages. The first is *knowledge-based assets*, which include all forms of innovatory activity including both process and product innovation and managerial capabilities. The second is *economies of common governance*, which include economies of scale and scope, economies of learning, and broader access to financial capital throughout the MNE organization. The third is *monopolistic advantages* in the form of privileged access to input and output markets (e.g. patent rights, brand names, ownership of scarce natural resources), which act as barriers to entry, enabling the MNE to earn monopoly rents.

In the traditional view of the OLI paradigm, the L explains where the firm goes. Because foreign factors are needed in order to realize maximum potential rents from the firm's O advantages, the MNE will choose to invest or not invest in different host countries depending on their environmental, social and policy-oriented characteristics (Dunning, 1993a). However, instead of seeing L as a menu of existing and potential *host country* attractions, in this chapter we hypothesize that it should be seen as *firm-based advantages (and disadvantages) of having a multinational network.* By turning the L variable on its head – that is, from a country-based to a firm-based focus – we can integrate the multinationality – performance literature into the OLI paradigm and thereby provide the relationship with a solid theoretical foundation.

Let us reconceptualize L in the OLI paradigm as the advantages and disadvantages of multinationality. The MNE goes abroad to take advantages of cross-border opportunities that are not available to domestic firms. Dunning (1993a) argues that MNEs engage in four basic types of FDI: market seeking, resource seeking, rationalization or efficiency seeking, and strategic asset seeking. Through FDI, MNEs can exploit sources of competitive advantage not available to domestic firms, but are also open to costs and risks that do not face domestic firms. These cross-border locational *advantage*s include:

- *Differences in cultures, demands and income levels.* Market-seeking FDI is designed to exploit profitable opportunities in higher income markets, generating rents on the firm's ownership advantages. FDI can also be used to shift sales towards lower income markets, extending the life of an obsolete product line. In international trade theory, these are the gains from exchange since they are generated by country-based differences in demand.
- *Differences in basic and created factor endowments.* Through resource-seeking FDI, a firm can shift production locations to take advantage of differences in basic factor endowments across countries. In addition, differences in knowledge-based assets and skilled labor across countries motivate strategic-asset-seeking FDI, allowing MNE to use foreign knowledge bases to generate world-wide learning within the enterprise. These represent specialization gains for the MNE.
- *Differences in government policies.* Differences in government regulation (e.g. taxes, subsidies) can also create locational advantages and cross-border potential gains for the MNE through cross-border arbitrage.

Lastly, both specialization and exchange gains are created by efficiency-seeking FDI, where an existing MNE reorganizes its production, distribution and sales networks to better arbitrage differences in endowments, markets and government regulations.

The three categories of cross-border differences outlined above offer the MNE a source of competitive advantage over domestic firms; that is, the ability to use FDI to arbitrage differences between, and take advantage of new opportunities in, foreign countries. The higher breadth and depth of multinational involvement, the greater the potential rent-creating opportunities for the MNE. Cross-border arbitrage opportunities therefore offer the MNE *static, efficiency-motivated benefits* from multinationality.

Cross-border arbitrage opportunities can also provide *dynamic, strategic benefits* from multinationality. MNEs can take advantage of multiple locations to adapt flexibly to changes/shocks in the external environment. A wider MNE network provides the enterprise with real options that create excess market value (Allen and Pantzalis, 1996; Kogut and Kulatilaka, 1995). Global scanning increases the firm's ability to compete against other oligopolists in world markets. MNEs are better able than domestic firms to scan the global market looking for opportunities or avoiding threats. In addition, MNEs, due to their ability to move assets quickly between countries, have more bargaining power relative to location-bound actors, such as governments, trade unions and domestic firms.[5]

Cross-border arbitrage opportunities are not cost or risk free. As the number of foreign countries in which the MNE operates and the percentage of its operations that take place overseas increase, we expect the following cross-border locational disadvantages:

- *Costs and risks of multiple sources of value.* As Sundaram and Black (1992) argue, MNEs operate with multiple sources of value that create foreign exchange risks. Foreign sales are negatively affected by transaction exposure; market value and ability to raise capital are negatively affected by translation exposure; and the MNE's operations as a whole suffer from economic exposure.
- *Costs and risks of multiple levels of authority.* As the MNE expands into more countries, it is faced with higher cross-border transactions costs and higher interaction costs with a wider variety and number of governments. Multiple levels of authority also create higher political risks for the MNE (Sundaram and Black, 1992; Kostova and Zaheer, 1999).
- *Costs of greater cultural diversity.* As the number of foreign markets and production locations increase, the MNE is faced with the costs of adapting to new cultures. Institutional theory suggests that the liability of foreignness increases as firms move to more culturally distant countries (Gomes and Ramaswamy, 1999). As the number of institutional environments rises, it may be more difficult for the MNE to maintain legitimacy (Kostova and Zaheer, 1999).

As the number of foreign countries and the relative share of foreign operations increase, the costs of operating at a distance and the complexity of managing the MNE also rise. The MNE must adopt more expensive global organizational structures to maintain strategic control of the MNE network. In addition, higher coordination costs and greater cultural distance suggest greater difficulty with resource (particularly tacit knowledge) transfers throughout the MNE network.

Multinationality therefore implies both advantages and disadvantages for the MNE. Given these costs and benefits, each firm chooses an optimal configuration of its resources and activities. That configuration is firm specific and a source of advantage to the MNE relative to its competitors. No two MNEs are likely to have exactly the same configuration because their goals, strategies and institutional histories differ. Cross-border arbitrage opportunities are bundled into a configuration of MNE activities and resources that give the multinational network both depth and breadth. Each MNE chooses its optimal degree of breadth and depth of multinational involvement, taking into account their benefits and costs.

We hypothesize that depth of multinationality can be conceptualized in two ways – depth and breadth. Depth includes both foreign market penetration and presence. *Foreign market penetration* is the dependence of the firm on foreign markets. The higher the foreign market share, the greater the gains from exchange and the ability to leverage rents on the MNE's ownership advantages; however, it also means more exposure to multiple sources of value and authority. *Foreign production presence* assesses the degree to which the enterprise is engaged in production-based activities across borders. The higher the foreign production share, the greater the gains from specialization and the dynamic gains from flexibility; however, it also means higher economic exposure, cross-border transactions costs and cultural diversity costs. *Country scope* is the geographic range or breadth of multinationality. The higher the country scope, the greater the cross-border arbitrage opportunities, suggesting higher potential static and dynamic gains; however, the higher also are the costs of multiple levels of authority and value.

We argue that a true MNE must score high on both dimensions of depth and breadth of multinationality. Given the existing breadth of the MNE network, the MNE can choose to allocate a higher or lower percentage of its total activities to foreign operations. In addition, vice versa, given its existing depth in foreign sales and assets, the MNE can allocate this depth across fewer or greater numbers of countries. Thus, we agree with Allen and Pantzalis (1996) that there may be a tradeoff between breadth and depth of multinationality.

We are now ready to assemble our theoretical model linking multinationality to firm performance. We argue that the OLI variables are linked, through their impact on FDI, to firm performance as outlined in Figure 3.1. New FDI that alters the MNE's breadth or depth of multinationality will

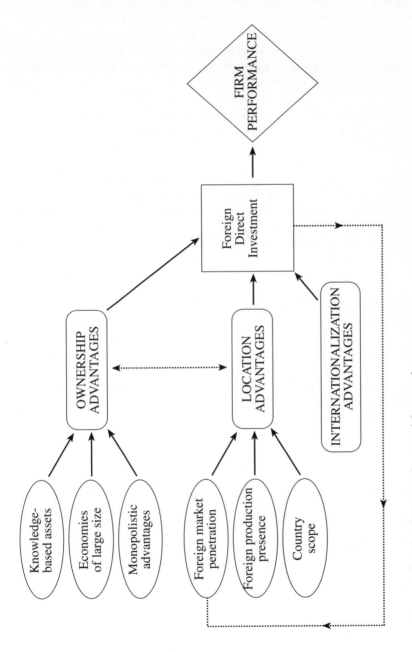

Figure 3.1 The OLI paradigm and firm performance

have second-round impacts on performance. Therefore, over time one would expect the OLI–performance relationship to be dynamic, with feedback effects and the potential for virtuous or vicious circles.

Following the OLI paradigm, we assume *a priori* that a multinational enterprise's performance is positively affected by each of the MNE's three types of ownership advantages.

> *H1: Ownership advantages (knowledge-based assets, economies of large size, monopolistic advantages) have direct, positive impacts on MNE performance.*

We hypothesize that multinationality – defined as breadth and depth of locational advantages – contributes positively and directly to MNE performance. This hypothesis allows us to address the conclusion reached by Morck and Yeung (1991), Mishra and Gobeli (1998) and Gomes and Ramaswamy (1999) that multinationality is not an dependent predictor but rather moderates the ownership–performance relationship. H2 assumes that this conclusion is incorrect.

> *H2: Location advantages (foreign market penetration, foreign production presence, country scope) have direct, positive impacts on MNE performance.*

Following the OLI paradigm, we also hypothesize that combining O advantages with L advantages generates higher performance. Using moderated regression allows us to test whether O moderates L (Itaki, 1991) or L moderates O (Morck and Yeung, 1991; Mishra and Gobeli, 1998) as a performance predictor. Our third hypothesis suggests that both views are correct; i.e., the interaction of O and L induces a second-round positive impact on performance (Dunning, 1993a).

> *H3: Ownership advantages combined with location advantages have additional synergistic, positive impacts on MNE performance over and above their individual direct impacts.*

As a test of Sullivan's (1994) index of multinationality, we hypothesize that:[6]

> *H4: An index measure of multinationality is a better predictor of MNE performance than its decomposition into individual location advantages.*

Lastly, we hypothesize that multinationality has both benefits and costs, with costs eventually dominating so that the positive impact on performance tapers off (see Hitt, Hoskisson and Ireland, 1994; Hitt, Hoskisson and Kim, 1997; Riahi-Belkaoui, 1998; Gomes and Ramaswamy, 1999):

H5: The relationship between locational advantages and firm performance is curvilinear, rising and then declining, reflecting that multinationality carries both benefits and costs.

METHODOLOGY

Sample

Our sample was drawn from the S&P 500 for 1990–4. We limited the sample to manufacturing firms (primary SIC code: 2000–3999), resulting in 247 firms. We eliminated firms that were not headquartered in the United States and that did not have at least one foreign affiliate, according to Dun and Bradstreet (1996). Several firms had missing data, resulting in a pooled cross-section times-series data set of 151 firms over five years.

Measures

Our analysis uses two measures of MNE performance: return on assets (ROA) and excess market value (EMV). ROA is the most commonly used measure of financial performance in studies linking MNE performance to multinationality. Our second proxy, EMV, is a measure of excess market valuation of the firm over and above the value of its physical assets used as a proxy for Tobin's q.[7] High values for EMV suggest the existence of intangible assets, and an implicit valuation of the firm's ability to capture the benefits of these ownership advantages in its long-run market performance.[8] We see ROA as a measure of short-run financial performance, whereas EMV is a proxy for long-run market-based returns.

We have three measures for ownership advantages.[9] The most common proxy for knowledge-based assets used in international business research is the R&D-to-sales ratio (RDS).[10] The size of the firm, measured by total assets, is a common proxy for economies of common governance. We log the variable to linearize the data (LNASSET). As a proxy for monopolistic advantages, we use selling and general administrative (SG&A) expenses divided by total sales (SGAS). Since SG&A costs can also proxy for the overhead or fixed costs associated with the firm's global activities, if there are firm-level economies of scale, SGAS should decline as global sales increase.[11]

Our key multinationality measures are *foreign market penetration* as measured by the foreign sales ratio (FSTS), the most common proxy for multinationality; *foreign production presence* as measured by the foreign assets ratio (FATA); and *country scope* as measured by the number of countries where the MNE has foreign affiliates (NFCO).[12] Since foreign affiliates can be concentrated in particular countries, we chose NFCO instead of NFA as a proxy for country scope.[13] In addition, since most MNEs have foreign affiliates in OECD rather than developing countries, we define *developed country share* as the share of OECD-member countries in the total number of foreign countries where the MNE has operations.

Our fifth location variable, an index of multinationality (LOC), is used to test Sullivan's (1994) proposition that an index outperforms individual measures of multinationality. Following Gomes and Ramaswamy (1999), a composite index of multinationality is created by principal components analysis of FSTS, FATA and NFCO, using eigenvalues as weights. The Cronbach's alpha for the three variables is .8172, suggesting that the composite measure has validity.[14]

We introduce two types of control variables. The firm's debt–equity ratio (DERATIO) is included as to capture a portion of firm's value and financial indebtedness. A set of industry dummy variables is added to control for industry-specific impacts on performance.[15]

Data Analysis

Because our study employs pooled cross-section time-series regressions, we first ran F-tests to assess the feasibility of pooling the data across years. The results indicated that there were important year effects so we included year dummy variables, where 1994 is the (excluded) base year, in each regression. In addition, all independent variables except the industry dummies were centered at mean 100 to reduce multicollinearity, which reduced the variance inflation factors (VIFs) to acceptable levels. We also found evidence of heteroscedasticity (but not autocorrelation) and corrected for it by running OLS regressions with White-corrected standard errors.

We use moderated multiple regression analysis to ascertain the direct and indirect impacts of the location variable on firm performance. Our equations test the following model, where V is firm performance, in hierarchical stages:

$$V = \beta_0 + \beta_1 O + \beta2 L + \beta_3 O*L$$

In stage 1, we test for the independent direct impacts of O and L on V; in stage 2, for their joint direct impacts, and in stage 3, for their moderator

impacts on firm performance. These represent hypotheses 1–3. We also substitute the composite measure LOC for the individual L variables and add
a squared term LOCSQ in order to test hypotheses 4 and 5, respectively.

Results

Descriptive statistics are reported in Table 3.1. Regression results are
reported in Tables 3.2 (ROA) and 3.3 (EMV). Because our variables are
centered at mean 100, each coefficient should be interpreted as the conditional effect of the predictor variable at the mean of all the other predictors
(Aiken and West, 1991, p. 39). Control variables are not reported in the
tables. In general, OECD is positively and significantly related to ROA and
EMV, whereas DERATIO is consistently negative and significant. Of the
industry dummy variables, FOOD and METALS are consistently significant and positively related to performance. The year dummy variables are
generally negative and significant for ROA, but positive and significant for
EMV. We turn first to the ROA regressions in Table 3.2.

The general fit of the regressions is good, with R-squared values ranging
from .1737 to .2999. The F statistics are all significant at $p < .0001$. In the
first stage, we test for the independent effects of the O and L variables on
performance. In stage 1(a), only SGAS is significant among the O variables,
whereas in stage 1(b), FATA and NFCO are both significant (although
FATA has a negative sign, contrary to expectations). The LOC composite
index is also significant in stage 1(c), although adding the quadratic term
in stage 1(d) causes both to lose significance.

In stage 2, we introduce both O and L as predictors of MNE performance. Stage 2(a) appears to be a combination of stages 1(a) and 1(c) in
that all variables significant in those regressions remain so. In addition,
LNASSET now attains significance; however, it is negatively related to
ROA, contrary to our expectations. Comparing stage 2(b) with a combination of stages 1(a) and 1(c) yields similar conclusions, as does a comparison of stages 2(c) with 1(d); i.e., the LOCSQ variable remains insignificant.

Stage 3(a) includes nine interaction terms, representing combinations of
O*L. Because of the high VIFs, we do not interpret the individual coefficients; however, it is clear that most of the interaction terms are significant,
as are almost all of the O and L variables. When we substitute the LOC
composite index for the individual L variables, the interaction terms lose
their significance as do all the O variables and the L index itself. This suggests that an index measure may be a poor method to test moderator effects.

In Table 3.3, we show the relationships between the O and L variables
and performance as proxied by EMV. Note first that the R-squares range
from a low of .0760 in stage 1(b) to a high of .4241 in stage 3(a), much

Table 3.1   Descriptive statistics and Pearson correlation coefficients

	No.	Mean	S.D.	1	2	3	4	5	6	7	8	9	10	11	12	13	14	15
1 ROA	755	5.89	6.73	1														
2 EMV	755	1.57	3.24	0.35*	1													
3 RDS	755	100	0.04	0.11*	0.46*	1												
4 SGAS	755	100	0.13	0.29*	0.37*	0.60*	1											
5 LNASSET	755	100	1.25	-0.11*	-0.34*	-0.22*	-0.33*	1										
6 FSTS	755	100	0.17	0.08*	0.03	0.26*	0.34*	0.14*	1									
7 FATA	755	100	0.14	0.02	-0.04	0.04	0.22*	0.12*	0.82*	1								
8 NFCO	755	100	9.74	0.15*	-0.00	0.13*	0.28*	0.45*	0.51*	0.46*	1							
9 OECD	755	100	0.16	-0.06	0.09*	0.04	-0.15*	-0.33*	-0.29*	-0.23*	-0.65*	1						
10 LOC	755	100	4.91	0.15*	-0.00	0.13*	0.28*	0.45*	0.54*	0.49*	1.00*	-0.65*	1					
11 LOCSQ	755	100	1000.99	0.15*	-0.00	0.13*	0.28*	0.44*	0.54*	0.48*	1.00*	-0.65*	1.00*	1				
12 DERATIO	755	100	96.82	-0.18*	-0.18*	-0.23*	-0.17*	0.32*	-0.17*	-0.09*	0.07*	-0.04	0.07	0.07	1			
13 FOOD	755	0.09	0.28	0.19*	-0.00	-0.26*	0.11*	0.00	-0.04	0.01	-0.03	-0.04	-0.03	-0.03	0.11*	1		
14 WOOD	755	0.07	0.26	-0.11*	-0.11*	-0.21*	-0.20*	-0.01	-0.13*	-0.03	-0.14*	0.15*	-0.14*	-0.14*	0.09*	-0.09*	1	
15 CHEM	755	0.32	0.47	0.20*	0.05	-0.02	0.05	0.24*	0.11*	0.07	0.24*	-0.28*	0.24*	0.24*	-0.07	-0.21*	-0.19*	1
16 METAL	755	0.06	0.24	-0.11*	-0.07*	-0.19	-0.24*	-0.05	-0.04	0.05	-0.00	-0.05	-0.00	0.00	-0.02	-0.08*	-0.07	-0.17

Note: Asterisks denote pairwise correlations where p < .05.

Table 3.2 *MNE performance and multinationality: ROA regression results*

	O	L	LOC	LOC + LOCSQ	O + L	O + LOC	O + LOC + LOCSQ	O + L + O*L	O + LOC + O*LOC	O + LOC + LOCSQ + O*LOC
	1(a)	1(b)	1(c)	1(d)	2(a)	2(b)	2(c)	3(a)	3(b)	3(c)
RDS	0.29				−5.51	−1.04	−1.69	15266.18*	−104.69	−84.87
SGAS	11.04***				8.67**	7.54**	7.71**	7520.22***	56.64	29.44
LNASSET	−0.34				−0.83**	−0.79**	−0.81**	839.10***	−2.29	−5.88
FSTS		2.98			2.03			3750.83		
FATA		−7.86*			−8.33*			20004.07**		
NFCO		0.19***			0.21***			−136.61H		
OECD		7.07***	6.20**	6.22**	6.96***	5.78***	5.91**	5.58**	5.93**	5.89**
LOC			0.29**	0.54		0.30***	1.80		−56.42	−63.87
LOCSQ				0.00			−0.01			−0.01
FSTS*RDS								38.88		
FSTS*SGAS								−76.53**		
FSTS*LNASSET								0.15		
FATA*RDS								−192.54*		
FATA*SGAS								1.01		
FATA*LNASSET								−8.59**		
NFCO*RDS								0.9		
NFCO*SGAS								0.42H		
NFCO*LNASSET								0.05*		
LOC*RDS									1.05	0.84
LOC*SGAS									−0.40	−0.22

Table 3.2 continued

	O	L	LOC	LOC + LOCSQ	O + L	O + LOC	O + LOC + LOCSQ	O + L + O*L	O + LOC + O*LOC	O + LOC + LOCSQ + O*LOC
	1(a)	1(b)	1(c)	1(d)	2(a)	2(b)	2(c)	3(a)	3(b)	3(c)
LOC*LNASSET									0.01	0.05
INTERCEPT	−1092.35	−230.62	−642.58***	−669.24**	−312.92	−1173.01	−1284.63**	−2362373.00***	4413.81	5286.1
NO OF OBS	755	755	755	755	755	755	755	755	755	755
R SQ	0.2006	0.1862	0.1737	0.1738	0.238	0.2212	0.2223	0.2999	0.2228	0.2242
F DIST	21.52***	15.42***	18.03***	16.90***	18.64***	20.44***	19.79***	9.49***	14.57***	19.55***

Notes: Asterisks show significance levels using a 2-tailed t-test where H < .10, * < .05, ** < .01, *** < .001. Control variables are not reported.

Table 3.3 *MNE performance and multinationality: EMV regression results*

	O	L	LOC	LOC + LOCSQ	O + L	O + LOC	O + LOC + LOCSQ	O + L + O*L	O + LOC + O*LOC	O + LOC + LOCSQ + O*LOC
	1(a)	1(b)	1(c)	1(d)	2(a)	2(b)	2(c)	3(a)	3(b)	3(c)
RDS	33.20***				33.32***	32.68***	33.21***	10941.97**	292.00***	302.17***
SGAS	−0.31				−0.48	−0.92	−1.06	1245.43*	−20.32	−34.29H
LNASSET	−0.72***				−0.78***	−0.80***	−0.78***	174.85***	−11.21***	−13.05***
FSTS		1.46			−2.35H			10531.56*		
FATA		−2.96			0.29			1774.76		
NFCO		0.04*			0.05***			19.66		
OECD		3.48**	3.20**	3.07**	1.80*	1.62*	1.51H	1.06	1.19	1.17
LOC			0.06**	−1.56**		0.07**	−1.15**		232.03***	228.21***
LOCSQ				0.01**			0.01**			−0.01H
FSTS*RDS								−72.45		
FSTS*SGAS								−31.72***		
FSTS*LNASSET								−1.18		
FATA*RDS								−36.21		
FATA*SGAS								19.10H		
FATA*LNASSET								−0.64		
NFCO*RDS								−0.43		
NFCO*SGAS								0.18*		
NFCO*LNASSET								0.06***		
LOC*RDS									−2.63***	−2.73***

Table 3.3 continued

	O	L	LOC	LOC + LOCSQ	O + L	O + LOC	O + LOC + LOCSQ	O + L + O*L	O + LOC + O*LOC	O + LOC + LOCSQ + O*LOC
	1(a)	1(b)	1(c)	1(d)	2(a)	2(b)	2(c)	3(a)	3(b)	3(c)
LOC*SGAS									0.2	0.34*
LOC*LNASSET									0.11***	0.12***
INTERCEPT	−3216.65***	−201.13*	−323.90**	−150.22	−3184.22**	−3263.36****	−3172.83****	−1236045.00**	−26166.60***	−25718.64***
No of Obs	755	755	755	755	755	755	755	755	755	755
R SQ	0.3127	0.0822	0.0760	0.0816	0.3262	0.3177	0.3208	0.4241	0.3646	0.3661
F statistic	12.67***	7.29***	8.85***	9.91***	14.27***	15.22***	20.19***	7.64***	11.04***	10.40***

Notes: Asterisks show significance levels using a 2-tailed t-test where H < .10, * < .05, ** < .01, *** < .001. Control variables are not reported.

46

greater variation than in the ROA regressions. All the regressions have F statistics that are significant at $p < .0001$. In stage 1, we examine the independent effects of O and L. Stage 1(a) shows that RDS and LNASSET are both significant, although LNASSET is negative (as it was in the ROA regressions). In stage 1(b), only NFCO is significant. LOC is positive and significant in stage 2(c). When the quadratic term LOCSQ is added in stage 1(d), the sign on LOC changes and the LOCSQ variable is significant. This suggests that, in terms of EMV, there is a nonlinear relationship between multinationality and performance. Note, however, the large drop in predictive power in the three location-only regressions (stages 1(b, c and d)) where no ownership advantages are present, as compared to the other EMV runs. This suggests that ownership advantages are important predictors for EMV.

In stage 2, when both O and L variables are included, as in the ROA regressions, the results are a combination of stages 1(a) and 1(b), with the exception that FSTS is now significant (although negatively related to EMV, contrary to our hypothesis). Stage 2(b) is similarly a combination of stages 1(a) and 1(c), with LOC again having a positive sign. Lastly, in stage 1(c) we see a nonlinear relationship between multinationality and performance.

In stage 3, we add the interaction terms between the O and L (or LOC) variables. Four of the nine moderator O*L terms in stage 3(a) are significant, as are all the O variables; however, only FSTS is significant among the L variables and even OECD loses its significance. When LOC is substituted for the individual L components in stage 3(b), two of the three moderators are significant as is LOC; however, the R-squared drops compared to stage 3(a). The addition of LOCSQ in stage 3(c) suggests again that the relationship between LOC and EMV is nonlinear.

Discussion

The purpose of our research is to develop a theoretically based model of the relationship between multinationality and firm performance. Using the OLI paradigm, we have developed five hypotheses about this relationship. We explore each in more detail below.

Our first hypothesis is that the three ownership advantages – knowledge-based assets (RDS), economies of common governance (LNASSET) and monopolistic advantages (SGAS) – should have direct and positive impacts on firm performance. We first test this hypothesis by examining the O variables in equations (1a) and (2a–c) in Tables 3.2 and 3.3. In general, the SGAS and LNASSET measures are significantly related to ROA, although LNASSET has a negative sign. In the EMV regressions, RDS and

LNASSET are significant, and LNASSET again has a negative sign. This suggests that knowledge-based and monopolistic advantages have a positive, direct impact on MNE performance. The common governance variable, however, appears to have a negative impact.

To further explore this relationship, we tried a quadratic form of LNASSET (available on request). In the ROA regression, adding the squared term causes the coefficients for LNASSET and its square to become insignificant. In the EMV regressions, however, both LNASSET and its square are highly significant, suggesting a U-shaped relationship.[16] We conclude that economies of common governance may only be a positive advantage for the largest MNEs in our sample.

We next performed a Wald test of the joint significance of our linear hypotheses about the O advantages. These results are reported in rows 1 and 2 of Table 3.4, which shows the change in F statistic from adding the O variables in stage 1(a) and in a comparison of stages 2(a) and 1(b). The F test results show that O advantages are direct, important explanatory variables of performance.[17]

Based on all these tests, we conclude that ownership advantages do independently and positively contribute to MNE performance, providing positive support for H1.

Our second hypothesis is that the three location components – foreign market penetration (FSTS), foreign production (FATA) and country scope (NFCO) – should be significant and positive predictors in equations 1(b) and 2(a) in Tables 3.2 and 3.3. First, note that FSTS is generally not significant. FATA also performs poorly; the coefficient is negative in the ROA regressions and not significant elsewhere. The negative sign is surprising since we anticipated that all L components would be positively correlated with ROA. Our third location variable, NFCO, is the best performing in terms of hypothesis 2 as its coefficient is positive and significant. A Wald test of the joint significance of the three L variables clearly shows that they positively contribute to MNE performance (see rows 3 and 4 of Table 3.4).

One reason for the mixed results on the L variables may be statistical. In our data set, FATA and FSTS are highly correlated although the low VIFs in all equations suggest that multicollinearity is not a problem. To further explore this issue, we ran separate regressions (available on request), each with one L variable for ROA and EMV in stages 1(b) and 2(a). Only NFCO was positive and significant in all four regressions; the coefficients on FSTS and FATA, on the other hand, were not significant in seven of the eight regressions. When NFCO was included with either FSTS or FATA, the foreign share variable became significant and negative. This implies that FSTS and FATA are only important once breadth of multinational involvement is taken into account; then, conditional on NFCO being at its

Table 3.4   Does multinationality matter?

No.	stages compared	Significance test	Change in F statistic	
			ROA	EMV
H1: Ownership matters				
1	S1(a)	Contribution of O variables	17.85 ***	26.64 ***
2	S2(a) – S1(b)	Contribution of O variables	19.91 ***	23.51 ***
H2: Location matters				
3	S1(b)	Contribution of L variables	14.31 ***	2.76 *
4	S2(a) – S1(a)	Contribution of L variables	15.56 ***	5.29 **
5	S1(c)	Contribution of LOC	24.45 ***	7.38 **
6	S2(b) – S1(a)	Contribution of LOC	29.68 ***	10.40 **
H3(a): Ownership moderates the relationship between MNE performance and location advantages				
7	S3(a) – S2(a)	Contribution of all moderators	5.03 ***	11.68 ***
8	S3(a) – S2(a)	Contribution of RDS moderators	2.71 *	5.13 **
9	S3(a) – S2(a)	Contribution of SGAS moderators	7.32 **	4.14 **
10	S3(a) – S2(a)	Contribution of LNASSET moderators	8.22 ***	19.68 ***
H3(b): Location moderates the relationship between MNE performance and ownership advantages				
11	S3(a) – S2(a)	Contribution of all moderators	5.03 ***	11.68 ***
12	S3(a) – S2(a)	Contribution of FSTS moderators	5.64 **	9.74 ***
13	S3(a) – S2(a)	Contribution of FATA moderators	3.87 **	1.67
14	S3(a) – S2(a)	Contribution of NFCO moderators	5.71 **	15.62 ***
15	S3(b) – S2(b)	Contribution of LOC moderators	0.60	10.72 ***
H4: Individual measures of multinationality are superior to an index measure				
16	S1(b) vs S1(c)	Comparison of L variables vs LOC	3.32 *	1.74
17	S2(a) vs S2(b)	Comparison of L variables vs LOC	4.56 *	2.81 H
H5: The relationship between MNE performance and location advantages is non-linear				
18	S1(d) – S1(c)	Contribution of LOCSQ	0.03	8.03 **
19	S2(c) – S2(b)	Contribution of LOCSQ	1.32	7.90 **
20	S3(c) – S3(b)	Contribution of LOCSQ	1.65	3.23 H

Note: Significance of change in F is reported as H < .10, * < .05, ** < .01, *** < .001.

mean, the impact of either depth variable on MNE performance is significant and negative. We therefore conclude that breadth is more important than depth as a contributor to MNE performance, as argued by Allen and Pantzalis (1996). In summary, our analysis of the location components provides positive but mixed support for H2.

Using moderated regression analysis, we can test whether O moderates L (Itaki, 1991) or L moderates O (Morck and Yeung, 1991) or O and L interact to positively affect MNE performance (Dunning, 1993a). Due to the high multicollinearity induced by the interaction terms, generally we cannot interpret the signs on the variables in stage 3(a). It is interesting to note that in the ROA regression all the O variables and two of the three L variables are significant. In the EMV regression, all three O advantages and FSTS are significant.

The Wald test can be used to measure the joint significance of the interaction terms. These results are reported in Table 3.4. We perform two sets of tests. The first groups the nine interaction variables into three subgroups of O advantages and then tests the significance of each O advantage as a moderator variable. We find strong support in rows 7–10 for the joint significance of RDS, SGAS and LNASSET as moderators. We then sort the nine interaction terms into subgroups of L advantages. As reported in rows 11–14, with the exception of FATA in the EMV regression, there is strong evidence that location advantages also moderate the relationship between O and performance. The joint conclusion we reach from these two tests is that O and L synergistically provide additional and positive contributions to MNE performance over and above their individual contributions. That is, MNEs with strong ownership advantages gain additional rents from their location advantages, over and above multinationality *per se*, and vice versa. Thus, H3 is supported.

In order to determine whether a composite index of multinationality performs better than its individual components, in stages 1(c), 2(b) and 3(b) we substitute our composite index, LOC, for the individual L variables. Generally, the coefficient on LOC is significant and positive in both ROA and EMV regressions, suggesting that an index can be a useful measure of multinationality. However, in order to properly test which method is superior (the composite or its components), we test the combined linear constraints imposed by the principal components analysis used to construct LOC. These results are shown in rows 16 and 17 of Table 3.4. Interestingly, the individual L variables are superior to the LOC composite index in three of the four cases. This may be an artefact of the method used to compute the LOC variable. On the other hand, since each variable is subject to some measurement error, it may simply be that a composite variable compounds these measurement errors and the resulting 'noise' obscures the multinationality–performance relationship. We conclude that H4 receives mixed support.

Lastly, we test whether the relationship between multinationality and performance is curvilinear by adding a squared term, LOCSQ, in stages 1(d), 2(c) and 3(c). In the ROA regressions, the term is not significant, implying that the ROA–LOC relationship is positive but linear. On the other hand, in the EMV regressions the relationship is clearly nonlinear. In stage 1(d), the coefficients for LOC and LOCSQ imply a U-shaped relationship, bottoming out well below the minimum LOC value in our sample, and then rising. In stage 2(c) where ownership advantages are present, we find a similar U-shape.

Given these surprising results, we conducted a second test (available on request) using piecewise linear regression, following Riahi-Belkaoui (1998). The LOC–ROA relationship was positive but linear; however, four of the five LOC segments in the EMV regression had significant coefficients, first positive, next negative and then positive. Since the coefficients are the slopes of the EMV–LOC relationship, conditional on all other variables being at their mean values, these EMV piecewise linear regressions provide further evidence that the multinationality–performance relationship is U-shaped for our sample firms.

These results are somewhat surprising given other studies that found an inverted-U relationship. One explanation might simply be differences in data sets, variables and empirical tests. Hitt, Hoskisson and Kim (1997) and Riahi-Belkaoui (1998), for example, use measures of multinationality that are based on foreign sales; since our LOC measure is a composite, this may explain why our LOC–ROA results are different. However, Gomes and Ramaswamy (1999) use a composite measure similar to ours, but still find an inverted-U shape. The conflicting results might be explained by the fact that their regression equations include no ownership or control variables.

A second explanation might lie in the individual L components. Allen and Pantzalis (1996, p. 645) explain the inverted-U shape as the result of too much depth (within-country expansion) relative to breadth (cross-border expansion). Building on this insight, we individually regressed quadratic forms of all three location variables on ROA and EMV to see whether individual L variables were linear in their relationships with firm performance. These results (available on request) show that FSTS and NFCO are linearly related to ROA. FATA, on the other hand, has the traditional inverted-U shape, implying that the returns to foreign production presence taper off. In the case of EMV, however, five of the six quadratic terms (all but FSTS in stage 1(b)) are positive, suggesting increasing returns to both depth (NFCO) and breadth (FATA and FSTS), at least in the presence of ownership advantages.

Why should multinationality be nonlinear and increasing in its relation with EMV, but not with ROA? Our third explanation is that EMV measures long-run expected performance of the firm, taking into account both intangible and tangible assets. EMV is a proxy for Tobin's q, which captures the potential rents from the firm's intangible assets. ROA, on the other hand, is more directly related to short-run financial performance based on the firm's capital assets. That is, EMV is future oriented, while ROA is past oriented. In this sense, EMV better captures the *potential* benefits from multinationality, particularly when the firm also has high ownership advantages. If this were the case, then one would expect that the returns to multinationality might be more closely tied to EMV than to ROA. To the extent that our conjecture is correct, this suggests that even the largest US multinationals may not have exhausted the returns from increasing the depth and breadth of their international operations. The long-run expected market returns from multinationality may be much larger than the short-run financial returns.

Lastly, the theoretical argument for an inverted U-shaped relationship is not that clear cut. The static and dynamic gains from exploiting cross-border differences in resources, markets and capabilities should, in theory, taper off, but the level at which this occurs for an individual firm is not apparent. The costs and risks of multiple authorities, values and cultures should rise as their number and diversity increases. However, as the MNE becomes more familiar with its existing pattern of affiliates and countries, the liability of foreignness should fall, encouraging further expansion of the MNE network. In addition, over time innovations reduce transportation and communication costs, permitting a non-trivial increase in the optimal degree of multinationality for all firms. Thus, one might expect the net benefits to vary across a cross-section of MNEs, with net benefits tapering off for the most multinationalized group, but as time passes, the average optimal degree of multinationality should increase.

CONCLUSIONS

This study used the OLI paradigm to explore the impacts of multinationality on firm performance. Our study contributes to this literature in several ways. First, we developed a theoretical model of the benefits and costs of multinationality, linking multinationality to MNE performance through the OLI paradigm. We reinterpreted the 'L' in OLI as *firm specific, not country specific, advantages*. We decomposed L into three components, two measuring depth (foreign market penetration and foreign production presence) and a third breadth (country scope). Second, using a data set of US manufacturing MNEs in 1990–94, we found that O and L advantages both independently and interactively affect MNE performance, thus providing one of the first empirical tests of the OLI paradigm. Third, we found that a composite index of multinationality was generally inferior to its individual components. Fourth, we found that the net benefits of multinationality are positively related to financial performance, but taper off. Long-run market performance, however, continues to demonstrate positive net benefits even at high levels of multinationality, perhaps because it is more sensitive to ownership advantages. Our research therefore provides support for Dunning's recent observation that 'more attention needs to be given to the importance of location per se as a variable affecting the global competitiveness of firms' (Dunning, 1998, p. 60).

NOTES

1. This solves the level-of-analysis problem that has plagued the OLI paradigm, where O and I are conceptualized as firm-level advantages whereas L advantages are country level.
2. His five components are FSTS, FATA, the ratio of overseas subsidiaries to total subsidiaries, top managers' international experience, and psychic dispersion of international operations.
3. UNCTAD, in the *World Investment Report*, also uses a composite measure based on the average of the unweighted sum of three ratios (foreign assets to total assets (FATA), foreign sales to total sales (FSTS), and foreign employment to total employment (FETE)). Foreign assets are treated as the primary indicator of multinationality, with the top 100 MNEs being ranked by the size of their foreign asset holdings. See, for example, UNCTAD (2001a).
4. Tallman and Li (1996) test the ratio of foreign sales to total sales and the number of foreign countries, however, only number of foreign countries (breadth) is positively related to performance.
5. Note that, unlike Hitt, Hoskisson and Ireland (1994) and Gomes and Ramaswamy (1999), we do not see economies of scale and scope as locational advantages but rather as ownership advantages, based on the separation of O from L in the OLI paradigm.
6. Gomes and Ramaswamy (1999) develop a similar index for their study of the multinationality–performance relationship, but do not compare its effectiveness with the individual measures.
7. EMV is computed as (market value of equity + book value of debt – total assets)/total sales (Allen and Pantzalis, 1996, p. 638).
8. We also tested several other measures of firm performance (available on request). The regression results for ROS (return on sales), ROE (return on equity) and EPS (earnings per share) are similar to those for ROA, as were those for MVA (market value-to-assets ratio) to EMV. Therefore, we report only ROA and EMV. A principal components factor analysis shows that the performance variables load on two measures: the first we call short-run financial performance (ROA, ROS, ROE and EPS) and the second, long-run expected market performance (EMV and MVA), with no unique factors. The Cronbach's alpha for all five measures is .8155, suggesting they represent one common category.
9. We tested whether the three measures were congruent, using Cronbach's alpha. The value was .6538, suggesting positive support for grouping these variables as measures of ownership advantage.

10. R&D expenditures have one major limitation as an O measure; i.e., the total dollar outlays must be expended immediately whereas the revenues from R&D occur much later in time. Thus, RDS is likely to be more highly related to firm performance measures that are long run in nature and take intangible assets into account in the firm's market valuation, such as Tobin's q or EMV.

11. We wanted to use advertising expenses; unfortunately, there were many missing values. Rather than assume firms that do not report advertising expenses engage in no advertising, as do Morck and Yeung (1991, p. 170, fn.15) or delete these firms completely, we substituted SGAS.

12. Allen and Pantzalis (1996) use the log of NFCO as their breadth measure; however, in our analysis the logged form of NFCO performed poorly and we therefore used the more traditional measure. Because of the difficulty in collecting data on the number of foreign affiliates and foreign countries, we collected data for 1994 only. Thus, NFCO varies by firm but not by year in our data set.

13. NFCO has been used by Morck and Yeung (1991), Allen and Pantzalis (1996), Mishra and Gobeli (1998) and Gomes and Ramaswamy (1999), among others. Also, in early tests, we found that the degree of multicollinearity between NFCO and NFA was very high and dropped NFA from our empirical tests.

14. We also used factor analysis to develop a second index, finding similar results although the weights were quite different. Lastly, we created a third composite index that included OECD as a fourth component; however, its performance was marginally inferior to LOC and the Cronbach's alpha lower. We also developed a second composite measure that included OECD; however, it was marginally inferior to LOC.

15. The primary SIC codes reported by each firm were grouped into the following categories: FOOD (food, textiles, leather and other, SIC 20–3, 31 and 39), WOOD (wood and paper products, SIC 24–7), METAL (primary and fabricated metals 33–4), CHEM (chemicals, SIC 28–30 and 32) and MACH (machinery and equipment, SIC 35–8). The 755 observations were split as follows: FOOD (65), WOOD (55), METAL (45), CHEM (242) and MACH (348). In order to maximize heterogeneity across the industry dummies, we computed individual Cronbach's alphas, dropping a different industry each time. Dropping MACH (the largest category) resulted in the lowest alpha so MACH was chosen as the omitted variable.

16. In stage 1(d), the coefficients for LNASSET (-99.193) and its square (0.491) imply that the relationship reaches its minimum at LNASSET $= 101.01$. For MNEs with LNASSET above 101.01 (the top 20% of firms in our sample), the relationship is positive. The results were almost identical for stage 2(a).

17. The CNSREG program in STATA 6.0 estimates constrained linear regression models but does not compute the change in F statistic. We thank Christopher Baum at Boston College for writing a program to solve this problem, which is now available on the STATA website.

4. The eclectic theory in Latin America

Robert Grosse[1]

Dunning's eclectic theory is essentially a 'kitchen sink' theory. That is, it includes everything that could explain (economic) aspects of international firms, including the kitchen sink. The theory does not give any hint as to priorities among factors in explaining international business activity, nor does it offer a dynamic perspective, except as it has been extended by various authors (e.g. Agarwal and Ramaswami, 1992; Banerji and Sambharya, 1996). In brief, the eclectic theory is too eclectic to be a compelling theory – yet it is persistent in its appearance in the literature, and it is long-lasting relative to other theories of the multinational firm – and it offers a wide range of strategy and policy guidelines that remain valuable today.

Why is this so? Despite various efforts to debunk the theory (e.g. Itaki, 1991), and alternatives that are more elegant (such as the internalization theory (Buckley and Casson, 1976; Rugman, 1980) and the theory of competitive advantage (Porter, 1985), not to speak of extensions of Ricardo's comparative advantage theory (Ricardo, 1817; Ohlin, 1933; Jones, 1956) the eclectic theory has held up remarkably well. Apparently there is something fundamentally useful about this conceptual structure. Perhaps this can be seen most readily in an empirical context.

As one broad example, consider international business in Latin America. In this context it is clear that the eclectic theory offers a very useful perspective on foreign direct investment patterns during the second half of the 20th century. This statement should be qualified by noting that the application of the eclectic theory produced different results as times changed, particularly in waves of relatively low regulation during 1945–60 and 1982–90, high levels of regulation between those two periods, and then a major shift in the 1990s with the technological revolution in telecommunications and computing. This brief sketch of industrial-country MNEs and their activities in Latin America is intended to open the discussion to further exploration of the usefulness and problems with applying the theory in empirical contexts today.

THE ECLECTIC THEORY IN LATIN AMERICA 1945–60, 1982–90

Market-seeking MNEs entered the region most frequently through imports, to serve the local markets in countries such as Mexico, Brazil, and Argentina, as well as the smaller nations of the region. This pattern of activity fit well with the eclectic theory, considering that the attractive markets were served by MNEs with *Ownership* advantages such as proprietary technology and marketing skills (typically proxied as advertising spending). Production was generally fully internalized in the MNE, but carried out outside the Latin American region except in cases of low-value consumer goods and some other manufactures that were required to include local content (such as autos).[2]

In a sense one could argue that the eclectic theory also explained FDI into natural resource exploration and production (particularly in oil, copper, and other metals, as well as in agricultural products such as bananas and pineapples). The investment took place because the *Location* advantage of available natural resources pushed the foreign MNEs to enter and produce locally, with their main markets remaining in industrial countries, particularly the United States. This activity often pre-dated the Second World War, with natural resources investments by Exxon, Anaconda, and Kaiser, as well as United Fruit and Dole, going back to the late 19th and early 20th centuries.

A weakness of the theory during the 1945–60 and 1982–90 periods is that it did not account very well for the low percentage of total business done through non-internalized forms such as licensing, franchising, and other contracting. While this part of the total spectrum of operational forms has always been a part of the theory, contracting strategies were relatively underutilized during this time period.

THE ECLECTIC THEORY IN LATIN AMERICA DURING 1960–82

In the 1960s and 1970s, MNEs in Latin America found themselves opposed by public opinion and by national governments, as the era of nationalism pervaded the region. Government policies heavily restricted MNE activities, all the way from initial investment limits (such as local ownership requirements as well as prohibition of investment in some sectors) to limits on profit remittance and on other payments such as royalties and interest on intra-company loans. The eclectic theory could be used in this context to note that the *Location* conditions did not favor direct investment in the region in general, and the MNE production was best located elsewhere (especially in the industrial countries).

Dunning did not pursue this line of reasoning at the time, although later he did explore the government as a key factor affecting company decisions and outcomes. For example, in Dunning and Narula (1996c) the authors looked at the relations between multinationals and national governments. That analysis, however, uses a different model (not the eclectic theory) for analysing government/company relations in the context of a cycle of direct investment. Also, in the late 1990s, Dunning participated in a large project on government relations with multinational firms (Dunning, 1999), but again the focus was not specifically on the eclectic theory.

This is a major problem with the eclectic theory, as it is centrally focused on inter-company competition, with countries largely presented as sources of cost conditions for production. The fact that country governments inter-vene in the business environment to set and change rules is obviously a complication to such thinking. And even more problematic is the fact that changing government policy has led to major shifts in corporate strategies in this region during the past 50 years. The division of time periods in this brief sketch is made precisely to emphasize that opportunities and conse-quent strategies have changed dramatically in response to government policy conditions. These policy conditions have not appeared out of nowhere, but rather they do follow economic conditions (such as recession, debt crisis, boom, oil/commodity price shock) that could help in under-standing the corporate strategies that followed. The eclectic theory is not able to respond to this challenge, because it takes the regulatory and macro-economic environments as given.

THE ECLECTIC THEORY IN LATIN AMERICA SINCE 1990

The 1990s were more akin to the periods of relatively low regulation of MNEs in Latin America, although the technological and financial revolu-tions led to much greater use of mergers and acquisitions to achieve FDI, and much greater use of strategic alliances took place than before (ECLAC, 2000, Ch. 1B). This period is less usefully described by the eclectic theory, because the use of strategic alliances is not as readily fit into the theory as are exports and FDI. Nevertheless, it remains that most business analysts view MNEs' ability to compete as depending on *Ownership* advantages, and that *Location* advantages contribute greatly to determining the pattern of international production based on cost and regulatory conditions. The problem is that business has moved more to a focus on networks of firms that both compete and cooperate, and that may share partial ownership as well as some of their resources. These more complex patterns are difficult to explain in the eclectic framework, perhaps emphasizing the difficulty of making the *Internalization* decision today.

One feature of MNE activity in Latin America during the 1990s that does fit the eclectic theory quite well is the use of 'maquila' plants. Especially in Mexico, industrial-country MNEs have established both owned and licensed assembly operations to manufacture their clothing, autos, electronics products, and other goods. This activity represents a splitting of the production process to take advantage of low-cost labor (a *Location* advantage) in Mexico, Central America or the Caribbean, for products that are ultimately sold mainly in the US and Europe.

Another weakness of the eclectic theory that was mentioned above, and that has been more or less remedied by Dunning over the years, is the fact that the theory tends to focus on company characteristics and those of rivals, but not on the regulatory and/or social-political environment. This is consistent with other theories related to corporate strategy and to a certain extent with theories exploring the economics of multinational enterprise. In any event, Dunning began to look at the impact of regulation in particular on international business activity in the late 1980s, and his work in the 1990s shows a clear emphasis on the extension of the eclectic theory in the area of government/business relations (e.g. Dunning, 1999). This comes particularly from the *Location* advantage base of the theory, in which locations may be preferable on the traditional economic cost basis, but also on the basis of providing better regulatory treatment.

The issue of regulation was enormous in Latin America during the 1960s and 1970s, as the legitimacy of the multinational was challenged, and as many countries followed Raul Prebisch and the UN Center for Latin America (CEPAL) in Chile in laying out highly restrictive policies toward MNEs (see Prebisch, 1950). So it often turned out that importing was a superior strategy for serving local markets in the region, even when cost conditions favored direct investment, because the government either disallowed or heavily restricted foreign direct investment. How could this phenomenon be incorporated into the eclectic theory? Not easily, at least not easily in the traditional economic framework of marginal cost measurement.

A similar theoretical challenge occurred in the 1990s era of deregulation. The Latin American governments not only opened the doors to foreign direct investment and multinational enterprises in general, but they also de-nationalized (i.e., privatized) a wide range of state-owned companies. Almost all of the telephone companies in the region were privatized during 1988–98. Likewise, electric power, banking, and transportation were largely opened to private-sector competition, and government-owned firms were sold off. How does this fit with the eclectic theory? About all the theory can say is that MNEs with the right ownership advantages would be well positioned to buy the utilities and other infrastructure businesses. This phenomenon contributed to the overall pace of acquisitions in Latin America in the 1990s, which is poorly explained by the eclectic theory.

This point perhaps opens the door to an understanding of what is at once the key strength and an important weakness of the eclectic theory. The theory is a kitchen sink theory. Virtually anything can be included in its purview; and the fact that government regulation is not easy to model in a traditional microeconomics framework does not disallow its inclusion as a *Location* factor in Dunning's theory. The impact of regulation may be to raise costs (e.g. through taxes), or to reduce revenues (e.g., through quotas and prohibitions on FDI) or to change the risk profile of a business environment. And it may also be to de-regulate industries and to de-nationalize firms – both of which have led to a wave of acquisitions in the region.

THE ECLECTIC THEORY AS A STRATEGIC TOOL

Another application of the eclectic theory that is often ignored by economic analysts is its use in the formation of business strategy. In this context the eclectic theory has a very favorable record in comparison with alternative models of global strategy. Here, instead of explaining past behavior of firms or of direct investment and trade flows, the goal is to design company strategy for operating internationally. Instead of demonstrating that ownership advantages enable the firm to compete, the goal is to use those advantages to build global corporate strategies.

This application of the eclectic theory is probably the closest thing to a recipe for global strategy that one can imagine. The recipe states that the firm must first assess its competitive (ownership) advantages relative to the key rivals in the market(s) of concern. Then the firm must decide whether production of its products and/or services should take place in a country where the firm already is producing those outputs, or in a new country. And finally the firm has to decide whether to produce the products/services itself or contract them out to be produced by a third party. This perspective is tremendously useful as a strategy tool, for framing the firm's decisionmaking on global competition.

Keeping to the Latin American application of the theory, the strategy of Intel may be a useful example to reflect on. Intel produces computer processor chips, mostly in locations on the US West Coast and in China and Malaysia. Intel's production is highly automated and highly dependent on economies of scale. In Latin America markets are relatively small compared to the US, EU, and Japan, but those in Mexico, Brazil, and Argentina are still significant in global terms. Given the huge scale economies needed for competitive production, Intel only produces in a limited number of locations around the world, and then imports chips to customers everywhere. The Latin American markets are attractive for chip sales, which Intel largely carries out through imports.

When the need arose for a new chip manufacturing plant in the early 1990s, Intel looked widely for alternatives and then settled on a Latin American location, in order to achieve low labor costs and to produce chips relatively close to the US market. The location decision was narrowed down to a choice between Brazil, Chile, and Costa Rica. The ultimate decision appears to have been made largely on the basis of the government subsidies offered by Costa Rica that surpassed those offered by Brazil and Chile. Apparently adequate production conditions could have been achieved in any of the three locations, and the policy factor was the final criterion that mattered.

How did the eclectic theory help Intel? (Or how could it have helped Intel?) Intel's main *Ownership* advantages are its proprietary technology for producing computer processor chips, and arguably its distribution network for getting chips to its customer base, which has become enormous over the years. In fact the distribution network may be less important than the customer relationships that Intel maintains, in terms of generating a competitive advantage. The fact that Intel operates huge production facilities that cost billions of dollars to construct and operate is possible a competitive advantage, but it is not proprietary, since any firm could, in principle, obtain the financing from institutional backers to invest in such facilities. It would be difficult to argue, therefore, that this is an *Ownership* advantage. Nevertheless, the large-scale production facilities are a major barrier to entry by smaller firms.

Intel's *Location* advantages come from its headquarters location in the United States, the largest country market in the world and a center of technological innovation that Intel both contributes to and learns from. Additional *Location* advantages come from Intel's possession of production facilities in China, Malaysia and the Philippines, which enable the firm to cut labor costs and achieve low total production costs of its chips.

And finally, Intel's *Internalization* advantages come from its ability to produce computer processor chips efficiently, with a high level of quality control, and with regular success in innovating new, more powerful chips. Without producing the chips itself, Intel probably would not be able to realize those advances in chip design. Even so, in theory Intel could consider the alternative of concentrating solely on chip design, and then contract out the actual routine production activity. In the final analysis, Intel's

Ownership advantage of the proprietary technology is probably intertwined with its *Internalization* advantage of producing the chips itself.

Now, when Intel came to the point of needing a new chip production facility, the initial decision was made to look for a location in low-wage Latin America. How did the eclectic theory help in the decision? First, it established that the *Internalization* advantage would require Intel to carry out the production itself – but it raised the issue of possible contracting out, and forced Intel to consider such an alternative. Second, it required that Intel consider its own *Ownership* advantages relative to the key rivals in the market of interest. The market of interest was global, and the key rivals were and are Advanced Micro Devices and Motorola. A chip plant in Latin America would potentially give Intel a competitive advantage over these rivals by pushing production costs lower than theirs for similar chips. And finally the *Location* advantage was relatively similar across the three countries being compared, given that their wage costs were low relative to the US and that transport costs would be fairly low to the main industrial-country markets from any of the three countries (although Costa Rica is closer geographically to the US and Asian markets). Government regulatory conditions favored Costa Rica, by lowering the operating costs through various subsidies that were offered. So, as long as regulation is included in *Location* advantages, then the *Internalization* and *Ownership* advantages were neutral but the *Location* advantage favored Costa Rica in this site selection decision.

The lesson here is that Intel did profit or could have profited from the use of the eclectic theory in its decision making. The recipe for make the decision is clear, and the relevant factors were largely measurable. The eclectic theory tends to offer this kind of easy applicability in many international business decisions, from plant location to choice of making a product/input or buying it from an outside supplier.

Probably the largest weakness of the eclectic theory in this context of corporate strategy is its inability to offer guidance on market demand conditions.[3] As with most microeconomic analysis, the eclectic theory focuses primarily on the supply side, and on cost minimization. The idea of measuring or projecting demand for a product remains outside of the theory's scope, though very relevant to corporate decision making.

OBSERVED COMPANY STRATEGIES AND THEIR CONFORMANCE TO ECLECTIC THEORY

Market-serving direct investment has evolved into many consumer and industrial sectors since the early beginnings in transportation and public utilities. All of the major global competitors in consumer products are actively involved in Latin America; Nestlé and Unilever rank among the largest firms in the region, along with several automakers. Much of the market-serving investment is used to carry out final assembly of products (for example, local assembly of auto kits, formulation of pharmaceuticals and chemicals), rather than basic production. When economies of scale are less important, full local production is often undertaken (for example, by the food processing companies, and by clothing companies that import designs but use local fabrics). General Motors has more than a dozen auto assembly plants through the region, using many imported parts but local labor to assemble the vehicles. By contrast, Nestlé has more than one hundred plants in Latin America, typically producing entire ranges of products locally and importing others for local sales.

How can the eclectic theory help in explaining the pattern of MNE investment in Latin America? Table 4.1 shows the 25 largest MNEs operating in Latin America (measured by sales) at the end of the 20th century.

These firms are led by the major oil and auto companies, along with a number of infrastructure companies (telecom and electricity). Additionally, several food and electronics companies are present among the largest foreign MNEs in the region. Beyond these concentrations, moving through the largest 100 MNEs in Latin America, the rest are spread across a wide variety of industries.

The firms present in this group (the top 25) are generally producers of capital-intensive products, more or less half in infrastructure and half in transportation (including fuel). The eclectic theory can be used to explain their choices of location of activity – with R&D for example generally centralized outside Latin America in the home country and/or other industrial-country centers. The local activity in Latin America tends to be exploration and production of raw materials, and provision of infrastructure such as telephone or electricity service. Only the food companies among the top 25 have numerous and extensive local market-serving affiliates in Latin America, consistent with the much lower cost of operating such affiliates than the capital intensive investments in oil, electric power, or car manufacturing.

Interestingly, the *Ownership* advantages of these largest firms tend to be lower-tech than one typically thinks about with respect to successful multinationals. That is, the oil companies and car companies have achieved their competitive success in Latin America probably less based on proprietary technology and more based on marketing skills, customer relationships, operation of global distribution networks, and the like. This likewise can be said for the infrastructure companies and the food companies. In fact, the main advantages seem to be the possession of a powerful, well-recognized

Table 4.1   The 25 largest MNEs in Latin America, 1999 (ranked by consolidated sales in the region)

#	Company	Origin	Sector	Argentina	Brazil	Chile	Colombia	Mexico	Other	Total sales ($US m)
1	Telefonica de España	Spain	Telecom	4,634	5,010	698	–	–	2,097	12,439
2	General Motors	USA	Autos	600	3,895	370	181	7,340	39	12,425
3	Volkswagen	Germany	Autos	1,020	3,976	–	–	6,906	–	11,902
4	DaimlerChrysler	Germany	Autos	784	1,610	–	–	7,352	–	9,746
5	Carrefour	France	Commerce	5,092	4,469	–	–	–	–	9,561
6	Ford	USA	Autos	1,144	2,406	–	13	4,689	–	8,252
7	Repsol/YPF	Spain	Petroleum	7,980	14	99	16	–	–	8,109
8	Fiat	Italy	Autos	1,160	6,499	–	–	–	–	7,659
9	Royal Dutch Shell	UK/Netherlands	Petroleum	1,834	3,658	768	–	–	189	6,449
10	ExxonMobil	USA	Petroleum	1,675	2,625	1,019	948	–	136	6,403
11	IBM	USA	Electronics	586	1,500	–	–	3,393	–	5,479
12	Endesa España	Spain	Electricity	814	466	3,790	294	–	111	5,475
13	AES	USA	Electricity	753	2,214	512	–	–	1,703	5,182
14	Walmart	USA	Commerce	500	534	–	–	3,782	–	4,816
15	Nestlé	Switzerland	Foods	430	1,770	650	105	1,811	–	4,766
16	Renault/Nissan	France	Autos	1,139	285	33	38	2,684	–	4,179
17	Unilever	UK/Netherlands	Foods	1,213	1,734	485	170	524	–	4,126
18	Motorola	USA	Electronics	208	1,000	–	9	2,600	–	3,817
19	Cargill	USA	Foods	2,059	1,482	–	–	–	–	3,541
20	Intel	USA	Electronics	–	840	–	–	–	2,700	3,540
21	PepsiCo	USA	Foods	630	189	–	40	2,673	–	3,532
22	Royal Ahold	Netherlands	Commerce	2,117	811	514	–	–	–	3,442
23	CocaCola	USA	Foods	1,620	395	272	95	891	63	3,336
24	Olivetti/Ital Tel	Italy	Telecom	2,326	308	385	–	143	–	3,162
25	General Electric	USA	Machinery	–	–	–	94	3,048	–	3,142

Source: ECLAC, *Foreign Investment in Latin America and the Caribbean* (2000, p. 62).

brand name, operation of well-structured global supply chain networks, and access to enormous amounts of capital to carry out the investments.

As noted above, the *Location* choice for selecting the Latin American markets seems to be more based on availability of raw materials, or necessity of having a local production presence, than on any criterion of cost minimization. The telephone and electric power distribution companies have to operate with local facilities in order to provide the local service. The oil companies have to operate locally either to explore for oil and produce it or to sell gasoline to consumers. The car companies provide an interesting counterpoint to this location-bound feature – but even they are producing (really assembling) cars locally largely due to historic demands by the governments to either produce locally or lose market access. It is only when we get to the less capital intensive industries such as foods and pharmaceuticals, and consumer products in general, that the cost factor may be determining the choice of local production versus imports in the way the eclectic theory usually poses that decision.

As far as the *Internalization* decision is concerned, this is almost a non-factor in the early 21st century in Latin America. Certainly in South America this is true. In Mexico, Central America and the Caribbean the widespread operation of maquila plants, many owned by local investors and operating under license from the multinationals, provides an interesting application of the eclectic view. The choice of owning the manufacturing facility versus contracting out for manufacturing service is one that clearly appears in each maquila operation, and it may readily be analyzed in the eclectic framework.

LATIN AMERICAN COMPANIES AND THE ECLECTIC THEORY

Another interesting problem to explore with the eclectic theory in Latin America is the international expansion of firms from that region. How useful is the eclectic theory in either explaining the internationalization of Latin American firms or in guiding Latin American firms in their global business strategies? The answers are fairly neutral in both cases. The expansion of Latin American firms overseas has been mostly through exports, which would be consistent with the theory based on the low production costs that tend to exist through the region. Also, the lack of competitive (*Ownership*) advantages for competing in industrial-country markets limits the ability of firms from the region to expand internationally into such target markets – and also pushes them to pursue markets in other developing countries. With respect to strategy development, the lessons from the theory are quite applicable, and they just depend on the characteristics of the firm in question. As with previous comments on government policy, a very distinguishing feature of the Latin American competitive context is the influence of governments on business, so if the eclectic theory offers relatively little guidance on dealing with governments, then it likewise misses this key aspect of strategy development.

By the end of the 1990s, with the process of economic opening largely completed in many countries of the region, the large family-based corporate groups from Latin America were investing overseas as US and European industrial leaders did through the 20th century. These direct investments are not yet numerous, but they are increasing, and they are placing several Latin American firms in the ranks of global leaders. Beyond the natural-resource-based groups, which are generally not family-based organizations, there are dozens of powerful groups from Latin American countries. They include the Grupo Diego Cisneros from Venezuela; Grupo Alfa from Mexico; Grupo Luksic from Chile; and Perez Companq from Argentina (Peres, 1998).

The Cisneros group has expanded overseas with several of its major companies, including the Venevision television network, which is the largest in Latin America (and its US affiliate, Univision), and several telecom ventures based on its Telcel domestic cellular phone company. In 1999 the group jointly invested with America Online to own half of the AOL-Latin America business. The group was originally based in retailing, holding the main Pepsi franchising operation for Venezuela, and banking. After the Venezuelan economic crisis of the early 1990s the Cisneros group has moved heavily into media and telecommunications and away from its traditional food and beverages activities.

Grupo Alfa is just one of the major holdings of the Garza Sada family in Mexico. This group holds major investments in steel (Hylsamex), petrochemicals (Alpek), telecommunications (Onexa, a joint venture with AT&T), and food (Sigma). Each of these firms has overseas FDI; for example, Hylsamex owns the SIDOR steel company in Venezuela. As with many of the other leading groups in the region, Alfa is moving into less cyclical, less resource-based businesses to stabilize its financial position and to promote growth.

Grupo Luksic from Chile has realigned its businesses extensively during the 1990s, such that today the group is heavily involved in copper (Madeco), beer (CCU), telecommunications (VTR), and banking (Banco Edwards). Luksic investment in banking formerly included two of the largest banks in Chile, but under government pressure after the merger of two Spanish banks that were also involved, the Luksics sold their interest and subsequently bought the smaller Banco Edwards. This group has placed a significant part of its resources into telecommunications in recent years.

Perez Companq in Argentina has pursued a restructuring very similar to those of the comparable leading groups in other countries of Latin America. Once largely a shipping company that diversified into other assorted businesses, in the 1990s Perez Companq focused increasingly on the oil and gas, telecommunications, and electric power sectors. After YPF (now Repsol), Perez Companq has been and remains the second-largest energy company in Argentina, with investments abroad in several mostly southern-cone countries. Moving downstream, Perez Companq owns key electric power generation and distribution companies, including Central Costanera and Edesur. When the Argentine telecom sector was opened to competition in 1990, Perez Companq bought a major interest in one of the two main operating companies, Telecom.

The strategies of these firms tend to be based on the following key *Ownership* advantages: knowledge of and access to local markets; and ability to deal successfully with governments, including in the context of privatizations. They also generally possess the *Location* advantage of being able to produce relatively low-cost products, given their production locations in low-labor-cost countries. It is clear that they are never leaders in creating new technology in the global context, but still these firms tend to be able to jump in and manage the lower-tech aspects of high-tech sectors – such as sales, distribution, negotiating with governments, and financial management (Peres, 1998; Dawar and Frost, 1999).

In addition to the private-sector groups, state-owned companies that remain in natural resource ventures are becoming more active in foreign direct investment. These include such firms as the three oil giants: Pemex, PDVSA (from Venezuela), and Petrobras. All three have important businesses in the United States, ranging from PDVSA's ownership of Citgo Oil to Pemex's petrochemical plants in several states. The largest of both state-owned and private firms based in Latin America are shown in Table 4.2.

How does the eclectic theory apply to these firms' activities? The state-owned firms, since they must respond to goals other than just economic ones, probably fit less well into the eclectic theory's scope. However, the family-based groups certainly do follow the logic of serving foreign markets through alternatives such as exporting and local production based on their ownership advantages and the locational characteristics of home and host country. They tend to be more prone to use joint ventures and other strategic alliances than similar industrial-country MNEs, probably because of size and thus financial limitations. Nevertheless, the Latin American family-based groups tend to possess ownership and location advantages

Table 4.2   The 25 largest MNEs in Latin America, 2000 (ranked by consolidated sales)

#	Company	Origin	Sector	Total sales ($US m)
1	Pemex	Mexico	Petroleum	36,361
2	PDVSA	Venezuela	Petroleum	32,600
3	Petrobras	Brazil	Petroleum	16,541
4	Telmex	Mexico	Telecom	10,115
5	CFE	Mexico	Electricity	8,188
6	Eletrobras	Brazil	Electricity	6,115
7	Petrobras Dist	Brazil	Oil & gas dist	5,140
8	Cemex	Mexico	Cement	4,822
9	Grupo Carso	Mexico	Holding	4,269
10	Alfa	Mexico	Holding	4,237
11	Femsa	Mexico	Beverages	4,057
12	CVRD	Brazil	Mining	3,901
13	Ipiranga	Brazil	Oil & gas	3,883
14	Ecopetrol	Colombia	Petroleum	3,860
15	Telemar	Brazil	Telecom	3,478
16	CBD	Brazil	Commerce	3,259
17	Furnas	Brazil	Electricity	3,208
18	Copec	Chile	Oil & gas	3,176
19	Odebrecht	Brazil	Holding	3,170
20	Bimbo	Mexico	Food	3,023
21	Codelco	Chile	Copper	2,886
22	Comercial Mex.	Mexico	Commerce	2,853
23	Cintra	Mexico	Airlines	2,735
24	Vitro	Mexico	Glass	2,718
25	Savia	Mexico	Food	2,663
26	Grupo Modelo	Mexico	Beverages	2,581

Source: America Economia, 'Las 500 de America Latina, 2000', *America Economia*, 27 July 2000.

that emphasize low-cost production, and so they are particularly appropriate for the eclectic theory's lessons.

The use of strategic alliances has long been a key part of Latin firms' strategies. These firms regularly have used equity and contractual links to US and European multinationals to obtain products for local distribution, technology for producing their own local brands, and access to foreign markets. This activity is expanding rapidly, and the eclectic theory may be applied to understand it through particularly the choice of internalizing activities or contracting them out.

(LATIN AMERICAN) CHALLENGES TO THE ECLECTIC THEORY IN THE 21ST CENTURY

This sketch of international business activity in Latin America at the turn of the century, and the use of the eclectic theory to explain it and to guide firms in decision making has demonstrated that the theory does indeed have reasonable applicability in this context. At the same time, the sketch shows that some phenomena, such as the widespread use of strategic alliances, and the heavy influence of government in business in the region, place great challenges to the theory's usefulness.

There is no doubt that the economic factors that contribute to explaining international business phenomena are well emphasized and helpfully understood through the eclectic theory. The difficulty in utilizing the theory to explain 21st century business in Latin America has perhaps more to do with the political and organizational issues that fall mainly outside its scope. There is no doubt that enterprising writers can tailor ad hoc explanations of the networks of company operations today, or the ways in which firms can and should deal with governments, but the fundamental usefulness of the theory is to highlight the three bases of MNE decision making. If those three bases have to be augmented in order to understand international business activity, then perhaps a new theory is needed. Even so, given that Ricardo's narrow focus on comparative cost conditions has been able to survive for two centuries of valuable application to explaining international business phenomena, I expect that Dunning's eclectic view also has a few more years of valuable life in it.

NOTES

1. Thanks to Marie Gant for her excellent research assistance on this project.
2. Exceptions include products such as soap, cheese, and a range of other consumer products where the lack of important scale economies in production and relatively high transportation costs compared with the value of the products called for local production. Firms such as Colgate-Palmolive and Nestlé were in Latin America at that time producing some products locally and importing others from the US and Europe.
3. Ignoring the major problem of the theory's inability to handle government policy outside cost factors such as taxes.

5. A theory of systemic adjustment and economic growth: the case of Finland

Timo J. Hämäläinen

INTRODUCTION

The world economy is currently going through a major techno-economic paradigm shift. The rapid development and diffusion of new information technologies and organizational arrangements has challenged the old economic and social structures of industrialized countries. The structural change, in turn, is calling into question the established social theories and ideologies which were developed in very different circumstances. Indeed, borrowing from Thomas Kuhn, there are today clear signs of a paradigm crisis in many disciplines of social sciences including economics, sociology and management science (see e.g. Heilbroner and Milberg, 1997; Beck, 1998). According to Kuhn, debates among different schools of thought, such as the recent on the 'New Economy', are typical for periods of paradigm crisis (Kuhn, 1975).

The current transformation has not left the established growth theories intact. In particular, the systemic change that touches all parts of society challenges theories which focus only on few determinants of growth and competitiveness and neglect many other important factors (Hämäläinen, 2002). The neoclassical growth theories have tended to assume that the market mechanism organizes economies efficiently. This has led to an emphasis on the accumulation of different types of productive resources: natural, physical and human (Rostow, 1990a). This input-driven approach tends to gloss over the technological, organizational, political and institutional factors that determine the efficiency with which those inputs are used in the economy (Gray, 1999). This is problematic in the highly specialized, complex and knowledge-intensive modern economies where market imperfections are pervasive and productivity improvements are the key determinant of economic growth (Stiglitz, 1989). No wonder that the empirical studies of neoclassical scholars have left a large unexplained residual – total or multifactor productivity growth – which Moses Abramovitz has termed as a 'measure of their ignorance' (1993).

The endogenous growth theories acknowledge the existence of market failures in modern economies and focus on the increasing returns related to education, R&D, learning-by-doing and knowledge spillovers. However, these models are quite difficult to test empirically. The measurement of some key independent variables is hard and the assumption of increasing returns makes the use of standard regression analysis problematic. Moreover, from the perspective of institutional economics, the endogenous theories use a rather simple approach to economic organization – i.e. the traditional market-vs-government dichotomy. Clearly, modern economies include many other organizational arrangements, such as networks, associations, corporate hierarchies, which can be efficient in different situations.

Both neoclassical and endogenous growth scholars pay very little attention to the socio-cultural and institutional variables identified by their classical predecessors. Perhaps these variables have been too difficult to model rigorously in mathematics. Moreover, neither of these two approaches pays sufficient attention to the characteristics of product markets and international business activities as determinants of growth. These factors have become increasingly important as user-oriented product innovation has become a key competitiveness factor and the globalization of business activities has become more extensive (Schienstock and Hämäläinen, 2001; Dunning, 1992a).

Modern growth research has tried to meet the challenge of the new techno-economic paradigm, or 'New Economy', by focusing on the economic impacts of new information and communications technologies (ICTs) (see e.g. Gordon, 2000; Stiroh, 2001; Pohjola, 2001 or the OECD Growth Project). However, it has not been very successful in explaining the economic growth of industrialized nations – a large unexplained residual still remains. It has become increasingly evident that the systemic change calls for more systemic explanations of economic performance. More holistic theoretical frameworks are clearly needed. Without such frameworks, the growth researchers will resemble the famous blind men who were touching different parts of the same elephant without understanding the true nature of the beast.

The systemic nature of the change creates other challenges, too. The adoption and use of new ICTs tend to have a high correlation with changes in other parts of the economic system: particularly in productive resources (increasing importance of created and advanced resources), organizational arrangements (from hierarchical to cooperative arrangements), and product market characteristics (increasing competition as well as differentiation and sophistication of demand) (see Hämäläinen,

2002). In such a highly correlated system, it is hard to tell which independent factor(s) should deserve the credit for the growth impacts of the 'New Economy'. Indeed, if tested separately, one could probably reach similar conclusions with any of the above growth factors.[1] Unfortunately, the data for these other growth factors are usually even more scarce than those for the ICT investments. The established statistics are still largely based on old economic theories and variables that reflect the postwar techno-economic paradigm.

This chapter examines the economic performance of advanced economies during major techno-economic transformations, particularly the present information and communication technology (ICT) revolution. The second section provides a theory of catching up and forging ahead during major paradigm shifts in the world economy. This section underlines the importance of rapid and comprehensive structural adjustments to economic growth during a major techno-economic transformation in the world economy. The third section analyses the structural transformation of Finland in the present paradigm shift. Finland provides an interesting example of a country that was catching up with the leading economies during the previous techno-economic paradigm after the Second World War but is now forging ahead to the information society as one of the leading countries (Castells and Himanen, 2001). The fourth section concludes the chapter by arguing that the structural adjustment challenge is ultimately a mental one and depends on the collective learning processes of nations.

THEORY OF CATCHING UP AND FORGING AHEAD

The neoclassical growth theory suggests that, over time, poor countries will catch up with the wealthier ones because they can learn from the leading countries' more advanced production methods and technologies. The initial scarcity of capital in the poor countries also increases their returns on investment compared to the more advanced nations. However, empirical evidence has supported this 'catching up effect' only among the relatively wealthy countries; really poor developing countries have been falling further behind (Barro and Sala-I-Martin, 1995). Moreover, in recent years, even the differences among industrialized countries have tended to increase. In particular, the leading country of the new paradigm, the United States, seems to be leaving others behind. This suggests that the catching up phenomenon may be related to a particular phase in long socio-economic cycles. Indeed, after the first Industrial Revolution in the early 19th century, it was the United Kingdom that was forging ahead of all the other developed countries (Freeman, 1995). Hence, there seems to be a need for a more sophisticated theory of catching up and forging ahead for techno-economic paradigm shifts.

Historically, the catching up phenomenon has been related to the mature stages of a techno-economic paradigm (late 19th century and the post-Second World War period). At this stage, both the advance of the techno-economic frontier begins to slow down and the imitation of best practice becomes easier. The economic growth of the leading countries is slowed down by the fact that radical innovations become increasingly difficult to make along the established technological trajectories and that these countries are the first to experience the accumulating problems of a mature paradigm (shortages of key resources, increasing organizational problems, changing patterns of demand, institutional rigidities, etc.). At the same time, the core production technologies and methods of the old paradigm become increasingly mature and standardized and, hence, easier to transfer across borders and to imitate. This is a period of decreasing returns in socio-economic development.

Once the techno-economic paradigm shift really begins, the catching up process is further facilitated by the fact that the leading economies have heavy investments in the structures of the old paradigm (established infrastructure, production equipment, labor skills, core technologies, organizational arrangements and market structures). These 'sunk costs' slow down the diffusion of the new paradigm because individuals and organizations are unwilling to 'cannibalize' their old assets by shifting to the new production paradigm (Christensen, 1997). The resistance to change can also be increased by the leading societies' long success with the old socio-economic paradigm that creates mental inertia and provides financial buffers against the accumulating problems of the old paradigm. As a result, these societies can easily become 'locked into' the old paradigm (see also Freeman, 1995; Schienstock, 1999). Only strong incentives for change, such as highly competitive markets or an economic crisis, can break such mental rigidities for structural change. The importance of economic crises for the improvement of socio-economic structures and economic competitiveness was particularly evident in the early 1990s, as we show in the next section.

Hence, a techno-economic paradigm shift gives the more flexible catching-up economies a 'window of opportunity' to pass by and forge ahead of the old leading economies (Abramovitz, 1986; Perez and Soete, 1988). The most advanced catching-up economies naturally have the best chance of becoming the leaders of the new paradigm. Societies further behind the techno-economic frontier will have greater difficulties in catching up to the new paradigm.

During and after a major paradigm shift in the world economy, the competitiveness and growth of national economies depends upon their particular socio-economic starting point – their existing resources, technologies, organizational arrangements, product market structures, international business activities, institutions and government role – and their adjustment capacity relative to the emerging techno-economic and socio-institutional paradigms (Abramovitz, 1995; Lipsey, 1997).

A good starting point (i.e. close to the new 'best practice' paradigm) and adjustment capacity give a society a clear advantage in socio-economic development due to the 'increasing returns' associated with the quick and balanced adjustment to the new paradigm. The increasing returns to adjustment stem from the systemic interdependencies and positive feedback loops within the new techno-economic paradigm. More specifically, they come from the (Arthur, 1994; Freeman, 1995; Lipsey, 1997):

- increasing specialization and scale of production within the new paradigm,
- rapid learning of producers and consumers (about new products, production methods and organizational arrangements),
- growing external benefits in production (emergence, growth and clustering of complementary industries and activities) and consumption (network externalities), and
- external economic benefits of socio-institutional adjustment.

The societies that are unable to adjust in the early stages of the new paradigm, or can only adjust in an unbalanced way, will not gain the increasing returns of the new paradigm and begin to fall behind the leading countries.

In the early stages of the new paradigm, the increasing returns associated with the rapidly advancing techno-economic frontier make catching up very difficult for late-adjusting societies. The new resources, technologies and organizational innovations initially emerge in unstandardized form and, hence, are difficult to transfer, especially across borders. As a consequence, the new leaders of the world economy tend to forge ahead the other advanced economies after major technological revolutions. For example, the United States increased its economic lead over the other industrialized countries in the early part of the 20th century, just as Great Britain had done in the early 19th century (Freeman, 1995). As we have noted above, the same phenomenon also seems to take place in the current paradigm shift.

We next illustrate our theory with the recent transformation and growth experience of Finland.

POSTWAR GROWTH EXPERIENCE IN FINLAND: CATCHING UP AND FORGING AHEAD

The postwar growth experience of Finland resembles the contemporary growth miracles of Japan and West Germany. After the lost war and heavy war reparations the Finnish economy industrialized very rapidly on the back of heavy investments in export-oriented basic industries such as paper and pulp, basic metals and chemicals. There was a national consensus on the investment-driven growth strategy that rapidly brought Finland closer to the world technological frontier and created new technological capabilities among Finnish firms (Pohjola, 1996). The acquisition of foreign machinery and equipment played a key role in the technological catching up process. Equally important was the determination with which the national education system was developed. The growth strategy was also supported by tightly regulated capital markets (low interest rates); generous tax exemptions for investments; flexible exchange rate policies; and the highly profitable barter trade with the Soviet Union. The Finnish welfare state was modeled according to the successful Swedish example.

At the end of the 1980s, Finland had reached the league of the wealthiest countries in the world as measured by the GDP per capita. Her catching up process was perhaps even more impressive than those of West Germany and Japan because Finland was not an industrialized economy before the war like these two other countries. However, at the same time, the structural inefficiencies and distortions created by the investment-driven growth strategy also began to emerge. The deregulation of financial markets (increasing real interest rates) and the collapse of the Soviet Union revealed the structural inefficiency of the Finnish economy in the new techno-economic environment. The fact that Finland was the most expensive OECD country both in 1989 and 1990 in PPP comparisons reflected this inefficiency.

Table 5.1 shows how the overall structural competitiveness of Finland deteriorated from 9th place to 14th place among the OECD countries between the early 1980s and early 1990s. The overall competitiveness index is an average of seven competitiveness factors in the new economic paradigm. These factors were synthesized from the vast competitiveness and growth literature in economics, strategy, management and innovation (see Hämäläinen, 2002).

1. New productive resources (venture capital, human capital, scientific knowledge, ICT infrastructure),
2. New technologies (R&D inputs, innovations, adoption of ICTs),
3. New organizational arrangements (allocative, technical, coordination and dynamic efficiencies),

Table 5.1 Structural competitiveness of nations in the new techno-economic paradigm

Competitiveness rank:	Early 1980s		Late 1980s		Early 1990s		Mid 1990s		Late 1990s	
1	Canada	0.62	USA	1.27	Japan	0.82	Sweden	0.85	USA	1.1
2	Switzerland	0.46	Switzerland	1.19	USA	0.69	Finland	0.71	Finland	0.88
3	Australia	0.43	Japan	0.7	Sweden	0.47	USA	0.62	Switzerland	0.72
4	USA	0.42	Germany	0.65	Netherlands	0.45	Canada	0.59	Canada	0.55
5	Sweden	0.41	Great Britain	0.62	Canada	0.42	Switzerland	0.56	Netherlands	0.55
6	Japan	0.23	Sweden	0.6	Switzerland	0.38	Great Britain	0.5	Denmark	0.42
7	Germany	0.2	Canada	0.52	Denmark	0.34	Japan	0.44	Australia	0.41
8	Netherlands	0.18	Netherlands	0.52	Germany	0.29	Norway	0.41	Sweden	0.36
9	Finland	0.15	Belgium	0.14	Great Britain	0.27	Denmark	0.34	Ireland	0.28
10	Great Britain	0.11	Australia	0.08	New Zealand	0.2	Netherlands	0.32	Norway	0.24
11	New Zealand	0.1	France	0.01	Belgium	0.16	Australia	0.22	Japan	0.23
12	France	0.01	Finland	-0.02	Australia	-0.04	New Zealand	0.21	Great Britain	0.22
13	Norway	0.01	Denmark	-0.06	Norway	-0.05	Germany	0.1	Belgium	0.11
14	Austria	-0.01	Austria	-0.12	Finland	-0.08	France	0.01	Germany	0.06
15	Denmark	-0.02	New Zealand	-0.17	Austria	-0.12	Belgium	-0.02	New Zealand	-0.09
16	Belgium	-0.06	Norway	-0.24	France	-0.13	Ireland	-0.04	Austria	-0.28
17	Greece	-0.27	Ireland	-0.3	Ireland	-0.18	Austria	-0.09	France	-0.38
18	Ireland	-0.27	Portugal	-0.79	Portugal	-0.63	Portugal	-0.75	Portugal	-0.46
19	Spain	-0.38	Italy	-0.8	Turkey	-0.63	Spain	-0.83	Spain	-0.62
20	Portugal	-0.62	Spain	-1	Greece	-0.66	Italy	-1.06	Turkey	-1.33
21	Italy	-0.63	Greece	-1.18	Spain	-0.9	Greece	-1.47	Italy	-1.34
22	Turkey	-1.05	Turkey	-1.6	Italy	-1.1	Turkey	-1.62	Greece	-1.64

Source: Schienstock and Hämäläinen (2001).

4. New product market characteristics (sophistication of demand, product market institutions, user–producer cooperation),
5. Degree of economic internationalization (foreign direct investment, international trade, cross-border alliances),
6. Institutional incentives (taxation, regulation, returns to education), and
7. Role of government (expenditure on efficiency and competitiveness vs. equity related tasks).

The numerical values for each competitiveness factor were calculated as a weighted average of several normalized indicators. The normalization made possible the comparison and combination of indicators with very different measurement scales.

In the Fall 1990, the Finnish economy collapsed to the most severe depression in independent Finland's history. Numerous firms filed for bankruptcy, thousands of over-borrowed households defaulted on their debts and the banking system went into deep crisis. The unemployment rate topped at 20 percent and the state ran a massive budget deficit. Very soon, the state finances were at the mercy of international lenders. The crisis was too deep to be brushed under the carpet; ad hoc explanations would not anymore return people's trust in the old institutions and ways of doing things.[2] It became clear the Finnish economy and society required major structural changes.

In the early 1990s, Finnish firms laid off their workers *en masse*, reorganized their business processes, and considerably improved their productivity and competitiveness. And all this took place nearly without new investments. The government made drastic cuts in public expenditures that had not been possible in better economic times. At the same time, the export competitiveness of Finnish firms was re-emphasized as a key policy goal. Also, individual citizens changed their behavioral patterns: people began to pay back their debts, work harder and many sought new training opportunities to upgrade their skills.

As we can see, the Finnish economic crisis came with a silver lining: it reduced the society's mental rigidities to adjustment. Moreover, being a late-industrializing country, Finland had not become so deeply embedded in the old techno-economic paradigm as many older industrialized countries. Thus, Finnish society has been quite flexible in its adjustment to the new techno-economic environment. Some observers even think that Finland is a leading information society in the world (Castells and Himanen, 2001).

The positive impact of economic crises on structural adjustment capacity is confirmed by the data from other OECD countries in the early

1990s, the time of the previous recession in the world economy. Table 5.2 ranks the OECD countries according to their average economic growth rates between 1991 and 1993. There is a clear negative correlation between the growth rates of the poorly performing economies (in the early 1990s) and the subsequent change in their competitiveness rank (between the early and mid-1990s).[3] Finland, Sweden and Switzerland were the worst performing countries during 1991–3 but 11 OECD countries had an average economic growth rate below 1 percent during that period. The negative correlation between economic growth and structural upgrading is strongest among the worst performing countries but even the sample of all OECD countries shows a clear negative correlation between economic growth and structural adjustment in the following years.[4]

Table 5.2   Average change in economic growth rates between 1991–93

	Average growth 1990–93	Change in competitiveness rank	Correlation of growth and competitiveness
Finland	−3.6	12	5 worst performing countries:
Sweden	−1.6	2	correlation: −0.84
Switzerland	−0.5	1	
United Kingdom	0.3	3	10 worst performing countries:
Italy	0.4	2	correlation: −0.85
Canada	0.4	1	
France	0.5	2	All OECD countries:
Denmark	0.6	−2	correlation: −0.59
Belgium	0.7	−4	
Greece	0.7	−1	Countries with growth between
Spain	0.8	2	1–2 %:
New Zealand	1.0	−2	correlation: 0.02
Portugal	1.2	0	
Japan	1.5	−6	Countries with growth over 1 %:
Netherlands	1.7	−6	correlation: −0.04
USA	1.7	−1	
Austria	1.8	−2	
Australia	1.8	1	
Ireland	2.7	1	
Norway	3.2	5	
Germany	4.8	−5	
Turkey	5.0	−3	

Source: Schienstock and Hämäläinen (2001).

On the other hand, there is very little correlation between the economic growth rates and structural adjustment in countries with growth rates over 1 percent. Thus it appears that only a relatively severe economic slowdown will reduce the mental rigidities of decision makers to structural change. This may explain, for example, why the long but relatively mild recession of Japan during the 1990s did not lead to major structural reforms.

The internationalization of Finnish firms during the 1990s had an important impact on the competitiveness and growth of the Finnish economy. There were major changes in international trade patterns, portfolio investments and foreign direct investment (FDI) flows.

In the 1990s, Finnish exports were characterized by increasing knowledge-intensity. The share of high technology products of total exports increased from 6 percent in 1991 to 21 percent in 1999. Most of this increase can be attributed to the rapid growth of the telecommunications cluster. At the same time, the share of exports in GDP nearly doubled from 22 percent in 1991 to 43 percent in 2000. The rapid growth of high technology production and exports has created a 'third leg' for the Finnish economy besides the traditional forest and basic metal industries. Global markets have facilitated the specialization of Finnish firms into their core activities and narrow product niches which resulted in increasing scale and learning economies.

Finnish capital markets also became more international in the 1990s. The liberalization of the Finnish capital markets began in the mid-1980s and the last restrictions on cross-border capital flows and foreign ownership were removed in 1993 (Pajarinen, Rouvinen and Ylä-Anttila, 1998). Since then, the foreign ownership of Helsinki Stock Exchange (HSE) listed shares has increased rapidly and approached 70 percent in November 2001 (HSE, 2002). This makes the HSE one of the most internationalized stock exchanges in the world.

The rapid growth of foreign portfolio investment has improved the availability of equity capital for Finnish firms and made the Helsinki Stock Exchange a more liquid market place (Pajarinen, Rouvinen and Ylä-Anttila, 1998). The increasing foreign ownership has also pushed the corporate governance practices of large Finnish firms toward the Anglo-Saxon 'shareholder value' approach. Thus many firms have terminated their supervisory boards and restructured their management boards. In the latter, external expert members have increasingly replaced management representatives. The Finnish firms have also created new incentive mechanisms (e.g. stock options) for their managements to meet the demands of international investors (Huolman *et al.*, 2000). The new efficiency-oriented governance practices mark a clear break from the stakeholder-oriented and corporatist governance structures of the 1980s.

Both outward and inward direct investment began to grow more rapidly in Finland in the mid-1980s. However, the outward FDI flows outpaced the inward flows as many large Finnish firms operating in sheltered domestic markets (e.g. insurance companies and banks) as well as some state-owned companies holding monopolistic market positions (chemicals, oil) increased their foreign investments. The poor financial performance of these investments and the subsequent disinvestments suggest that many of the original investments were made without the necessary ownership-specific advantages underlined by the established FDI theories (see Dunning, 1993a). These investments can be better explained with some less well-known theories of FDI that emphasize the monopolistic rents of large firms in domestic markets and their exploitation by the management in foreign countries (Cowling and Sugden, 1987).

After a brief pause in the early 1990s, the rapid growth of outward and inward FDI resumed in 1993. The outward flows continued to outpace the inward flows during the rest of the decade. In the late 1990s, the stock of outward investment was about two times larger than the stock of inward investment. Pajarinen, Rouvinen and Ylä-Anttila (1998) discuss the impacts of FDI on the Finnish economy during the 1990s. The economic impacts of outward FDI are not very clear but empirical research suggests that the cross-border expansion of large Finnish firms improved their international competitiveness in most cases. However, at the same time, the investments also somewhat reduced the firms' domestic employment. The growth of inward FDI had more positive than negative effects on the Finnish industry. On average, foreign-owned firms in Finland have grown faster and they have been more profitable than indigenous firms. Foreign firms have also provided new technology as well as new marketing and organizational skills to their Finnish subsidiaries. All this has reinforced the competitiveness of the Finnish economy.

The role of government in the Finnish economy was also reshaped after the crisis of the early 1990s. A consensus on the new growth strategy began to emerge somewhere in the mid-1990s once the immediate problems of the economic crisis began to subside. Instead of inputs and investments, the new strategy emphasized economic efficiency and innovation (MTI, 1996). In terms of Dunning (1992b), Finland moved towards a 'macro-organizational' policy approach that emphasizes the reduction of market failures as the core responsibility of the government. With the severe economic crisis in the background, this strategy was easy to understand. The Finnish economy was increasingly exposed to foreign competition and could not compete without world-class efficiency, productivity and value-adding capacity. And the popular welfare state could not be financially supported without an efficient and competitive economy. Having a strong engineering orientation, the Finnish value-adding strategy was based on technological innovation. Policy makers wanted Finland to become a true 'knowledge-based society' and the early success of the telecommunications cluster showed the potential of this strategy. As a result, the role of technology policy became central in the new growth strategy. Perhaps as a reflection of the old input-driven strategy, increasing national R&D inputs became the central goal of technology policy in the late 1990s.

This section has described the rapid systemic adjustment of Finnish society to the current techno-economic paradigm shift in the world economy. As we saw, the systemic adjustment increased the structural competitiveness of the Finnish economy very rapidly in the early 1990s. The increasing returns of systemic adjustment were also reflected in a high multifactor productivity growth rate of the economy during the 1990s. According to OECD calculations, this rate, as adjusted for changes in the quality of human capital, jumped in Finland from 2.2 percent in the 1980s to 2.8 percent between 1990 and 1996. The corresponding figures for the United States were 0.8 and 0.9, for Germany 1.6 and 2.0, and for France 1.9 and 0.5. The rapid systemic adjustment, increasing overall competitiveness and high MFP growth of the Finnish socio-economic system supported strong economic growth in the late 1990s.

CONCLUSIONS

The good performance of the Finnish economy in recent years, and particularly the exceptional growth of its telecommunications cluster (with Nokia as the flagship), has attracted a lot of foreign attention. Numerous delegations of foreign policy makers and researchers have visited Finnish firms and authorities in order to find out the drivers of Finnish success. However, there seem to be many different success factors and no one can provide a comprehensive explanation. Based on our analysis, it looks as if a small and culturally homogeneous country like Finland could have a competitive advantage in the systemic adjustment required by the transformation of the world economy. The 'massive externalities' (Lipsey, 1997) and increasing returns of the new paradigm can more easily be reached when key decision makers in related fields can easily be gathered around one table, and their previous social relationships and mutual trust facilitate the coordination of complementary activities (see also Lundvall, 1999). Such systemic adjustment is likely to be more difficult in larger and culturally more diverse societies.

Despite this competitive advantage, maintaining the momentum of systemic upgrading is not easy in Finland. The memories of the crisis in the early 1990s are already fading away and the rapid economic growth of recent years is leading to increasing demands on government expenditures.[5] In this environment, continuous structural upgrading demands increasing attention to the remaining and future structural challenges of the Finnish economy and society. Unfortunately, Finnish economic policy discussions have traditionally focused on macroeconomic issues such as interest rates, currency, state budget, inflation, and so forth (see Schienstock and Hämäläinen, 2001). Macroeconomic discussion does not help the structural adjustment process very much. Much more attention and analysis would be needed on structural competitiveness issues. These are typically microeconomic by nature.

The structural adjustment challenge of the new techno-economic paradigm applies to all economies in the world. This chapter has argued both theoretically and with historical examples that the new leaders of the world economy will be countries and regions that first embrace the new paradigm and adjust their structures to it in a systematic way. The real challenge for policy makers is to facilitate the systemic adjustment before a major crisis. For this, they need good information on the key policy challenges and their changed context. However, new wine in old bottles is not sufficient. The development of new structures and institutions also demands new perspectives and mental maps from decision makers. These, in turn, are closely linked with their beliefs and assumptions, value systems and behavioral norms. Thus major structural changes, such as comprehensive regulatory reform or major reallocations of public expenditure, may require a 'mental paradigm shift' from decision makers (Hämäläinen, 2002). Moreover, in a democracy, major structural changes cannot be implemented without public support. Such changes must be consistent with the widely shared mental frames, values and behavioral norms in society. Hence, the systemic adjustment capacity of a society ultimately depends on its collective learning and unlearning processes (see Hämäläinen, 2002; Harrison and Huntington, 2001).

NOTES

1. As an example, our own study of the OECD countries in the 1980s and early 1990s found product market conditions to be a far more important determinant of growth than technological competitiveness (which included the adoption of modern ICTs). However, reflecting the systemic nature of change, there was a high correlation between product market conditions and technological competitiveness (Hämäläinen, 2002).
2. In psychological terms, the crisis created a widely shared 'cognitive dissonance' or mental distress among the Finnish people (Festinger, 1957; Hämäläinen, 2002). This unpleasant feeling of uncertainty was related to the growing mismatch between the old mental frames, values and norms of people and their new experiences in the rapidly changing techno-economic environment.

3. The change in these countries' competitiveness rank is calculated as the difference between a country's overall competitiveness index ranking in the mid-1990s and early 1990s (see Table 5.1).

4. However, as our calculations for the whole 1990s showed, the positive impact of economic crisis on structural adjustment tends to decrease after a few years. Thus long economic booms create a special challenge for maintaining the momentum of the structural adjustment process.

5. The chairman of the Finnish Nokia corporation, Jorma Ollila, recently noted that the tone of public policy discussion in Finland changed after 1999: 'There is now a general assumption [among Finns] that the world has been completed. All necessary [policy] measures have already been taken. The only thing that remains to be done is to divide the fruits' (*Helsingin Sanomat*, 2002).

6.   Is trade or FDI the more important contributor to globalization?

Zu Kweon Kim

INTRODUCTION

The movement toward globalization is defined as a process by which an economic entity in a country establishes close economic linkages and interdependence in terms of international trade in goods and services, foreign direct investment (FDI), and other economic activities with other economic entities throughout the world (McGrew and Lewis, 1992; Dunning, 1993a, 1994b, 1995, 1997b; Gray, 2002b). Globalization can incorporate many diverse but interlinked activities. These include multinational enterprises' (MNEs) strategies to move production factors such as capital, skilled labor and technology across national boundaries to sustain and increase their competitiveness at the global level; liberalization and/or deregulation by governments to stimulate their domestic economies and attract mobile investment within their territories; and supranational institutions encouraging or enforcing economic liberalization such as the General Agreement on Tariffs and Trade (GATT) and the World Trade Organization (WTO) in trade, and the International Monetary Fund (IMF) in financial markets (Garrett, 2001; Rajan, 2001; Solinger, 2001)

A second idiosyncratic attribute of globalization is that it promotes the structural transformation of firms and nations derived from newly created interrelationships (Dunning, 1994b). For instance, the relative importance of trade by arm's length transactions in the process of globalization has been replaced by foreign direct investment by MNEs. This chapter investigates the role of trade and FDI in a globalizing economy since the year 1970.

GLOBAL TRENDS

Table 6.1 explains global trends in foreign direct investment based on six time periods from 1970 to 1998. Since the first period, 1970–1974, worldwide FDI

Table 6.1   Average value, share and growth of FDI and TGDP, 1970–98

	1970 to 1974			1975 to 1979			1980 to 1984			1985 to 1989			1990 to 1994			1995 to 1998		
	Value US b$	% of total	% of growth	Value US b$	% of total	% of growth	Value US b$	% of total	% of growth	Value US b$	% of total	% of growth	Value US b$	% of total	% of growth	Value US b$	% of total	% of growth
World																		
FDI inflows	18.1	100	29.08	29.7	100	9.63	57.6	100	8.24	128.8	100	29.53	202.0	100	6.62	447.0	100	26.66
FDI outflows	18.9	100	17.16	37.7	100	23.09	49.8	100	–0.94	140.0	100	34.85	233.4	100	5.12	462.6	100	23.46
FDI inward stocks	508.5	100	3.90	633.1	100	4.88	877.0	100	7.12	1305.6	100	10.58	2211.7	100	10.11	3631.8	100	13.80
FDI outward stocks	401.6	100	5.10	542.2	100	7.28	785.7	100	6.87	1215.8	100	12.46	2257.5	100	11.70	3785.1	100	13.74
Exports	501.0	100	28.81	1196.6	100	14.55	1928.5	100	3.67	2347.6	100	12.11	3754.3	100	6.99	5357.1	100	6.53
Imports	512.2	100	27.85	1221.4	100	14.65	1984.5	100	3.99	2407.6	100	12.16	3844.2	100	6.65	5426.2	100	6.68
GDP	3855.6	100	14.41	7192.4	100	13.58	10930.0	100	3.89	15438.6	100	10.30	23883.1	100	7.29	29145.1	100	3.04
Developed countries																		
FDI inflows	14.0	77.8	23.89	22.2	74.5	10.57	39.4	68.5	7.94	106.6	82.8	35.25	135.9	67.3	–0.80	288.3	64.5	35.40
FDI outflows	18.8	99.7	17.08	37.0	98.9	23.22	47.4	95.1	–1.56	130.9	93.5	34.92	208.6	89.3	3.24	406.8	87.9	26.09
FDI inward stocks	355.5	69.9	4.31	447.7	70.7	5.14	623.4	71.1	6.89	954.3	73.1	12.09	1645.8	74.4	9.22	2528.8	69.6	12.57
FDI outward stocks	375.9	92.6	5.44	515.0	95.0	7.60	751.2	95.6	6.84	1154.1	94.9	12.25	211.0	93.6	11.17	3437.2	90.8	13.20
Exports	346.7	69.2	25.36	787.5	65.8	14.84	1233.7	64.0	3.24	1603.8	68.3	15.54	2657.4	70.8	6.62	3623.4	67.6	6.10
Imports	369.3	72.1	27.48	840.5	68.8	14.35	1327.9	66.9	3.41	1701.4	70.7	14.04	2702.6	70.3	5.56	3650.7	66.9	6.66
GDP	2800.3	72.6	14.53	5232.6	72.8	13.64	7840.7	71.7	4.14	11953.4	77.2	11.68	17843.1	74.7	6.54	21349.6	73.3	2.11
Developing countries																		
FDI inflows	4.1	22.2	50.28	7.7	25.5	10.04	18.2	31.5	28.68	22.2	17.2	11.90	66.1	32.7	30.10	158.7	35.3	14.80
FDI outflows	0.06	0.3	121.34	0.4	1.1	31.07	2.4	4.9	115.08	9.1	6.56	41.80	24.8	10.7	31.14	55.8	12.2	7.20
FDI inward stocks	153.0	30.1	2.95	185.4	29.3	4.25	253.6	28.9	7.75	351.3	26.9	6.64	565.9	25.6	12.75	1103.0	30.4	16.86
FDI outward stocks	25.7	6.4	0.27	27.2	5.0	1.51	34.5	4.4	7.53	61.7	5.1	16.50	145.5	6.4	19.75	347.9	9.2	19.88
Exports	154.3	30.8	37.26	409.1	34.2	14.17	694.8	36.0	4.57	743.8	31.7	6.68	1096.9	29.2	7.97	1733.7	32.4	7.52

Imports	142.9	27.9	28.85	380.9	31.2	15.74	656.6	33.1	5.48	706.2	29.3	8.23	1141.6	29.7	9.38	1805.5	33.1	6.82
GDP	1055.3	27.4	14.28	1959.8	27.2	13.48	3089.3	28.3	3.30	3530.2	22.8	6.21	6040.0	25.3	21.17	7795.5	26.7	5.90
NIEs																		
FDI inflows	0.8	4.4	32.28	1.7	5.7	11.23	4.5	7.8	20.92	10.3	8.0	28.32	34.3	17.0	33.66	71.5	16.0	5.93
FDI outflows	0.02	0.1	218.14	00.1	0.3	39.08	0.9	1.8	62.15	6.3	4.6	49.82	21.2	9.1	34.54	43.5	9.4	-0.40
FDI inward stocks	48.8	9.6	1.80	55.6	8.8	3.13	72.1	8.2	6.63	106.9	8.2	10.34	215.4	9.7	18.07	479.2	13.2	18.04
FDI outward stocks	12.8	3.2	0.20	13.1	2.4	0.85	15.5	2.0	6.0	32.2	2.7	22.85	99.0	4.4	25.79	268.9	7.1	20.79
Exports	48.5	9.7	26.53	122.4	10.2	18.51	235.1	12.2	7.37	314.3	13.4	20.06	658.8	17.5	12.58	1065.4	19.9	7.42
Imports	57.9	11.3	29.34	135.5	11.1	15.65	148.3	2.5	6.11	339.8	14.1	22.70	711.5	18.5	11.30	1096.9	20.1	4.73
GDI	229.1	5.9	18.14	475.3	6.6	15.25	820.1	7.5	6.08	985.4	6.4	8.29	1814.8	7.6	11.78	2558.7	8.8	3.67

Notes:

Developed countries include USA, Canada, Japan, Australia, New Zealand, South Africa, EU countries.

Developing countries include all other countries except developed countries.

NIEs include China, Hong Kong, Indonesia, Korea, Malaysia, Philippines, Singapore, Taiwan, and Thailand. They are a subset of developing countries.

Sources: UNCTAD Handbook of Statistics.

inflows and outflows have increased by more than 23 times, to reach an average $447 and $ 462.6 billion, respectively, during 1995–8.

Average growth rates of worldwide FDI inflows and outflows, however, have not been steady during all time periods. These fluctuations are identified during the recessions of the early 1980s and 1990s where average GDP growth rates were single digits except 1995–8. In particular, during 1980–4, FDI outflows grew at an average annual rate of 115 percent in developing countries but were negative 1.6 percent in developed countries (Table 6.1). Because FDI outflows in that period were predominantly accounted for by developed countries, over 95 percent in worldwide FDI outflows, and average growth rates of FDI outflows by major investing nations such as the United States, the United Kingdom, Germany, France, Canada, Netherlands recorded negative numbers, worldwide FDI outflows grew by negative 0.94 percent during the same period. Similarly, negative growth rates of FDI inflows in most of developed countries except the United States and Canada, resulted in only 6.62 percent increases in worldwide FDI inflows during 1990–4 (UNCTAD, 1991, 2000).

The period 1995–8, was extraordinary. Worldwide, and in particular in developed countries, FDI inflows and outflows jumped to at an average annual rate of over 20 percent while GDP grew at the lowest rate compared to the five other time periods. The NIEs recorded negative growth in FDI outflows (Table 6.1). Four reasons account for much of this. First, the financial crisis in Asia in 1997 cut down the continued high economic growth and FDI outflows, mainly in NIEs. Second, the financial crisis stimulated developed countries' FDI outflows by giving them very favorable foreign exchange rates in Asia. For instance, a rapid rise in acquisitions by foreign firms took place in Korea, Philippines, Taiwan and Thailand during 1997–9. Cross-border M&A sales in Korea reached over $9 billion in 1999, which is 16 times more than those in 1996 (UNCTAD, 2000). Third, Japan which has been suffering from the worst economic recession since the mid-1970s, experienced a negative growth in GDP. Fourth, strong economic recovery in the United States, European Union and Latin America could motivate more FDI inflows and outflows (UNCTAD, 1998, 2000).

The distribution of worldwide FDI between developed and developing countries has changed since the year 1970. Developing countries, primarily newly industrialized economies, have been getting more weight in worldwide FDI. Korea and Taiwan started to increase their FDI outflows quite rapidly from the period 1980–4 and other countries in NIEs such as China, Singapore, and Thailand joined Korea and Taiwan from the next period (UNCTAD, 2000). Even though the biggest recipient of NIEs' FDI was still the United States, the downstream FDI activities by NIEs in East and

South-East Asian intra-region, supported by Ozawa's (1995) wild-geese-flying paradigm, were growing (Altomonte *et al.*, 2000). As a result, the predominance of developed countries in worldwide FDI flows has declined from 99.7 percent in the first period to 87.9 percent in the last period, 1995–8. This pattern has also appeared in FDI inflows (Table 6.1). These consequences could represent globalization strategies by third world MNEs through international production and governmental efforts to attract more FDI through liberalization and deregulation.

Another noticeable trend in Table 6.1 is the unparalleled growth rates in FDI, trade and GDP. In the 1970s, world trade (exports plus imports) had increased at the rate of growth of 21 percent a year, which was followed by 19 and 14 percent in worldwide FDI flows (inflows plus outflows) and GDP, respectively. However, in the 1990s, worldwide FDI flows had increased at the rate of growth of 15 percent, more than two times faster than that of the growth of world trade and more than three times that of the growth of GDP (Table 6.1). This changed pattern could imply that the role between trade and FDI in a globalization process has been changed.

THE RELATIVE ROLES OF TRADE AND FDI IN GLOBALIZATION

The degree of economic integration among countries, which is the definition of globalization used here, can be measured by the relative importance of world trade (imports plus exports), world FDI stocks (inward plus outward) and world FDI flows (inflows plus outflows) to world output (GDP) (UNCTAD, 1998, p. 7). For the world as a whole, the ratio of world trade to world GDP has stayed relatively constant since 1970, and the ratio of world FDI stocks to GDP has increased steadily since 1980. The ratio of world FDI flows to GDP has bee increased, but not steadily with two big leaps in the mid-1980s and 1990s. In particular, the relative importance of world trade to world output has been outstripped by that of world FDI flows since the mid-1980s (Figure 6.1). The leading position of world trade by arm's length transactions in the process of globalization has been replaced by foreign direct investment by MNEs.

In the early 1970s, the end of fixed exchange rate mechanism established by Bretton Woods, stimulated more capital mobility at the global level and started to build the global financial market system (Solinger, 2001). During the 1970s, however, MNEs had followed normal sequential processes to engage in international production activities, which are from domestic production to FDI through export based on their own accumulated ownership

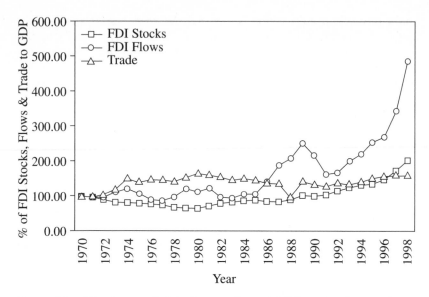

*Figure 6.1   The degree of globalization through FDI stocks, flows and
              trade, 1970–1998 (1970 = 100)*

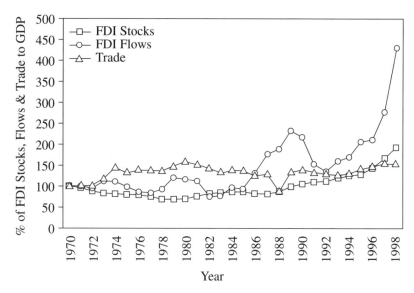

*Figure 6.2   The degree of globalization in developed countries, 1970–1998
              (1970 = 100)*

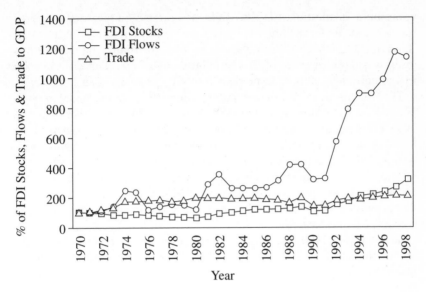

Figure 6.3   The degree of globalization in developing countries, 1970–1998 (1970 = 100)

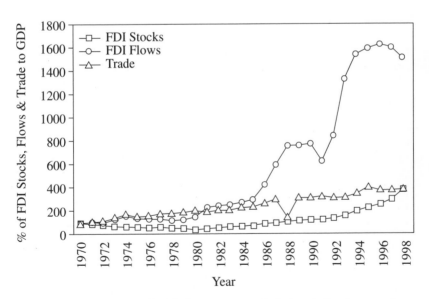

Figure 6.4   The degree of globalization in newly industrialized economies (NIEs), 1970–1998 (1970 = 100)

advantages. In addition, FDI by MNEs had often been regarded as substitute for trade under the product-cycle paradigm with a single product view (UNCTAD, 1996). As a result, the process of globalization in the 1970s was led by world trade instead of FDI by MNEs (Figure 6.1). This phenomenon was similar in developed, developing and NIEs (Figures 6.2, 6.3 and 6.4).

The liberalization and deregulation of markets, improvements in communication technology since the 1980s have given MNEs further opportunities to integrate transborder economic activities (Dunning, 1997b). East Asian countries in particular have adopted the strategy of open industrialization, which means they opened domestic markets to global competition to improve their competitiveness (Altomonote *et al.*, 2000). The strategy has placed relatively more importance on FDI rather than on trade since the beginning of 1980s, except after the 1997 financial crisis in Asia (Figures 6.3 and 6.4).

Since the mid-1980s, the world's liberalization and globalization can represent the environment for trade and FDI in the world economy. Improvements in technology have reduced production costs and stimulated the dispersion of production and service networks. Liberalized trade policies, which began in the post-war years, have further accelerated the processes with GATT and WTO. Unilateral liberalization of national FDI policies derived from bilateral investment treaties and the creation of sectoral, multilateral, and regional agreements, have been prevalent phenomena. In addition, most MNEs have established their foreign affiliates, which are almost stand-alone through the results of sequential processes. For example, manufacturing firms supply foreign market exports at first and then engage in international production through the intermediate processes such as using intermediate markets and non-equity contracts. These kinds of liberalization of trade and FDI have had many implications for MNEs. First, MNEs have more choices in terms of the types of trade and FDI by the ameliorated access to foreign markets and to foreign factors of production. Second, MNEs, which can capitalize on the tangible and intangible assets by using their own intra-firm systems, can maximize overall efficiency. Third, newly created large markets by the liberalization processes pressing on MNEs by the expectation of global consumers, the emergence of global competitors, and other phenomena such as escalating R&D costs and shortening product life cycle, are among the common causes which lead MNEs to establish global interdependencies (Dunning, 1994a). Fourth, the importance of different factors, which had determined the destinations of FDI, has changed. It means that because of relatively relaxed movements of production factors, FDI location decisions do not have to rely heavily on traditional objectives: seeking national markets for manufacturing goods and services or seeking a destination for location-specific resources at the right price (UNCTAD, 1996). As a result, in all cases, world, developed, developing and NIEs, big leaps in the importance of FDI by MNEs as regards gross domestic product rather than trade have occurred since the mid-1980s (Figure 6.1, 6.2, 6.3 and 6.4).

The increased degrees of international involvement of MNEs can also partially support the important role of FDI in the process of globalization since the mid-1980s. FDI by MNEs is a major force to lead towards global-ization by transferring proprietary assets internationally at lower costs and by practicing global-based strategies (Gray, 1999). Multinationalization or transnationalization is defined as a function of the extent to which a firm's economic activities are located outside its national boundary (UNCTAD, 1998). According to UNCTAD (1998), the average transnationality index of the world's 100 largest MNEs increased from 51 percent in 1990 to 55 percent in 1996. Multinationalization is recognized as one of the most important strategies to sustain firms' competitiveness in the world business environment. Higher involvement or higher levels of firms' capabilities to deal with overseas markets are broadly accepted as a major means of increasing their performance in the deeply inter- and intra-active world competition (Wolf, 1977; Rugman, 1979; Michel and Shaked, 1986; Morck and Yeung, 1991).

In addition, the common foci of macroeconomic policies among coun-tries on economies of scale, agglomeration effects, and knowledge spillover give more evidence on the increasing importance of FDI by MNEs in the process of globalization (Button, 1998; Romer, 1986). It means that more understanding of the positive influences of FDI by all governments has created more FDI by MNEs (Dunning, 1993a, 1995).

CONCLUSION

Dynamic business environments in a global context have changed the major impetus to the process of globalization from trade by arm's length transactions to foreign direct investment by MNEs since the mid-1980s.

Other critical points to understanding the true role of FDI by MNEs in globalization are intra-firm trade within their hierarchies and the effects of earlier FDI on trade. According to Gray (1999), the changed initial motive for FDI, developments or expanded capabilities of subsidiaries and efficiency-seeking FDI to supply the parent and/or other subsidiaries in other countries can stimulate intra-firm trade. In addition, a substantial portion of the increase in trade can be seen as the fruit of earlier FDI (Gray, 2002b; Fry, 1996). It implies that FDI by MNEs contributes to the global-ization process in a double way.

7. Institutions, exclusivity and foreign investment

Sarianna M. Lundan

INTRODUCTION

In this chapter we revisit the issue of investment attraction and retention from the perspective of a region wishing to attract foreign investment. Conceptualizing the MNE as a learning or knowledge network, as has been done in many contributions recently, allows us to refine the discussion of investment attraction, and in particular the issue of investment retention. We argue that the 'learning subsidiary' wants to belong, both to the internal MNE network, as well as to the institutional network of its host region, and that investment retention is conditional on the extent to which the MNE can appropriate the economic payoff from its insider status in the long run.

A large part of the international business literature to date has not been primarily concerned with the location-bound component, but rather with the issue of mobility. In the 1970s and 1980s the focus was on the development of theories of foreign direct investment as well as the firm's process of internationalization, with the so-called Uppsala or behavioral school focusing on the resources and limitations that allow for initial internationalization, while others considered the managerial issues related to the mode of entry. Along with the maturation of the investments made in the 1970s and 1980s, attention has shifted from the processes of expansion of the firm more toward the exploitation and further integration of the extant investments of the multinationals. In their highly influential work Bartlett and Ghoshal (1989) were among the first to discuss the management of an existing multinational in its efforts to become a transnational and to achieve an integrated network structure.

As the focus of research has shifted towards issues such as the management of headquarter-subsidiary relationships and the broad area of knowledge management within a multinational, issues related to institutional structure in the host region have also begun to rise towards the surface. While the literature on international expansion focused on the unique attributes (ownership-specific assets) of the investing firm, knowledge management is concerned with the firm's ability to access and appropriate valuable assets developed elsewhere. Such assets often reside inside another firm, and their process of development is of increasing interest. Of particular interest is the extent to which the knowledge-based assets of competing firms are the product of local interaction between firms, and to what extent do they rely on inputs and support from various government-related institutions, such as specialized research institutes or universities.

The increased focus on institutions as underlying the performance of multinational firms is but one aspect of the widening interest on location and economic geography. Dunning (1998) argued that location was a neglected factor in international business, which together with other high-level commentaries, such as Michael Porter's famous statement that anything that isn't location specific cannot confer a long-term competitive advantage, has resulted in a resurgence of interest in issues concerning the location-bound sources of competitiveness. There is increasing evidence that the ability of the firm to take part in local agglomerations of activity, whether in enjoying the externalities from the presence of other firms, such as in Silicon Valley or the pharmaceutical cluster in New Jersey, or whether taking part in government-sponsored research networks, has implications for firm performance. The importance of such localized economies is changing the way in which multinationals approach investment location decisions, and this in turn has implications for public policy with respect to investment attraction.

Our argument proceeds as follows. We first discuss the concept of social capital, and its two institutionalized forms, national business systems and national systems of innovation and their contribution to locational attractiveness. We then discuss the knowledge-based MNE, and the ways in which multinationals tap into the local infrastructure. We conclude by a discussion of the development of trust and the process of integration between the MNE subsidiary and its host.

CREATED ASSETS AND SOCIAL CAPITAL

Owing to its close relationship to trade theory, early theorizing about international business activity considered two major types of locational assets, namely natural and created assets. In the first category belonged all manner of natural resources, such as mineral deposits and forest resources, but also the available pool of unskilled labor. Natural assets were taken to be available in finite quantities and in any event not to be replenishable in the short to medium term. Over time, of course, more and more attention came to be focused on created assets, i.e. the various technological and organizational capabilities that resided within advanced economies and their pivotal contribution to a country's economic well-being.[1] Additionally, a convergence of the available stock of created assets could be observed in the advanced economies due to the transfer of management practices as well as technologies via foreign direct investment.[2] But how exactly were such assets created? Are they the aggregate outcome of individual achievements by firms, or is there a common basis for the managerial and technological improvements observed in a given country?

In his seminal work North (1991) discussed the importance of social capital to economic well-being. Social capital is comprised of the set of values and practices that make up a given culture, when applied to the context of economic activity. Beliefs about the importance of a work ethic, the value of intergenerational equity and saving, and the relationship towards authority all influence the possibilities for wealth creation. All other things being equal, firms resident in locations with high amounts of social capital would be more likely to be able to contribute to the generation of new resources within the economy. From this argument the logical next step was to argue that over time, cultures would institutionalize some of their practices, and that (economic) institutions were thus a manifestation of the underlying culture.

In order to find out if any lessons could be learned regarding the generation of successful institutions, one needed to look at the combinations of cultural values and the institutions accompanying them in a comparative context. Some heroic efforts to accomplish this can be found in the literature (Whitley, 1992a, 1992b). The shortcomings of such studies have been discussed elsewhere (Casson and Lundan, 1999) and we do not go into further detail here, except to note that a careful study of the emergence and evolving importance of institutions in a given national context tends to reveal an overwhelming number of historical idiosyncrasies, which makes the process of distillation a very difficult one indeed.[3]

A somewhat less ambitious, and possibly consequently somewhat more successful, stream of literature has focused on a subset of the question of social capital, and looked at institutions involved in encouraging and fostering innovation in business enterprises. This literature on so-called national systems of innovation has indeed produced some interesting research on the connections between firms and the local national and regional institutions that support them, such as independent research centers, universities and the like (see e.g. Nelson (1993) on the national level and Cooke and Morgan (1998) on the regional level). A well-functioning network of firms and institutions not only encourages domestic economic activity, but also creates an attractive hotspot for foreign multinationals, eager to benefit from the interaction.[4]

THE KNOWLEDGE-BASED MNE AND LOCATION-BOUND ASSETS

Up to this point the discussion has primarily dealt with what might be termed a closed system with countries and regions focusing on the sets of institutions that foster indigenous business activity. But of course there is another equally important aspect we have already alluded to in our discussion of institutions and economic performance, which is the interaction between multinationals through foreign direct investment and the local regional and national institutions created and supported by governments. The more than half century of progress in trade and investment liberalization following the Second World War has led to an enormous increase in the importance of multinationals as vehicles for the dissemination of management practices and technologies, and more and more attention is also being paid to the ability of multinationals to tap into various location bound resources globally.

Evidence of the importance of foreign sourcing of competitive assets by Fortune 500 multinationals, particularly in high technology sectors, has been presented by Dunning and Lundan (1998) and Dunning and Wymbs (1999). It is argued that in addition to size and consequent oligopolistic rents resulting from market domination,[5] one element contributing to the advantage of multinationality is the ability of multinationals to source various competitive resources around the world. In particular, the recent decades have witnessed a tremendous increase in various cooperative efforts by firms to gain access to the various geographically dispersed resources. The patterns of partnering activity present a picture of concentration, both in terms of a sectoral concentration in high technology, as well as a geographical concentration within the Triad. While in the earlier stages of internationalisation, the tendency was for firms to keep their R&D related activities closer to home, the increased partnering activity is an outgrowth of the internationalization of the R&D function, which has also resulted in the establishment of corporate R&D centers abroad (Lundan and Hagedoorn, 2001).

Hagedoorn and Lundan (2001) present further evidence of partnering activity since the 1980s, and argue that there is a clear shift, whereby companies seem to prefer contractual partnerships to joint ventures, and an explosion in high-technology partnerships. However, such trends mask a great deal of inter-industry variation, since the information technology and chemicals sectors alone account for slightly under and slightly over a half of all new alliances in the high and medium technology sectors respectively. Thus in seeking to explain the contemporary patterns of R&D partnering, a large part of the explanation arises from the behavior of the 'representative firm', which they argue is, at end of the 1990s, an American information technology company that forms a contractual alliance with a domestic (or international) competitor.

The underlying reasons for the expansion of such activity are related to intensified global competition and the consequent shortening of product life cycles and the need to keep the costs of new product development under control by collaborating with other firms. Thus, a firm may hope to partner in order to gain experience in a field where its current competencies are minimal, and where in-house development would be exceedingly expensive and time-consuming. On the other hand, a firm might wish to access the locally developed resources as an intact package, and the dramatic increase in mergers and acquisitions in recent years can be at least partially attributed to this desire.

There is therefore an increased interest on the part of multinationals to access different elements of the local network of institutions in their host locations, and to combine such elements within the multinational network of the firm. Recent research on knowledge management within MNEs has indicated that efforts to link the subsidiaries to the local institutional structure, and in particular to the system of innovation, promotes learning within the subsidiary, and to the extent that knowledge is transmitted within the MNE, this makes the subsidiary more secure within the MNE network (Simões, Biscaya and Nevado, 2002). In addition, such subsidiaries can grow to form the basis for a center of excellence within the multinational network (Holm and Pedersen, 2000).

These developments pose two distinct challenges for local, regional and national governments that would like to attract foreign investment, and learning (i.e. knowledge seeking) subsidiaries in particular. In the first instance, there is the problem of marginalization or of being left out of the mainstream of investment and outside the consideration of investing firms. The second problem is the possibility of poaching or hollowing out of the resources that were developed locally and rely on the local infrastructure, but where the economic benefit will ultimately flow to a multinational that has made little or no investment in regional development. These issues are discussed in the following section.

LOCATIONAL COMPETITION

The problem of marginalization appears in the context of an entire continent, such as Africa, which has been left with negligible flows of investment, as well as in many economically less advantaged sub-national regions within the Triad. In recognition of the dangers of being left out of the global economy, most developing countries (and regions) today have adopted a favorable outlook on foreign investment in a stark reversal of the import-substitution policies of a few decades ago. They are now likely to see foreign investment as the only means of upgrading of managerial and technological capabilities within their countries, and consequently investment promotion agencies have been set up in countless regions around the world in an effort to attract high-skill employment to a particular area (see e.g. Narula and Dunning, 2000).

The competition for foreign investment in so-called locational tournaments is a manifestation of the information asymmetries between the multinational investor and the host country or region. The host wants to attract firms that it believes will contribute to the upgrading of skills and technology within the local economy, and the firm is looking for the best institutional infrastructure it can find for its investment. In this context the infrastructure includes both the essential elements of the physical infrastructure, such as a reliable supply of electricity, communications infrastructure, roads and other transport, but also a desirable level of social capital that manifests itself in a work ethic that is conducive to economic prosperity (cf. Peck, 1996). The absence of these minimum conditions in terms of socio-economic infrastructure accounts for the marginalization of many developing countries, which do not have the skills or capital available to engage in locational tournaments.

As in all problems that take the form of matching applicants to jobs, if perfect information were available on the requirements of the job and the qualifications of the applicants, the matching would be quite simple. However, since both sides have an incentive to distort their true value in the marketplace, we get locational tournaments. The more important it is for a given location to highlight its institutional attractiveness, such as the high educational achievement of its workforce, or the excellent relations between firms and regulatory authorities, the more room there is for embellishment, and little possibility of checking the facts. Such a location would be likely to bid above the odds to attract foreign investment, or in other words it would offer incentives in excess of the true value of its institutional endowment. On the other hand, in the same tournament the multinational would play hard to get, while also claiming that the specific conditions offered by the bidding location would be of the right kind for the firm to realize the value out of its investment. Again the firm's claims will be very difficult to verify and thus it is very difficult for the host offering the inducement to decide whether Firm A or Firm B is the more worthy recipient of support. (See also Wheeler and Mody (1992) and Mudambi (1995) on the effect of incentives on investment location.)

For example, in an effort to experience the positive effects from foreign investment, the Northern Ireland investment agency has made several concerted attempts to increase its attractiveness to foreign investors. However, even if the local investment authority wanted to reflect the true and accurate value of Northern Ireland as an investment location, this would be exceedingly difficult to do, since the economic performance of Northern Ireland has been overshadowed by the importance of persistent economic transfers from the United Kingdom for the provision of security (Dunning, Bannerman and Lundan, 1998). The tremendous cost both in monetary and human terms of the 'Troubles' continues to bear down on the community, and while one understands that in a purely economic sense inducements offered to investors in such a situation are counterproductive in the long run, it is hard not to sympathize with the regional agency dealing with the very real need for high-quality jobs in the short and medium run.

From an economic perspective such inducements are futile, because they merely distort prices away from the true value, and consequently misdirect investment into less profitable uses. Although the overall welfare reducing effects of investment incentives are undeniable, there is a case to be made for the strategic attraction of foreign investment in the expectation that established foreign investment would create externalities that are attractive to other foreign investors in the same area. The trouble with this, as with all forms of strategic policy, is knowing ex ante which firms are the ones that are likely to attract further investment and when is the critical time for the initial investment to be made.

The second problem for local and national governments is that even if they avoid oblivion, there is a danger of multinationals poaching or hollowing out much of the core of the local capabilities. With respect to foreign multinationals investing in the area, the problem arises from the foreign investor being able to appropriate the bulk of the revenue that is attributable to locally generated capabilities. With domestic multinationals, the problem arises if they act as the investor, and move out of the institutional environment which allowed them to grow and develop their capabilities, transferring high-value activities to other locations, which from the perspective of the multinational seem better suited for their present needs. In both cases there is a loss of potential revenue to the home country that is not appropriated by (other) domestic firms, or more importantly by domestic taxpayers who are ultimately responsible for financing the economic infrastructure.

TRUST AND INTEGRATION

What then are the solutions to the problems of marginalization and appropriability challenges faced by governments? In most instances betting above your true value does not result in long-term gains. Based on the research on other kinds of partnering activity, it would appear that knowledge of what you are bringing to the market is essential in finding a successful marriage between regions and firms (see e.g. Kanter, 1994). Just as firms have come to realize that a high degree of self-awareness makes it easier to define what each partner is after in the relationship, it is in the interest of governments to determine in precise terms both what they are bringing into the market-place as well as what they are expecting a multinational to contribute.

It seems unlikely that such benefits could be of a very general nature and applicable to the whole economy, but rather that such benefits would need to be sector-specific, such as the provision of specialist education at university level (e.g. the training of paper engineers in Finland) or dedicated research institutes, a sophisticated regulatory mechanism and so forth. In this context it might be useful to apply the basic tenets of the resource-based theory of strategy, namely that any asset conferring a competitive advantage should be rare and difficult to imitate. Thus the location competing for foreign investment should offer an institutional infrastructure (interpreted in broad terms as before) that is rare and difficult to imitate. A literate labor force with reasonable computer skills is not rare, while a labor force with lower and advanced degrees in pulp and paper engineering is. The difficulty of imitation is of course a function of time and effort, but in the case of our paper engineers, as in most instances, the kinds of assets employing the indigenous social capital of a given country would be eco-nomically pointless for other countries to imitate.

The particular institutional conditions in each country give rise to differ-ent constellations of economic activity that can be valuable to a foreign investor. We have already alluded to the importance of clusters, such as the forest industry cluster in Finland or Sweden, or the shipbuilding cluster in the Netherlands, and their reliance on a long-standing set of connections between firms and government. Whether we are discussing cooperation between firms, or any kind of cooperation that lies outside the boundary of the firm, it is nowadays often talked about in terms of a network of con-nections. In such discourse, the network is outside the control of the firm, and the key question is how do you manage the connections, or what is the glue that holds the parts of the network together?

Two possible sources of network cohesion that have received a great deal of attention in the literature are culture and trust. The invention of corpo-rate culture, and the idea that firms could become like churches and foot-ball clubs that people join because they believe in them and want to belong was popularized by Peters and Waterman's study of successful firms that had strong corporate culture. While there may be some firms who can create a sense of belonging close to that of a voluntary organization (at least during an economic upturn), it is unlikely that any such bond would form between a host region and the investor since there are no mechanisms (symbols, rituals) for the dissemination of shared ideas.

The other remedy, trust, is not strictly separate from culture, but concentrates more on the quantifiable benefit arising from the reduced need to monitor agents if you can trust them to behave in the interest of the common good. The focus on trust was particularly keen when comparisons were being made between the Japanese and the American culture, and the resulting differences in supplier relations and the boundary of the firm.[6] Firms were encouraged to build long-term relationships with each other, and to generate mutual dependency in order to increase switching costs. For example, in Uzzi's (1997) study of the New York garment district, relationships based on trust were described as ones where the other party had gone out of their way to help the other firm sometime in the past, but where the reciprocity of good will was nonetheless constantly monitored, out of fear of becoming a 'sucker'. Thus even when anonymous contracting parties become known, trust continues to evolve with experience.

Mutual dependency and a balanced scorecard of favors clearly lower the costs of transacting, and in the case of the Manhattan garment firms, lead to the definition of an inside and outside group of firms, where the firms on the outside are dispensable, and used only for routine, perhaps one-off orders. We would argue that a constellation of economic activity, such as the inside group of businesses discussed here, fulfills the requirements of being difficult to imitate and rare due to the complexity of connections between firms. But more importantly, such groups are exclusionary, and a part of the value of tapping into such networks arises from the fact that they are not universally accessible. Rather they are accessible to insiders and exclusionary to outsiders, and part of their economic value lies in this very distortion of the free market. (See also Granovetter (1995) on the rationale for business groups.)

For a government wishing to attract and retain a foreign multinational, this would mean opening up the domestic network and an ever-increasing role for collaboration with multinationals as inside participants. Since the benefits of groups accrue to those on the inside, there is little moral hazard with respect to the multinational once it is let in. The more fully the multinational participates in the local network, the more it is in its interest to keep the network functional and exclusionary, which in the long run should result in the kind of value-adding collaboration the government was hoping to achieve in the first instance.

After all, as we have seen with the convergence of the technological capabilities within the Triad, we would argue that it is not so much the case that created assets are rare, or even particularly difficult to imitate, but that access to them is often restricted. The most tacit or embedded capabilities are difficult to imitate because they are difficult to access. Trade and investment takes place because conditions are not equal, and to increase the gains from trade, conditions need to be more, not less, unequal. In a world where trade and investment liberalization has already brought production conditions within the Triad close to convergence, the only way they differ is in terms of access.

There are many examples of cases in the literature where the existing institutional structures are exclusionary, and as we have argued in this chapter, this is in fact part of their purpose. The classical example in the 1980s was the difficulty many American firms faced in entering the Japanese market, which resulted in the US government undertaking protracted negotiations under the so-called structural impediments initiative to get Japan to change its opaque kind of capitalism to something more transparent and easier to access for American multinationals.[7] However, as Mason (1992) pointed out, the firms who had gained access to Japan before the trade conflict of the 1980s, and who had gained access the hard way by persistent efforts, were not inclined in any way to join in the Japan-bashing, and were in fact quite happy to operate in the Japanese market with little American competition. Similarly, Guillén (2000) studied the role of business groups in Argentina, South Korea and Spain, and argued that while business groups have emerged in response to deficiencies in the domestic market, their position is also upheld by economies that are not open to global competition. Any multinational wishing to enter the market would need to negotiate access in collaboration with the groups, and a reform-minded government would face the same scenario.

Of course in the context of the developing countries the situation is somewhat different, in that when we talk about governments taking an inventory of what they can offer to the potential investor, in the case of the least developed countries, we are discussing aspects of the basic physical infrastructure. In addition, in developing countries there have been numerous efforts by international organizations, such as the United Nations, the International Monetary Fund and the British Commonwealth, to improve corporate governance and to increase transparency in business and in government (Narula and Dunning, 2000; Lundan and Jones, 2001). In terms of the question of marginalization it is indeed vital for such countries to get both the physical as well as institutional infrastructure to a level where they can effectively participate in a liberalized world economy. Such efforts at institutional homogenization, however, can only save the countries from marginalization, and will not on their own create the conditions for tying foreign investment into a given location.

In some cases this may result in the creation of enclaves of economic activity where the improved infrastructure conditions are more easily met. Nonetheless, such enclaves are likely to suffer from not being rare or difficult for other developing countries to imitate. Somewhat paradoxically, for the developing countries liberalization of their economies along with increased transparency and improvements in corporate governance need to take place before they can engage in the kind of WTO-consistent deliberalization that the Triad economies are undertaking when investing in their locational attractiveness.

As regards the practical policy implications for regional governments, Young, Hood, and Peters (1994) advocated 'targeted attraction and aftercare policies' which build on the indigenous strengths of the area, while recognizing that it is unlikely that a region could attract a 'developmental' (i.e. learning) subsidiary, but that by working with the MNE, one might emerge over time. Similarly, a two-stage process was advocated by Mudambi (1999) for governments wishing to attract (and retain) foreign investment. During the first stage, countries should concentrate on making themselves known to potential investors, and in the second stage, they should bond the investor to the location with a tailor-made package of incentives.

We would argue that rather than offer monetary incentives, the host government can play an important role in facilitating the entry of the foreign investor into the local network, including research consortia and other collaborative ventures involving local firms. This contrasts with the overall provision of high-quality infrastructure in terms of a highly educated work force, for example, in that there should be asymmetrical benefits accruing to the firm that enters early into the network. A high quality infrastructure is necessary but not sufficient in ensuring that from among many potential investors, the investor with the best long-term potential will undertake the project. But even if the 'right' firm is attracted, without a degree of exclusivity arising from membership in the local network, the means governments have of tying the multinational into the local network amount to little more than moral persuasion. Thus participation should not be open for all, but be earned thought repeated interaction and a proven commitment to the region. In such a scenario, the costs of participating become increasingly high for the 'wrong' firm, while the payoff increases for the 'right' firm.[8]

CONCLUSIONS

We have argued in this chapter that in a free market, the locations that are truly attractive to investors are shady corners that are not fully open to competition. The shady locations discussed here offer a specialized infrastructure both in terms of the physical and institutional infrastructure, and require a degree of effort to penetrate. However, once on the inside, firms enjoy exclusive access to resources that can contribute to their long-run competitive advantage. We have argued that any cultural bases for economic performance are only found at the level of the industry, and consequently such attractive locations would seldom encompass entire countries. Instead, since many industries have their own pattern of geographical concentration, these specialized regions would tend to be industry-specific.

The specific nature of combinations of resources and firms contributes a degree of stability to the investment. Since there is an up-front cost for entry, at least in terms of search costs, the firm is reluctant to leave once on the inside. On the other hand, to the extent that entry is restricted, there is little incentive to break up the network, as this would deteriorate everyone's position. Such tailor-made matches of firms and locations reduce the importance of locational tournaments, and consequently reduce the need to offer financial incentives to attract firms. On the other hand, finding a successful match requires considerable search costs on both sides, but particularly on the part of the host government, which needs to know what precisely it is able to offer the investing firm, and how such offerings compare with other locations.

As firms have become more similar in the skills and technologies they posses and the strategies they pursue, investing in location-specific resources is a way to enhance both multinational competitiveness as well host region economic performance. Firms refrain from making long-term investments if the threats to appropriation are very high. In creating an infrastructure that is initially open, but becomes more exclusionary over time, governments make an investment in providing more information about the true value of the investment opportunities, and improve the functioning of the market. Thus attracting investment based on the 'fundamentals' is not costless, but compared to paying incentives, it has a better risk–return profile in the long run. In this scenario, the suitable multinational may not be so much attracted, but grown through sustained local interaction.

NOTES

1. Such created or knowledge-based assets are often based on the exploitation of an initial natural resource advantage.
2. Indeed, one could make the argument that globalization today is in fact a three-way game between the United States, Japan and the European Union (cf. Rugman, 2000).
3. Another way, advocated by Casson and Lundan (1999) is to look at the competitiveness and evolution of the collection of industries within the economy and to analyze on an industry level the recipes that contribute to performance.
4. 'Sticky places in slippery space' as Markusen (1996) put it.

5. I am indebted to the Editor for pointing out that oligopolistic rents are in fact quasi-rents, since they are perishable, as many an oligopolist could attest.
6. Trust in the closely prescribed Japanese context is of course different from the American highly individualistic context, and Williamson's focus on opportunism in a highly individualistic and highly mobile society may not have been entirely misplaced.
7. See Gray and Lundan (1994) on the clash of capitalisms.
8. To an extent, this is true of any investment, however attracted, due to the sunk costs. In fact Mudambi (1998) offers evidence that firms with a longer investment duration are more likely to make further investments.

8. Financial versus industrial firms in industrial and regional restructuring

Ann Markusen

A rich literature on industrial restructuring emerged in the last two decades of the 20th century. Work on particular industries – ensembles of firms which compete in distinctive product and service lines – helped us understand how auto, steel, machining, and various service industries locate, invest, expand, hire, fire, relocate, and close (e.g. Massey and Meegan, 1978; Bluestone and Harrison, 1982; Markusen, 1999a). A complementary literature explored the regional development implications of firm strategies within this process, and among regional scientists and economic geographers, studying firm behavior as key to regional development became widespread (Schoenberger, 1991; Healey and Rawlinson, 1993; Markusen, 1994).

Yet by and large, these accounts were unable to investigate firms' internal workings to explore internal hierarchies and struggles between and among managers with conflicting missions, some of which bear on spatial outcomes. An exception is Schoenberger's (1997) intriguing study of Lockheed's California operations in the early postwar period. Nor do these accounts pay much attention to the relationship between financial and industrial firms, with their quite different profit calculus. Furthermore, the interactions between these types of firms and the state remain seriously neglected, despite ample evidence in case studies of industries and individual firms that state regulation and subsidies are powerful shapers of firms' locational calculus and that firms spend considerable resources attempting to influence them.

The central argument of this chapter is that financial firms, seeking short-term returns, may induce economic and geographical restructuring which would not have otherwise taken place. They may, as well, be more successful in pressing for favorable government policies. In this chapter, I use the American aerospace industry as a template to examine the relationships between financial and industrial firms, and between these firms and the state, which bear on the resulting spatial distribution of the industry. Aerospace is a relatively mature industrial sector that is still experiencing

growth and considerable innovation, especially in the 'payload', or instru-
mentation, guidance and communications systems. It consists of an
increasingly small number of very large firms, the products of recent
mergers, who design, assemble and market aircraft to commercial airlines
and governments, and a large number of small and medium-sized firms
within whose ranks there is much ferment. While it is somewhat unique in
that governments form a major portion of the market – in 1996, military
sales accounted for about 55% currently of the value of American industries' aircraft sales, down from 74% during the Reagan defense buildup but
above the trough of 46% in 1992 (Aerospace Industries Association, 1997)
– and remain a major underwriter of research and development, in many
other ways the industry's experience is quite mainstream. It is particularly
instructive for understanding how the dominance of finance capital's role
in contemporary mega-mergers affects economic geographical outcomes.

FINANCIAL VERSUS INDUSTRIAL FIRMS

The distinction between capital invested in production and that invested in
circulation activities was well made by Marx. Unfortunately, the normative
priority Marx placed on industrial capital influenced a generation of economic geographers to focus chiefly on firms that directly produce goods
and services, rather than those which finance the processes of investment
and distribution. Scholarly comparisons of competitive performance of
Japanese, European and American firms in the 1980s and early 1990s began
to focus on a fundamental institutional difference between the three conti-
nents – that American firms were subjected to higher profit expectations
than their counterparts abroad (Poterba and Summers, 1991; Porter, 1992;
Harrison, 1994). Yet even in these accounts, financial firms tended to get
short shrift. Consider this summary of the Poterba and Summers' findings
by Harrison:

> They found that U.S. investors tend to demand considerably higher minimum
> acceptable rates of return for their capital – so-called hurdle rates – than do their
> foreign competitors. This behavior on the part of American investors is way out
> of whack . . . (1994: 184)

This statement not only confuses the agents of demand and supply for
capital, comparing investors to foreign competitors (it should be foreign
investors) and assumes that all investors in American firms are Americans,
but reads as if there are no firms occupying the space between atomistic
investors and firms who borrow money capital.

In reality, there are a large number of firms operating in the market for money capital. Industrial, construction or service firms who wish to borrow money to innovate, expand, acquire existing firms, build a new plant or office tower, or cover inventory turn to financial firms for the cash to do so, which can be procured through diverse means: initial or new stock offerings, bonds, loans of various sorts. They also use financial firms' services to invest retained earnings in anticipation of future investments or for short-term asset management. At the peak of this hierarchy '. . . are the "bulge bracket" underwriting and trading monsters like Morgan Stanley and Goldman Sachs. They bring forth new securities issues to their customers, and trade them for their own and their customers' accounts' (Henwood, 1997: 82).

Simply put, the fundamental difference between the two types of firms is that financial firms make money on the turnover of money capital and assets, while industrial and service firms make money by successfully creating and selling products and services which more than cover the costs of doing so. The short-termism so heavily criticized in the competitiveness literature is ascribable to the separation, or externalization, of finance from management in the American industrial firm, and its placement in a separate tier of firms. In Europe and Asia, at least to date, finance and management functions have been more heavily intertwined institutionally. This is about to change, which is why it is particularly important for scholars of regional development to understand the distinction. The huge megamergers now beginning to unfold in Europe are the handiwork of investment banking practices much like those that have dominated in the US for a decade or more.

The size of the financial sector is significant and has been growing over the past two decades. In 1991, the finance, insurance and real estate sector (FIRE) surpassed manufacturing's share of American GDP, and by 1993, accounted for $1.2 trillion in output, compared with manufacturing's $1.1 trillion.[1] In 1992, FIRE accounted for 16% of corporate revenue but 37% of US profits, a share which rose steadily from 14% in 1980 and 25% in 1985. Manufacturing profit shares fell concommitantly, from 53% in 1980 to 36% in 1992 (Henwood, 1997: 79–80). These figures suggest the ascendancy of financial capital over industrial capital in this period. A financial crisis might again alter these shares, but for the period in question, one of dramatic geographical industrial restructuring, this shift cannot be ignored.

This shift is the product of institutional changes associated with the now well-documented 'shareholder revolt' that has accelerated the trend toward the externalization of capital over internal corporate redeployment of retained earnings, reinforced via the transformation of managers into owners by tying executive compensation to stock performance (Dymski,

Epstein and Pollin, 1993). This shift in managerial affinity has had a corrosive effect on longer-term investment strategies, because current managers are tempted to side with stockholders in cashing out, taking their compensation today and reinvesting it elsewhere. In an example for the aerospace industry, CEO William Anders did just this in downsizing General Dynamics and was rewarded with compensation in excess of $200 million for a single year, catapulting him onto the front cover of *Business Week* as one of the nation's top ten in executive compensation. Whether or not industrial firms are actually better or worse allocators of financial capital than are external markets is a hotly debated issue in the finance literature, with inconclusive evidence (for a review, see Markusen, 1999b).

FADS AND FASHION IN THE FINANCIAL SECTOR

Finance capital would not be so significant if it operated according to neoclassical economists' and business school financial theorists' models. Then it would simply be quickening the pace of regional restructuring that would occur anyway. But there is ample empirical evidence that it does not. Rather than simply keeping managers in line, so that they maximize profits and forgo satisficing and empire-building, financial firms engage in extensive market manipulation, bribery to secure insider information, political influence-peddling to alter tax and regulatory mechanisms, and clever use of the press. 'They view investing as war', Henwood (1997: 105) cites Norm Zadeh, who rates money manager performance, as saying, 'and in war, all is fair'.

Financial industry leaders work to create 'fashions' in investment strategies which attract herding behavior on the part of others and can dominate for a decade or more. Investment bankers, in particular, populate a highly concentrated industry where lead firms wield considerable market power. Their clustering in major money market centers like Wall Street is tied to the relative absence of full information, free market competition in this segment of the capital market and the significance of consensus-forming face-to-face interactions.

Frequent merger waves over the past century and a half bear witness to this process of financial fashion-fashioning (Brealey and Myers, 1991). The buzz words in this most recent era are 'core competency' (a concept many economic development-minded scholars have adopted without reflection) and 'pure play'. Beginning in the mid-1980s, conglomerate firms, whose creation had dominated the 1970s merger wave (and provided billions in financial firm profits) were discredited, and a rash of hostile takeovers and divestitures ensued (further enriching investment banks).

For short-term returns, financial firms may induce economic geographical outcomes which would not have happened in the absence of their machinations. This can be illustrated in the American aerospace industry, where aerospace firms in the 1990s were subjected to intense merger pressures from investment banking firms. Just at a point when long-term minded aerospace managers awoke with a hangover from the Reagan military spending bubble (an increase in procurement spending of more than 70% in real terms from 1980 to 1989) and were attempting to move engineers, technologies and high tech facilities into commercial product lines, from satellites to intelligent highways and smart cars, Wall Street counseled the opposite. Rather than conversion strategies, aerospace firms, they claimed, should cope with the rapid decline of defense spending by divesting themselves of commercial divisions and acquiring other defense firms, transforming themselves into specialized 'pure play' defense giants (Oden, 1999b; Markusen, 1999b).

The Wall Street firms were able to succeed in their campaign through their extensive control of financial research, investor publications and influence over the financial and trade association press. The latter had written confidently about an era of defense conversion in the early 1990s (Miller, 1991; Morrocco, 1991; Schine, 1991; Velocci, 1991) and were taken aback by the 'pure play' offensive. Members of large consulting firms began writing their own articles in the business press and talking to journalists about the futility of defense conversion and uncertain returns to diversification (Lundquist, 1992).[2] They pooh-poohed conversion, citing one or two anecdotes of failures in the past, and counseled narrowing firm focus to profitable defense activities and spinning off units not closely related to these. Less publicly visible but already active in negotiating takeover deals were Wall Street investment banking houses such as Bear Stearns, CS First Boston, Saloman Brothers and Merrill Lynch.

Beginning in 1993, both analysts and the press began to use language quite reminiscent of game theory to characterize the merger dynamic. Two Booz/Allen vice presidents warned against 'fence sitters' in a 1993 trade press account on defense mergers.[3] 'The notion that management can wait out the coming consolidation is one of the popular myths among many industry executives', they argued, forecasting a rapid surge in activity lasting only a few years, during which 'the most attractive partners are taken out of action early in the process'. Citing consolidation in other industries like printing and publishing, they went on, 'We expect a similar pattern to evolve in aerospace, with preemptive moves by aggressive companies foreclosing opportunities for others.' Such mergers 'could establish world-class leaders and lock out other players from the first tier. We believe the acquisition lull in recent months represents the eye of the hurricane and will precipitate a sharp increase in consolidation activity' (Markusen, 1999b: 131). By early 1996, articles were appearing under headlines such as 'Mergers Becoming a Business Imperative' (*Jane's Defence Weekly*, 1996).

The Wall Street challenge was replicated in the corporate board room, where powerful shareholders pressed for higher short-term returns promised by the investment bank formula, and even in the corporate suite, where Chief Financial Officers, recent products of business schools and financial firms, fought with Chief Executives Officers who were engineers who had risen through the ranks. They were successful. Elsewhere, I show the sequence of defense-specialized giant-generating divestitures and mergers chalked up by the investment bankers, beginning with family-dominated General Dynamics, furthered through the meteoric success of LBO expert Bernard Schwartz of Loral, and capped by the capitulation of the previously resistant Lockheed/Martin top management (Markusen, 1999b). By 1999, the numbers of top defense contractors imploded from more than fifteen to four, all of whom were more defense dependent than at the outset of the decade (Markusen, 1999b, 1999c). The largest US contractors have remained highly defense dependent, while Boeing and Raytheon, by acquiring large military divisions or entire firms, have become more so, as have firms like Litton who have spun off their civilian divisions and new firms like Alliant Tech, created when Honeywell spun off its military work (Markusen, 1997). As we show below, although these mergers have not achieved the claims made for them, their emergence has dramatically reshaped aerospace industrial and managerial geography.

What is the evidence for the superiority of 'focus' or 'pure play' over conglomerate firm form? Although a number of business school theorists have written compelling theoretical rationales for the advantages of focus (see the review in Denis, Denis and Sarin, 1997), the empirical evidence is quite mixed. A number of studies have been done comparing conglomerate to focused firm performance, and most conclude that the latter have generated greater stockholder returns (Berger and Ofek, 1996; Comment and Jarrell, 1995; Denis, Denis and Sarin, 1997; Liebeskind and Opler, 1994). However, these studies rely on a controversial indicator of performance – stock values. The link between stock market prices and economic efficiency is tenuous, however, and relying on stock market signals may lead to suboptimal investments (Dow and Gorton, 1997). The value of a stock is not a measure of return to investment, since it is an evaluation of the entire firm including proprietary intangible capital rather than of a marginal investment. Moreover, stock prices do not necessarily reflect all available information so that managers may underinvest relative to the rate indicated by the stock price.

Nor do all scholars agree on the inferiority of conglomerates. In a careful historical study, Servaes (1996) shows that in the past, conglomerate mergers did not suffer a diversification discount, suggesting that a changing Wall Street consensus holds sway over stock market responses (see also Matsusaka, 1993).

I have gone to some lengths in this section to demonstrate that both in the finance literature and in our own research on the aerospace industry in the 1990s, financial firms with short-term profits in mind have dominated industrial firm strategies, suppressing longer-term investment and diversification options. The strategies dictated by the Wall Street analysts and investment bankers were embedded in a consensus about appropriate firm form that was temporal and with hindsight, unwarranted. In what follows, I demonstrate both the spatial consequences of this fad-driven restructuring and the ultimate failure of the strategy on its own terms, except for the generation of excessive short-term profits.

THE SPATIAL CONSEQUENCES OF FINANCIAL FIRMS' STRATEGIES

The American defense industry, within which the aerospace sector forms the largest and growing share, faced prime contract cuts of 64% in real terms between 1987 and 1996. For reasons which we have documented extensively elsewhere (Markusen *et al.*, 1991; Markusen, 1991), defense capacity was heavily concentrated in the 'Gunbelt', a crescent running from New England through the south and west coasts. In the rash of downsizing and plant closings which ensued, two spatial shifts were pronounced.

First, operations in relatively expensive locations such as the North East and Los Angeles were disproportionally shuttered in favor of relocations and existing operations in the south and mountain states. In Oden's (1999a) analysis, he shows that while all regions lost prime contracts, the negative regional shift component was highest for New York, California and Massachusetts, in that order (Table 8.1). In contrast, the South Atlantic, East South Central and Mountain states all experienced net positive regional shifts.

Second, several key corporate headquarters and a disproportionate share of new high tech aerospace and electronics activity relocated to the greater Washington, DC area, the latter principally to northern Virginia. Virginia was the only state to actually increase its prime contract receipts in this period (Table 8.1). General Dynamics moved its headquarters from St. Louis to the DC area, and the merged Lockheed/Martin shuttered its historic Los Angeles headquarters and consolidated corporate management in

Table 8.1   Changes in DoD prime contract awards by selected states and region (in the billions of real 1994 dollars)

	Average contracts 1988–87	Average contracts 1995–96	Change in average from 1986–87 to 1995–96		
			Total loss in real contracts	Change due to decline in national contracts	Changes due to regional shift
Connecticut	6.6	2.6	−4.0	−2.5	−1.5
Massachusetts	11.0	4.6	−6.4	−4.2	−2.3
NEW ENGLAND	20.0	9.0	−10.8	−7.5	−3.3
New Jersey	4.1	2.7	−1.4	−1.5	0.1
New York	12.3	3.4	−9.0	−4.7	−4.3
Pennsylvania	5.1	3.2	−1.8	−1.9	0.1
MIDDLE ATLANTIC	21.5	9.3	−12.2	−8.1	−4.1
Illinois	2.2	1.2	−1.1	−0.8	−0.2
Michigan	2.7	1.2	−1.4	−1.0	−0.4
Ohio	6.1	2.6	−3.6	−2.3	−1.3
EAST NORTH CENTRAL	15.2	6.8	−8.4	−5.7	−2.7
Minnesota	3.0	1.0	−2.0	−1.1	−0.9
Missouri	7.3	6.2	−1.0	−2.7	1.7
WEST NORTH CENTRAL	13.7	8.9	−4.8	−5.2	0.4
District of Columbia	1.4	1.2	−0.2	−0.5	0.4
Florida	7.2	5.8	−1.4	−2.7	1.3
Georgia	4.6	3.6	−1.0	−1.7	0.8
Maryland	5.9	4.2	−1.7	−2.2	0.5
Virginia	8.3	10.5	2.2	−3.1	5.3
SOUTH ATLANTIC	29.9	27.9	−1.9	−11.3	9.4
Alabama	2.0	1.8	−0.2	−0.8	0.5
Mississippi	1.9	1.7	−0.2	−0.7	0.5
EAST SOUTH CENTRAL	5.9	5.2	−0.7	−2.2	1.6
Louisiana	1.9	1.0	−0.8	−0.7	−0.1
Texas	12.3	8.6	−3.7	−4.7	1.0
WEST SOUTH CENTRAL	16.1	10.6	−5.5	−6.1	0.6
Arizona	3.7	2.6	−1.1	−1.4	0.3
Colorado	3.0	2.0	−0.8	−1.1	0.3
MOUNTAIN	9.0	6.3	−2.7	−3.4	0.7
California	33.0	17.6	−15.4	−12.5	−3.0
Washington	3.5	2.3	−1.3	−1.3	0.1
PACIFIC	38.2	21.4	−16.9	−14.4	−2.4
US TOTAL	169.3	105.4	−63.9	−63.9	0.0

Sources: Oden (2000, p. 28, Table 1). Prime contract data from *DoD Prime Contract Awards by Region and State* (P06) Fiscal Years 1985, 1986, 1987 and Fiscal Years 1994, 1995, 1996. Price deflators are from the National Defense Budget Estimates for FY 1998, Tables 5–8 Procurement Category.

Bethesda, Maryland. Several large (more than a $1 billion in annual sales) high tech defense service firms – BDM Corporation and SAIC Corporation – have the bulk of their employment in northern Virginia's 'Pentagon City' and nearby suburbs.

Financial firm pressures do not account for all of this spatial restructuring. Changes in the composition of defense spending protecting military readiness and operations at the expense of new and existing weapons systems favored regions specializing in troop provisioning, ongoing tactical aircraft programs, maintenance and engineering and information services at the expense of advanced weapons research and production centers (Oden, 1999b: 29). However, in intensive research on four aerospace regions, managers reported intense financial mandates to cut costs explicitly by moving and consolidating production in lower cost regions. Grumman responded to Navy aircraft contract cuts by transferring its remaining aircraft manufacture and upgrade work to lower-cost facilities in Louisiana and Florida in the early 1990s (Oden, Mueller and Goldberg, 1994). From Los Angeles, Hughes moved all its tactical missile work to Arizona, Lockheed relocated aircraft production to Georgia, and McDonnell Douglas transferred roughly 3800 C-17 aircraft jobs from Los Angeles to lower cost St. Louis (Oden *et al.*, 1996). Cost-cutting discipline helps to explain why Los Angeles and Long Island suffered deeper defense-related industrial job loss than St. Louis (Table 8.2). As recently as the summer of 1998, a business school intern at one of the top investment banking houses reported hearing his boss dictate to Boeing that it would have to lay off tens of thousands of workers before the firm would reverse its publicly proclaimed negative evaluation of Boeing's stock.

Table 8.2   Employment in defense-related manufacturing in four United States aerospace regions, 1989–1994

	Total employment 1989	Total employment 1994	Percentage change	Share of national 1989	Share of national 1994
Los Angeles–Long Beach	262749	133067	−49.4	11.2	7.6
Nassau–Suffolk, NY	58437	34062	−41.7	2.5	1.9
St. Louis	47678	31762	−33.4	2.0	1.8
Seattle–Bellevue–Everett	103887	83749	−19.4	4.4	4.8
Total four regions	472751	282640	−40.2	20.1	16.1
Total US aerospace	2348909	1753360	−25.4	–	–

Source: Oden (2000, p. 33, Table 3). Based on County Business Patterns data as compiled and estimated by Andrew Isserman, University of West Virginia, Regional Research Institute.

These consolidations often took place in the context of Wall Street insti-
gated mergers. Cost-cutting as a major means of extracting short-term
profit is widely acknowledged in the literature on mergers and the ascen-
dency of financial firms. Higher returns are realized chiefly through selling
off undervalued units and real estate, subcontracting out more routine por-
tions of production to lower labor costs at home or abroad and to avoid
unions, and cutting back on longer-term, more speculative corporate
research (Dymski, Epstein and Pollin, 1993). In a 1980s study of hostile
takeovers economy-wide, Bhagat, Shleifer and Vishny (1990) concluded
that lay-offs were an important source of windfall profits, as were tax
breaks from increasing indebtedness. Such cost-cutting often yields short-
term gains which are later less than functional for the firm, as we recount
below. But the spatial story is not complete without an appreciation for the
powerful role of the state, not so much as an autonomous actor, but as a
group of powerful politicians (including the President) and bureaucrats
heavily influenced by the money and views of the Wall Street financiers and
the lead firms in the aerospace industry.

STATE ROLES IN DEFENSE INDUSTRY SPATIAL RESTRUCTURING

The state's encouragement and more importantly, financial underwriting,
of the large aerospace mergers is key to understanding their contribution
to spatial restructuring.[4] At the outset of the decade, the Bush administration continued a long-standing Pentagon posture of discouraging mergers
in order to ensure competition, innovation and choice. Like Bush a major
beneficiary of lavish Wall Street and aerospace industry campaign funding
(Hartung, 1996; Project on Demilitarization and Democracy, 1995),
President Clinton shifted this strategy as payoff to the industry, especially
since he proposed additional major military spending cuts. Clinton's first
Secretary of Defense, Les Aspin, set up a new Office of Economic Security
in the Pentagon under the leadership of a Wall Street investment banker,
Josh Gotbaum, who brought with him an 'M&A' perspective. Bill Perry,
later Secretary of Defense himself, oversaw procurement issues from the
outset of the Aspin period. Perry had most recently been running his own
Silicon Valley investment banking/venture capital firm and was apparently
merger-friendly on joining the Pentagon (Markusen, 1998).

The Clinton Pentagon, however, never produced a defense industrial base
analysis to evaluate whether its future demand for individual weapons
systems could reasonably sustain one, two, three or more competitors,
despite the advice of experts like the Brookings Institution's Ken Flamm,

at the time a staffer in the Office of Economic Security, and Rand economists William Kovacic and Dennis Smallwood (Kovacic and Smallwood, 1994; Flamm, 1999). The Rand team laid out a robust procedure for preserving rivalry among contractors by monitoring proposed mergers and preventing them in cases where demand could sustain greater competition. Instead, Perry openly encouraged consolidation, in a famous 'last supper' speech in 1993, basing his advocacy on the promise of cost savings to the Pentagon.[5]

Perry embarked on an aggressive program which included special antitrust rules to permit greater consolidation of the defense and industrial base and succeeded in overcoming the antitrust reservations of the Department of Justice and the Federal Trade Commission, a move welcomed by industrial base Wall Street and business consultants. The Defense Science Board, comprised predominantly of defense contractors and consultants, recommended against formal Pentagon scrutiny of the mergers, which facilitated this backdoor approach – the Pentagon was presumably the most knowledgeable about the competitive impacts of the mergers, but in this way it did not have to issue formal reports. 'By publicly advocating the need for consolidation of the defense industry, the Defense Department accomplished a number of goals. Perhaps most important is that the government was able to isolate itself from the politically charged task of picking winners and losers by letting the market make those decisions' (Dowdy, 1997: 91–2).[6]

At about the same time, the Department of Defense played an active role in creating new financial incentives favoring 'pure play' mergers by subsidizing and aggressively promoting liberalized arms exports and by permitting defense contractors for the first time to include the costs of consummating mergers as part of current contracts, on the promise that they would generate future savings. Both of these moves provided billions in new subsidies which helped to tilt the balance for contractors in favor of remaining defense-specialized and engaging in the merger spree. These initiatives overwhelmed the significance of other Pentagon efforts to encourage dual use and civil/military integration.

The change in Pentagon practice to permit companies to charge the costs of making mergers work against their existing contracts was crucial in encouraging the mergers – Boeing at one point said it would not have acquired McDonnell Douglas without them (Markusen, 1999b) and it quickened the pace of spatial restructuring. During the mid-1990s, the Pentagon reimbursed the large aerospace firms billions of dollars for closing down lines and laying off people since this would supposedly save the military money in the future. These funds were not used for serious worker retraining, nor for moving engineers and technologies into commercial work, but for golden parachutes for top executives, meager severance pay for workers, and the costs of disposing of or demolishing property. In what bipartisan critics, including a conservative New Jersey member of the House of Representatives, dubbed 'payoffs for layoffs', Lockheed/Martin raked in more than $1 billion in taxpayer dollars to complete its merger, just one of 30 reimbursement requests to the Pentagon. A General Accounting Office study found that actual savings fell far below those promised, but firms were not required to reimburse the government for poor performance (US General Accounting Office, 1995). It is likely that fewer lines would have been closed and fewer relocations undertaken in the absence of these massive subsidies.

Politics and access to state bureaucracies have also contributed to recent aerospace industry spatial restructuring. The targeting of certain southern districts for consolidated operations – Newt Gingrich's Georgia district, for instance – was acknowledged by managers in the Rutgers interviews. The southeast, with its preponderance of Republican members of Congress in powerful appropriations and armed forces committees, was especially favored in the production shift (Oden, 1999b: 29–30). The gravitation of aerospace, military electronics, and defense service sector activities around Washington, DC, is a testimony to the increasing significance of government as market and can be considered the belated construction of a state-based agglomeration.

In this account, it is easier to detect the role of military industrial firms in shaping government policy than it is to uncover the role of Wall Street. My own experience running a study group at the Council on Foreign Relations with ongoing participation of investment firms has convinced me that many of the major innovations of this period, including the change in merger cost reimbursement practices, have been the brainchildren of financial firms, who have also been very active in their promulgation in Washington.

THE CONSEQUENCES FOR AMERICAN AEROSPACE

For several years following the mega-mergers, military industrial profits were extraordinarily high while defense workers were left behind (Powers and Markusen, 1998). These profits appear to have been associated principally with deep employment cuts, property sell-offs (many aerospace operations had been sited at what had become prime real estate, just south of the Los Angeles airport, for instance), and relocations, and of course, the up front reimbursements for such costs from the Pentagon. But by 1999, despite a reversal in the defense budget, the defense giant's stock plunged, as analysts increasingly reported failures in merging operations and corporate cultures and in finding new markets and product lines.

These failures should not have been surprising. Before the Boeing/ McDonnell Douglas merger, McDonnell Douglas CEO Harry Stonecipher acknowledged that size had its disadvantages and predicted that the mid-decade defense mega-firms might someday choose to split themselves into smaller, more manageable and entrepreneurial units (Mintz, 1995). Disparate corporate cultures (at Hughes and Raytheon, for instance) posed formidable problems to successful integration (Velocci, 1997). Even Boeing appears to have suffered from the diversion of its energies into the absorption of McDonnell Douglas, whose acquisition was widely interpreted as Boeing's effort to be a larger player in the military market (and not, as Europeans feared, to establish an American monopoly in commercial aircraft, which it more or less already enjoyed). For the first time, orders for the Airbus outpaced orders for Boeing commercial aircraft in 1999.

More recently, one wing of the Wall Street investment banking community has been vigorously crafting international mergers, but these have so far proved difficult to consummate for political reasons (Markusen, 1999c). It is quite possible that if these efforts remain blocked, breaking up the defense giants will become newly fashionable. After all, these would also generate impressive fees for the investment bankers.

Ironically, those aerospace firms which have maintained dual use capabilities, chief among them Boeing, have done much better than the 'pure play' giants. Even in the early years of the decade, Seattle's aerospace complex was much better positioned to absorb military spending cuts than were the Long Island and Los Angeles agglomerations (Table 8.2). This differential performance offers some evidence for the contention that a different route to restructuring in the 1990s, one driven by internally financed corporate diversification rather than dual use-destroying divestiture and defense specialization-building acquisition would have produced both a more spatially stable industry, with fewer permanently displaced engineers and blue collar workers, and a more successful one (Oden, 1999a, 1999b, 2000; Markusen, 1999b; Powers and Markusen, 1998).

ACKNOWLEDGING FINANCIAL FIRMS IN REGIONAL DEVELOPMENT

The prominence of financial firms in remaking the face of the aerospace industry produced long-term negative consequences long after the short-term profits from large merger fees and stock appreciation evaporated. It would be facile to argue that this was simply a case of a mature industry, previously protected by its special role in Reagan's defense buildup from the industrial restructuring forced on other sectors, suddenly subjected to Wall

Street financial discipline. The aerospace industry still accounts for an impressive share of the high tech science and engineering market and a disportionate share of government R&D funds, and it is still a growth market internationally. The particular path chosen by Wall Street investment banks for the industry was not the only one possible: it could have pressed for smaller, defense specialized firms, or larger, more diversified firms, either of which could form the basis for the next consensus.

The disturbing lesson from this analysis is that not only should financial firms, as suppliers of capital to other firms in the economy, not be left out of the analysis, but that even when incorporated, their behavior is not easily theorized a priori. The case of the aerospace industry in the 1990s underscores the point made eloquently by Lovering (1990) in response to Scott's (1988) work: contingency matters.

Although the aerospace industry is a special case in that the government is a major market for its output, in many ways it is similar to other relatively high tech producer and consumer durable goods industries, such as computers, computer software and communications equipment, who operate in less than fully competitive markets. Because of their special relationship to the Pentagon, aerospace firms are in many ways more transparent than are other firms, and the role of Wall Street in their restructuring is somewhat easier to research. But most other firms in the economy must rely on financial capital and are subject to the same vicissitudes of fads and fashions. Wall Street's stature and influence in Washington, in government at all levels (including international bodies like the World Bank and the IMF) is extraordinarily high and shows up in myriad government postures: tax law, commercial practices, trade policy, securities regulation, property rights, antitrust and so on. All of these may have important consequences for spatial outcomes.

Financial firms' motivation and behavior is hard to detect. Precisely because they are so shielded from competition, because they enjoy discretionary space and are skilled at market manipulation, and because they are so politically powerful, their modus operandi is deliberately kept under wraps. Regional economists and geographers, I believe, understate the role of financial capital because it is just plain hard to research. Even when the researcher obtains access, the sector's operations are not simple or straightforward, as are lean production practices in manufacturing. We understate the clout of financial capital because much of its power lies in its ability to shape national economic policy, through its domination of both the national banking system and the most powerful department, the Treasury. In the recent past and on into the foreseeable future, finance capital will play a significant role in how and where business operates at the global and regional scales.

NOTES

1. Peter Gray points out to me that these shares may be altered by the after-effects of 'irrational exuberance' through a sharp decline in the stock market indices with an effect similar to a financial crisis.
2. Lundquist, a former Air Force officer, White House Fellow and staff assistant to Sam Nunn, was a principal at McKinsey and Company's New York Office at the time he wrote this article.
3. In another press account, one of the same consultants is quoted as citing 'countless reasons why defence businesses should steer clear of conversion. Only the smallest businesses and the most basic technologies can readily move between one and the other. Big defence companies can no more adapt to the commercial world than can the products they churn out' (*The Economist*, 16 January 1993: 63–4.)
4. The following discussion draws upon Markusen, 1997 and 1998.
5. Perry was explicit, saying he hoped that 'several aircraft firms would disappear through mergers, as well as three of the five satellite firms in business then, and one of three missile companies' (Mintz, 1995).
6. Dowdy's article is the only one which has appeared in a major foreign policy journal on defense mergers – Dowdy is a partner in the Los Angeles office of McKinsey and Company.

9. The multiple dimensions of international involvement: an empirical test

Rajneesh Narula and Katharine Wakelin

INTRODUCTION

The post-war era has been a period of significant growth in both world trade and foreign direct investment (FDI) by multinational enterprises (MNEs). The two are closely interconnected as trade is increasingly internalised by MNEs, with almost one-third of world trade estimated to be conducted on an intra-firm basis (UNCTAD, 1994). Despite these facts, MNE activity is largely ignored by most international trade theorists. The competitiveness of a country, i.e. its ability to compete on international markets, is determined not just by its trade performance, but also by the activities of foreign-owned affiliates, and the investments of its MNEs overseas. However, the literatures on the theory and determinants of trade and FDI have remained largely independent of each other. This chapter seeks to address this shortcoming, by attempting to unite our understanding of trade and FDI and their interrelatedness by evaluating these issues within a common framework. We utilise a neo-Schumpeterian approach that regards technology as playing a central role in competitiveness.

This chapter aims to extend the neo-Schumpeterian approach to trade, which stresses the importance of absolute differences in technology in influencing export performance, to consider the absolute advantage of a country (and specifically the firms within a country) in a broader sense than its trade performance alone. For the purposes of this chapter, absolute advantage is seen to operate in two distinct ways. The first, and that emphasised by the neo-Schumpeterian school (see for instance Dosi, Pavitt and Soete, 1990; Freeman and Soete, 1997), is trade performance, and in particular the market share of a country on world export markets. The second, which has largely been neglected by the neo-Schumpeterian approach, is the outward foreign direct investment undertaken by a country's firms, and the inward foreign direct investment undertaken by foreign firms. Both the trade performance of a country and its position with respect to outward investment, are products of the absolute advantage of that country with regard to her competitors. By extending the neo-Schumpeterian framework to include foreign direct investment, a more coherent picture of the effects of technology on a country's competitiveness can be obtained, than by examining trade flows alone.

The technological capabilities of a country (its national system of innovation) affect the export competitiveness of firms within the country, and in particular the sectoral structure of export performance. In addition, technological capabilities influence the existence of MNEs in a particular country and affect the competitive advantage of those MNEs. As a result, outward investment from a country is also partly determined by the national system of innovation of the country. At the level of the firm, the technological capabilities of a firm, as well as leading to improved export performance (see Wakelin, 1997), bestow a particular competitive advantage on the firm, which the firm may wish to internalise through foreign direct investment rather than exports. Thus the technological capabilities of a country, and of the firms in that country, have an impact not only on export performance, but also on the outward investment pattern of a country, and provide a common determinant of both export performance and outward investment.

This chapter abstracts from firm specific characteristics, and considers the country level determinants of both export performance and FDI. A number of country determinants are considered in the model including technology (both that embodied in innovations, and disembodied in the skills of the workforce), the level of development of the country, relative market size, and resource availability. In the chapter we take absolute advantages as a proxy for national competitiveness. For the purposes of this chapter, absolute advantage is seen to operate in two distinct ways. The second part of the chapter outlines the theoretical background to the chapter, and in particular highlights the similarities between the relevant approaches to trade and FDI. The third sets out the empirical model to be tested and explains the data set used in the estimations. We then present and discuss the results, and finally give some conclusions.

THEORETICAL BACKGROUND

Understanding the role of MNEs has become critical to understanding economic growth and competitiveness, both as a result of the extent of foreign direct investment activities and their increasing domination of international trade. Since 1981, FDI flows have consistently grown faster than GDP or exports on a worldwide basis. In 2000 the global sales of MNEs exceeded $15.6 trillion, compared with world exports of goods and non-factor services in the same year of $7.1 trillion (UNCTAD, 2001). Despite the fact that fully one-third of world trade is estimated to represent intra-firm trade, trade theories have largely excluded FDI from their theoretical framework and from empirical analysis. On a theoretical level this is due to the assumptions of perfect competition which underpin neoclassical trade theory. Assuming constant returns to scale means that the size of the firm is of no importance, and firms are characterised as atomistic price takers. In order to consider both the role of technology in trade and the behaviour of MNEs, the heterogeneity of firms needs to be recognised, and this recognition is one of the unifying characteristics of both the FDI literature and the neo-Schumpeterian approach to trade. At the empirical level, the role of FDI has been neglected largely due to the difficulties in modelling the myriad of dynamic interactions and evolutionary processes that underlie MNE activities, and the lack of data with which to test them (Chesnais, 1995).

Our intention in this chapter is to demonstrate that the approach taken by the neo-Schumpeterian school to trade and competitiveness provides an excellent basis with which to bridge the gulf between the trade literature and the received approach to FDI and competitiveness. Despite the growing significance of FDI, little has been done to study its relationship to trade and competitiveness within a unified framework, with a few notable exceptions (see for instance Cantwell, 1989, 1991; Narula, 1996; Gray, 1999; Dunning *et al.*, 2001). This chapter aims to assess to what degree a neo-Schumpeterian approach to trade and competitiveness, as developed by Dosi, Pavitt and Soete (1990), can be applied to both FDI and export performance.

There are three main strands of the approach which have much in common with the literature on MNEs, that is the emphasis on technology, the importance of country specific determinants and the emphasis on absolute (or competitive) advantage. Each of these factors is discussed in turn below in some detail.

Technology

Differences in technology are increasingly taken as an important motivation for both trade and FDI. A conceptualisation of the innovation process as cumulative and firm specific underlies both some approaches to trade (Dosi, 1988), and to FDI (Cantwell, 1989). In the FDI literature (see for instance Dunning, 1993a, 2001; Gray, 1999; Cantwell and Narula, 2001) technology has been considered as conferring ownership advantages to firms. Technology may be said to consist of: (a) ownership advantages that are generally firm specific, both of the codifiable and non-codifiable variety, and which include knowledge pertaining to organising intra-firm transactions efficiently; and, (b) the knowledge inherent in industry and country specific structure of markets that relate to the organisation of efficient transactions (Narula, 1993). These ownership advantages provide one of the reasons for a firm preferring direct investment, which internalises these advantages, over arms-length transactions.

In the trade literature the cumulative nature of innovation and skills is used as an explanation for the continuing existence of technology gaps over time, in direct contrast to the automatic diffusion of technology assumed by neoclassical trade theory. Firms, sectors and countries can create specific competitive advantages through innovation, due to the cumulative nature of innovation and innovatory capabilities. Certain features of innovation highlighted by Dosi (1984, 1988) and Freeman (1982), lead to this accumulation. Among these are the often tacit and non-codifiable nature of technology; the importance of learning-by-doing and learning-by-using in technological change; and the potential to appropriate some of the benefits from innovation. These factors lead to the localisation of the benefits of innovation, and act against its automatic diffusion. Because of the localised nature of the search for innovation and its specificity to the innovating firm, there are costs associated with the adoption of innovation by non-innovating firms. In other words, technology is only partially appropriable by other firms, and the extent to which it can be appropriated depends on the similarity of the firms' environments and past technological capabilities. As present patterns of innovation are influenced by past experience and skills, present innovation occurs as a result of past innovation, and firms, sectors and countries can maintain particular competitive advantages over time giving a basis for trade.

Although technology is primarily a firm-specific phenomenon, it is possible to speak of national technological advantages, which are more than the summation of technological advantages across firms in a given industry in a particular country. Technology is localised in nature, not only at a firm level because of its path dependency, but also on a country-specific basis, since the interlinkages between users and producers in the innovatory process result in a unique technological profile for each country (Lundvall, 1992). The common institutional framework within the country also influences the development of a technological profile. These national systems of innovation are taken as an important determinant of both export performance of the country and the FDI behaviour of the country's firms. The emphasis on the innovation process as local, cumulative and firm, sector and country specific, provides one of the unifying features between the neo-

Schumpeterian approach to trade and the literature examining the behaviour of MNEs.

Country-specific Characteristics

The competitiveness of firms is influenced not only by their firm-specific technological capabilities, but also by the general economic structure of the country in which the firm is located. These are termed location advantages in the eclectic paradigm (Dunning, 1993a), since all firms in a given country have potential access to them. This 'structural competitiveness' of the country can affect the competitiveness of the firms in the country, as Chesnais (1992) put it:

> Their competitiveness will also stem from economy-specific long term trends in the strength and efficiency of a national economy's productive structure, its technical infra-structure and other factors determining the externalities on which firms can build.

In the trade literature much empirical work has been devoted to analysing the role of country characteristics in trade performance, both in terms of a factor proportions view of trade,[1] and more recently including differences in technology between countries as a determinant of trade (see for instance Fagerberg, 1988; Amable and Verspagen, 1995), the latter have found an important role for differences in technology in influencing the competitiveness of countries.

The importance of the different components of structural competitiveness in determining firm and national competitiveness varies both with the level of development of the country and the type of international economic activity undertaken. Less developed countries can be expected to be more influenced by natural resource availability and relative costs than by 'created assets' such as technology and skilled labour. As the economy of a country becomes increasingly capital and knowledge intensive, the technological assets of the firm may not be so closely linked to the natural assets of the home country from which its initial advantage was derived, but increasingly dependent on country-specific characteristics such as technology and infrastructure (Narula, 1996). In addition, firms located in industrialised countries may be less reliant on the characteristics of their home country, and more reliant on evolved firm-specific characteristics which provide the firm's competitive advantage. This is as a result of the longer period of time firms in industrialised countries have had to develop firm-specific characteristics, and the 'created' nature of most of the firm assets in industrialised countries. The firm-specific advantages of innovation have been shown to have a strong impact on the export performance of UK firms (Wakelin, 1997), although the sectoral pattern of innovation also played a role in UK firms' export performance. Thus the balance between firm-specific characteristics and country characteristics can be expected to change according to the level of development of the country.

The role of country-specific characteristics in determining the competitiveness of firms is also determined by the extent of multinationality of the firm and the nature of its international economic activity. On the one extreme, the ownership advantages of purely domestic-owned firms producing for the local market or for exports are likely to have a stronger relationship with structural competitiveness variables of its home country than a foreign-owned multinational firm based in that country. Such an MNE will have firm-specific assets that derive from the country-specific characteristics of its home and host country, and depending on the extent of its international operations, as well as other locations. This relationship with the home country may be even weaker for outward FDI, especially if the motivation for such outward investment is to acquire strategic assets (Dunning and Narula, 1996a).

In this chapter country characteristics are considered as determinants of export performance and FDI activity for a variety of countries, including both developing countries, newly industrialised countries and industrialised countries. These country determinants are expected to be more effective at explaining the behaviour of developing than industrialised countries. In addition, only the characteristics of the home country in the case of outward investment, and the host country for inward investment, are considered as determinants, neglecting the host and home country characteristics respectively. This represents only a partial explanation for FDI activity, since FDI is influenced by the balance between the ownership, location and internalisation advantages of the host and home country (Dunning 1988b, 1993a).

Absolute Advantages and Competitiveness

Both the FDI literature and the neo-Schumpeterian approach to trade also stress absolute (or competitive) advantage, based on firm-specific ownership advantages in the former approach and technological advantages in the latter. Hirsch and Bijaoui (1985) argue that firms' competitive advantages can be independent of factor intensities, but at the same time there is not necessarily a contradiction between the Heckscher-Ohlin approach to trade and firm-level advantages. The latter may be consistent with factor endowments, making more intensive use of the more abundant factors of production. Alternatively, competitive advantage may be based on the superior proprietary knowledge of a firm in a way unrelated to factor intensities. As a result both factor endowments and firm-specific advantages are determinants of a country's competitiveness.

The competitive advantage of firms is an absolute advantage over other firms. Comparative advantage acts at the level of the country and influences the pattern of trade specialisation of a country, and thus the sectoral structure. The competitive advantage of firms may be compatible, and interact with comparative advantage, or contradict it. In the work of Dosi, Pavitt and Soete (1990) absolute differences in technology are considered to be more important than endowment-based comparative advantage in explaining trade patterns. In their framework, within the trade pattern set out by absolute differences in technology, comparative cost considerations may be relevant, but it is absolute differences in technology which predominate. This view, that the 'competitiveness' of a firm or a country is defined by the presence of an absolute advantage, and not by comparative advantage has received similar treatment in these two complementary theoretical approaches. The competitive advantage of firms (locations) is an absolute advantage over other firms (locations), while comparative advantage acts at the level of the country and influences the pattern of trade specialisation of a country, and thus the sectoral structure. It is important to emphasise that competitiveness is both a firm-specific phenomenon, as well as a country-specific one. Although country competitiveness represents the overall ability of firms of a given nationality in a given sector to compete with firms located in a different country in the same sector, this is not simply the sum of the competitiveness of its firms (Lall, 1990). The competitiveness of firms is influenced also by the general economic structure of the country in which they are located including linkages among sectors, the national system of innovation and trade specialisation patterns.

The importance of the different components of structural competitiveness, in determining firm and national competitiveness, varies both with the level of development of the country and the type of international economic activity undertaken (Narula, 1996). Developing countries can be expected to be more influenced by natural resource availability, and relative costs than by firm-specific ownership advantages. Firms in industrialised countries have had a longer period of time to develop their own characteristics, and so may be less reliant on the characteristics of their home country. The balance between firm-specific characteristics and country characteristics can therefore be expected to change according to the level of development of the country.[2]

The extent to which competitiveness relates to technological capabilities and economic structure may be limited, since the competitiveness of a given firm is also determined by the extent of multinationality of the firm and the nature of its international economic activity. This has several implications. First, ownership advantages of purely domestic-owned firms producing for the local market or for exports, are likely to have a stronger relationship with the structural competitiveness variables of its home country, than a foreign-owned multinational firm based in that country. Second, countries which are home or host to MNEs that have considerable international operations (e.g. the industrialised countries) are more likely to be influenced by the country-specific characteristics of the other countries in which these MNEs operate, than countries with relatively less internationalised firms (e.g. developing countries). Third, different sectors of production have different scale economies or the demand may be heterogeneous across countries, thus having different propensities for internationalisation.

THE EMPIRICAL MODEL

The empirical model tested in this chapter aims to estimate the importance of country characteristics in explaining both FDI and exports. Three separate relationships are estimated: one for relative export market share and the other two for relative market shares of inward and outward investment respectively. The model is estimated across 41 countries,[3] with the data pooled across four years: 1975, 1979, 1984 and 1988. The countries have been selected on the basis of the availability of FDI stock figures for those years.[4] The export dependent variable used is each country's exports relative to the exports of the entire sample of 41 countries, normalised by the ratio of that country's population to the population of the whole sample. Likewise for FDI, the stock of outward investment relative to the stock for the whole sample normalised by relative population, and the stock of inward investment relative to the stock for the sample over relative populations are used. These dependent variables give an indicator of each country's export or FDI market share relative to the sample countries, with the latter taken as a proxy for the world market. The dependent variables are normalised by relative population in order to take account of the impact of varying country size on exports and FDI. Using market shares as the dependent variable measures the absolute advantage of countries on international markets, both in terms of exports and FDI.

The same explanatory variables are included in each model, with the addition of variables to capture the linkages between export intensity and FDI. The explanatory variables cover a number of country characteristics, including the level of development of the country, technological capabilities, primary resource availability, and market size. In order to be consistent with the notion of absolute advantage all the explanatory variables included in the model for a country are given on a per capita basis relative to the country with the highest per capita value in the sample for that year. For instance, in the case of the demand variable, demand in each country in the sample is given relative to demand in the US, and for the technology variable each country's technology is given relative to Switzerland. In each case the base country takes a value of one.

Technology is taken to be one of the fundamental determinants of international competitiveness in this model; although it is expected to be of greater significance in explaining the competitiveness of the industrialised countries in the sample than for the developing countries. Technology is divided into both embodied technology, i.e. innovation, and disembodied technology proxied by human capital. Previous studies have used R&D expenditures (Clegg, 1987) as a proxy for innovation. However, as such data is not available for a sufficient number of countries, we will use patents granted per capita in each country relative to patents granted per capita in the country with the highest value as an indicator of a nation's relative technological capability (RPAT).[5] We expect a positive relationship between RPAT and both export performance and FDI shares.

Second, human capital is included as a separate explanatory variable to indicate the level of skills available in the country. Papanastassiou and Pearce (1990) have used the proportion of scientists and engineers in total employment, but due to limited data availability, we are unable to use such an indicator. Instead, we take a ratio of the enrolment of students at the tertiary level per capita in the country in question relative to the country with the highest value (RHC). The development and availability of tertiary education varies widely among countries, and a large proportion of tertiary level students as a percentage of population indicates a well developed skill base. In general we hypothesise that a higher percentage of skilled personnel (RHC), will have a positive impact on competitiveness.

An indicator for the level of development of the country is also included in the model. That included is GNP per capita relative to the country with the highest GNP per capita in the sample. Other indicators for development such as gross fixed capital formation were also tried, but GNP had the highest explanatory power. A higher level of development is assumed to be associated with higher export shares and higher shares of outward and inward investment.

A variable for the availability of natural resources is also included in the model, based on the percentage of each country's exports made up of primary commodities (XP).[6] In the case of the developing countries in the sample, natural resources are expected to be an important source of competitiveness. However, countries which are specialised in primary resources are unlikely to have a large share of exports in terms of value, generally a specialisation in primary products is an indication of a less developed country. We would therefore expect a negative relationship between primary exports and the share in the world export market. Several studies have examined the effect of the relative abundance of natural resources on the extent and nature of inward and outward FDI. Rugman (1987) has found that the possession of natural resources influences the pattern of outward FDI activity by Canadian firms. Primary resources may provide an incentive for inward investment in order to exploit the resources, indicating a positive relationship between inward FDI and primary resources. Since a high primary export share implies a low manufacturing export share, we expect outward FDI to be lower given the limited scope for the development of ownership advantages of domestic firms. Therefore, the higher the home country's primary exports (XP) the smaller we expect its outward FDI share to be.

Although demand factors can be considered as consisting of two main features – *quality* of demand and *quantity* of demand (Narula, 1993), due to the complexity of measuring quality of demand in aggregate terms, we include a variable for the quantity of demand, or market size. Smaller countries are expected to have higher per capita shares in export markets due to the small size of the domestic market. Relatively large countries can be more dependent on the domestic market and less engaged in international trade. For FDI, the larger the market size of the host economy, the greater the attraction for foreign investors since the economies of large-scale production are likely to be captured. Therefore the stock of inward FDI to a country is likely to be greater when the size of the market is larger. Previous studies have used a number of proxies for market size including real lagged GNP (Culem, 1988). However, location decisions are based not on absolute market size but on relative market size. Our demand variable is aggregate private consumption in each country relative to the largest economy in the sample, the US, giving relative demand (RDEMD). In the case of outward FDI, large domestic markets present considerable opportunity for growth of sales. Therefore, the attraction of foreign markets, *ceteris paribus*, will be considerably less. This is especially true in the case of MNEs from industrialised countries. We expect that for industrialised countries the greater the home country market size the smaller the share of outward investment.

In addition to these explanatory variables which are common to all three models, the relationships between FDI and trade are also considered. For the trade and outward investment models, this means including the stock of inward investment per capita relative to the highest stock in the sample (RIWPOP) as an explanatory variable. Both export shares, and shares of outward investment are expected to be positively related to the level of inward investment. In the case of exports, firms frequently undertake inward FDI in a country and then subsequently export from that country.

In particular, this may occur when the country is part of a customs union (such as the European Union) or a free trade agreement, and has preferential access to markets. Only in the case where the domestic market of the host country provides a large enough market, would we expect inward investment not to be associated with exports. Countries which have a higher level of outward investment are also likely to attract high inward investment, with firms seeking out the highly developed assets of the country. Thus we would expect a positive relationship between inward investment (RIWPOP) and outward investment shares.

The development of a firm's ownership advantages is influenced by the extent to which it is exposed to international competition. For the model with inward investment share as the dependent variable, trade intensity (RTI), measured by the sum of exports and imports of each country over its population, relative to the highest trade intensity in the sample (Belgium in 1975 and Singapore in subsequent years) is included to capture the degree to which the country participates in international markets. Countries that have an import-substituting policy orientation will attract relatively less inward FDI than countries with export-oriented economy which tend to have a high trade intensity.

To summarise, the three models are given below. For the export relationship (1) the dependent variables is the ratio of export (X) share to population (pop) share; the market is defined as the sum over i, where i is all the countries in the sample, and the explanatory variables are as defined earlier. Logarithms are taken of all the variables and the models are estimated using Ordinary Least Squares (OLS). There are some missing data points, particularly for the patent data for some countries in some years. As a result the actual number of observations in the estimates n is lower than 164.

$$X/\Sigma_i X / pop / \Sigma_i pop = f(rgnp, rpat, rhc, xp, rdemd, riwpop) \qquad (1)$$

The relationships with outward and inward investments are given below where OW and OI are the stocks of outward and inward investment. Analogously, the equation for inward investment uses the relative trade intensity as an explanatory variable.

$$OW/\Sigma_i OW/ pop/\Sigma_i pop = f(rgnp, rpat, rhc, xp, rdemd, riwpop) \qquad (2)$$

$$IW/\Sigma_i IW/ pop/\Sigma_i pop = f(rgnp, rpat, rhc, xp, rdemd, rti) \qquad (3)$$

The heterogeneous nature of the countries in the sample means that a number of separate models were estimated. First, a restricted model including all the countries in a single model was estimated. Second, an unrestricted model allowing the estimated coefficients to vary according to two separate groups of countries, developing and industrialised countries, was estimated. For both the export estimation and the inward investment estimation the restricted model was rejected relative to the model allowing separate coefficients for the two groups, indicating that the determinants of FDI and export performance vary over these two groups of countries. The restricted model was not rejected for the outward investment model; as very little outward investment is undertaken by the developing countries the results are presented for the industrialised countries alone for the outward investment model. Even with separate estimations for developing and industrialised countries, there is a great deal of heterogeneity among the developing countries, which include both newly industrialised countries (NICs) such as Singapore and Taiwan, and relatively undeveloped countries such as Papua New Guinea. As a result, the model including all the developing countries together was taken as the restricted model, and an unrestricted model allowing the coefficients to vary over the two groups, NICs and developing countries, was estimated for both inward investment and exports. In both cases the restricted model was not rejected, indicating that there is no significant variation among the determinants of exports and FDI over these two groups of countries.[7]

RESULTS

a)   Exports

The model for export market share was estimated separately for developing and industrialised countries. For the industrialised country sample there is strong positive collinearity between the patent variable (RPAT) and inward investment per capita (RIWPOP), making it impossible to include both variables together. It appears that patents, inward investment and exports are all positively related. As a result the model is estimated twice including each of the variables separately; these are termed estimates (1) and (2) and are presented in the first two columns of Table 9.1.[8] As there may be potential endogeneity between inward investment and exports, with higher export intensity leading to greater inward investment, as well as inward investment leading to greater exports, estimate (1) excluding RIWPOP may be preferred as it does not include the potentially endogenous variable. Estimate (2) allows us to compare the results including inward investment. The results for the developing countries are given in the last column.

Table 9.1   Results for export market share

Variable	Industrialised countries (1)	Industrialised countries (2)	Developing countries
α	1.44 (5.57)***	2.59 (7.26) ***	2.51 (8.86) ***
RGNP	0.60 (2.60) ***	0.86 (3.70) ***	0.94 (6.90) ***
RPAT	0.13 (1.64)*	–	−0.07 (1.87) **
RHC	−0.02 (0.16)	0.12 (0.87)	0.06 (0.86)
XP	−0.02 (0.33)	−0.26 (2.98) ***	−0.42 (5.52) ***
RDEMD	−0.29 (7.03)***	−0.29 (7.22)***	−0.37 (8.08) ***
RIWPOP	–	0.20 (3.70) ***	0.23 (3.18) ***
Adj. R^2	0.50	0.52	0.92
n	59	69	43

Table 9.2   Results for the share of outward investment

Variable	Industrialised countries (1)	Industrialised countries (2)
α	2.62 (3.94) ***	5.35 (7.70) ***
RGNP	1.49 (2.31) **	1.17 (3.12) ***
RPAT	0.34 (1.92) **	
RHC	−0.15 (0.35)	0.56 (1.55)
XP	0.01 (0.05)	−0.60 (3.06) ***
RDEMD	0.20 (1.66) *	0.07 (0.64)
RIWPOP	–	0.61 (7.44) ***
Adj. R^2	0.14	0.43
n	59	69

Table 9.3   Results for the share of inward investment

Variable	Industrialised countries	Developing countries
α	0.77 (0.99)	1.36 (1.81) *
RGNP	−0.43 (0.86)	0.08 (0.12)
RTI	0.75 (2.80) ***	1.02 (2.11) ***
RPAT	0.72 (4.97) ***	0.09 (1.18)
RHC	−0.39 (1.31)	0.20 (1.22)
RDEMD	0.27 (2.44) ***	0.10 (0.41)
XP	0.81 (5.39) ***	0.65 (3.83) ***
Adj. R^2	0.50	0.65
n	59	43

Notes:
* significant at 1%
** significant at 5%
*** significant at 10%

As expected, the explanatory power of the model is considerably higher for developing countries than for industrialised countries. Thus country-level determinants explain a greater part of the export performance of developing than industrialised countries, indicating that factors not included in the model are of more importance in the context of industrialised countries. For developing countries their firms' competitive advantages may be more closely related to their country characteristics than is the case for industrialised countries.

The positive and significant explanatory variables for the industrialised countries are relative technology (RPAT), relative inward investment (RIWPOP) and the relative level of development of the country (RGNP). This confirms the importance of technological capabilities in export performance in accordance with other results (Fagerberg, 1988; Verspagen and Wakelin, 1997). It appears that even among the more industrialised countries those with a higher relative income per capita export more, indicating a greater involvement in export markets as economies mature. The results for the inward investment variable (which are the same for both industrialised and developing countries) suggest that inward FDI leads to greater exports from the host country, showing a complementary relationship between trade and FDI.

The human capital variable has the expected positive sign but is not significant. This may be partly due to weaknesses in the proxy, and the greater efficiency of RPAT in capturing technological capabilities. Relative demand (RDEMD) is negative and significant at the 1% level, confirming our hypothesis that countries which have a relatively small domestic market tend to have a higher propensity to export. This result is also confirmed for the developing countries. Exporting permits small countries to achieve economies of scale in their domestic production activities, while large countries – which are already able to achieve scale economies due to the size of their home markets – have less incentive to export. XP is negative but insignificant, indicating the level of natural resources is not an important factor in explaining the trade performance of industrialised countries.[9]

The primary resource variable (XP) has a negative and significant coefficient for the developing countries as we expected. Given that resource-intensive exports from developing countries tend to be of a low value-added nature, the market share in terms of value of these countries is low, relative to the capital and knowledge intensive exports of industrialised countries. Indeed, developing countries which have a relatively high market share of exports tend to achieve this through the exports of manufactured goods.

The main difference between the results for the two sets of countries is the role of technological capabilities in export performance. While the patent variable has a positive and significant impact on the export performance of industrialised countries, it plays a negative role in that of developing countries. It appears that only in the case of industrialised countries are technological capabilities important in improving export market share.

b) Outward Investment

As indicated earlier, industrialised countries account for almost 90% of outward FDI activity, while the majority of developing countries in the sample either have little or no outward FDI. As a result, the model for outward investment shares was estimated using only the sub-sample of industrialised countries, in order to facilitate comparison between the estimations.[10] The results are presented in Table 9.2. There is collinearity between the patent variable and inward investment so two estimates are made including each variable separately. As with exports, there may be potential endogeneity between inward and outward investment, indicating that estimate (1) would be preferred as it excludes the potentially endogenous variable.

However, the model including the inward investment variable has a much higher explanatory power than that including patents, showing the importance of the level of inward investment per capita in influencing outward investment. Both variables have positive and significant relationships with the share of outward investment, indicating that, as with the export results, technological capabilities have a positive effect on competitiveness. The positive relationship between inward and outward investment is partly due to the large proportion of FDI activity which takes place among industrialised countries; a high outward share of FDI is also associated with high levels of inward FDI activity.

Overall the results are similar to the export model results, with the exception of the relative demand variable RDEMD which is negatively related to export share, but is positive and significant at 10% in the outward investment share model. While having a small market led to increased exports this does not seem to be the case of outward direct investment share which appears to rise with country size.

c) Inward Investment

In the case of inward FDI market shares, the model including developing and industrialised countries together was rejected relative to an estimation separating the two groups of countries; thus the results are presented separately for industrialised and developing countries (Table 9.3). As with export shares, the explanatory power is higher for developing countries than for industrialised countries, although the difference is not so marked. This confirms that country-level characteristics play less of a role in explaining the inward investment share of industrialised countries.

The results for the two different groups of countries look quite similar with the exception of the patent and relative demand variables. The level of development of a country does not appear to influence its share of inward investment in either of the estimates, while relative trade intensity (RTI) and the level of primary exports (RXP), taken as a proxy for resources, are positive and significant for both groups of countries. Countries which are more open to trade appear to be more likely to attract inward investment, and the presence of natural resources also raises the share of inward investment.

For the industrialised countries, in addition to the above two factors the technological indicator (RPAT) is also positive and significant (it is insignificant for the developing countries). It appears that strong national systems of innovation also attract inward FDI, as well as raising exports and the share of outward investment. Relative market size, RDEMD, is also positive for the industrialised countries, indicating that large domestic markets lead to higher shares of inward investment. This does not seem to be the case for the developing countries which show no significant relationship between market size and the share of inward investment.

There are a number of common determinants which can be seen for the results for all three models. One is the importance of technology in influencing both exports and FDI. For the industrialised countries, exports, inward investment and outward investment are all positively and significantly related to technological capabilities. The other technology variable, human capital, is not significant in any of the models. It appears that particularly for the industrialised countries, technology, or the national system of innovation of the country, is one of the key country determinants of international competitiveness, and one of the determinants which can be used to explain both export behaviour and FDI.

The connections between FDI (both inward and outward investment) and exports, have also been explored in this chapter. Including inward investment as an explanatory variable for both export shares and shares of outward investment, indicates an important role for inward investment, particularly in influencing outward investment. Likewise, trade intensity is an important factor in explaining inward investment shares. In general, countries with high shares of inward investment also appear to have high shares of outward investment, and countries which have a high trade intensity are more likely to have high shares of inward investment.

CONCLUSIONS

This chapter aimed to explain both FDI and export behaviour using the same model of country determinants and highlighting the role of technology. For each group of either industrialised or developing countries, the extent to which the model explains inward FDI shares, outward FDI shares and export shares is very similar, although there is considerable variation between developing and industrialised countries. In particular, technological factors appear to be a unifying factor in explaining both export shares and shares of FDI.

Country-specific determinants are clearly the most important factors in explaining the competitiveness of developing countries, but the model is not so effective in the case of industrialised countries. This indicates that factors other than country-level determinants play an important part in the competitiveness of the industrialised countries. In the case of inward and outward investment, these may be the characteristics of the home and host country respectively, which are not included in the model. In addition, factors which are specific to firms, and are not captured by the country-level determinants may also be important. It seems evident that in the case of the industrialised countries, firm-specific competitive advantages may correspond less closely with the country's absolute advantages than they do for developing countries, thus providing one explanation for the greater explanatory power of country determinants in the case of the developing countries. It is interesting to note that firm-specific competitive advantages appear to be important in explaining both export and FDI behaviour, whereas their relevance has mainly been acknowledged only in the case of FDI. It seems clear, that studies of export competitiveness also need to take into account factors other than country-level determinants, and that firm-level studies may be able to shed light on the role of firm-specific factors in influencing trade performance.

Despite these limitations, the results do suggest some implications for policy makers. First, that the development of infrastructural facilities and the enhancement of national systems of innovation are of crucial importance in determining the international competitiveness of their industries. Despite arguments to the effect that globalisation among the industrialised countries has made country-specific factors such as structural competitiveness and national systems of innovation redundant in explaining the activities of MNEs, we have shown that this is in fact not the case. Indeed, perhaps more than ever, the role of government in facilitating the competitiveness of its domestic economy is ever more important, given the central role of technology (Narula and Dunning, 1998; Dunning, 1993a). Indeed, Chesnais (1995) suggests that the primary means by which governments in the industrialised world can maintain some degree of economic sovereignty in light of globalisation is by maintaining the effectiveness of their national systems of innovation.

Second, government policy towards FDI cannot be considered in isolation from trade policy. The growth of intra-firm trade, and the extent to which FDI is both trade-complementary as well as trade-substituting, requires that policy makers take a holistic approach. Contrary to Porter's (1990) view that high levels of inward FDI indicate a declining competitiveness, and outward FDI indicates an increasing competitiveness, our results suggest that in the case of developing countries at least, export competitiveness is significantly influenced by the activities of foreign-owned firms within the domestic economy, as are the outward activities of domestically owned MNEs from industrialised countries. However, it would be equally simplistic to argue that FDI activity always has a beneficial effect on the competitiveness of an economy. Several scholars (e.g. Dunning, 1993a; Cantwell, 1987, 1991; Dunning and Narula, 1994) have argued that the impact of inward FDI varies, *inter alia*, according to the motivation of the FDI, the level of development of the host country and the existing level of technological competence of the recipient industry. Although our results hint at this complexity, a rigorous test of this approach would require an analysis for several countries using time series data on a sectoral basis.

The same caveats are also true with regards to outward FDI. However, unlike inward FDI and exports, outward FDI is not always indicative of the competitiveness of the home country: there is increasing use of FDI to acquire assets, in addition to the use of FDI to exploit the existing assets of the MNE (see contributions to Dunning and Narula (eds), 1996b). This represents a means to promote the competitiveness of an economy, by exposing domestic firms to other national contexts and environments, thereby also allowing firms to avoid the constraints associated with developing technological capabilities suited solely to the home market. This underlies the growth of MNEs from the developing countries such as Thailand, Indonesia, Taiwan, India and China, to name but a few, who are engaging in FDI activity overseas with the active support of their home governments to acquire technological assets and competences in overseas locations with the intention of improving their competitive position.

APPENDIX

The countries included in the estimates are:

Industrialised countries:
Japan, Canada, Australia, New Zealand, United States, United Kingdom, France, Germany, Netherlands, Denmark, Norway, Finland, Sweden, Austria, Belgium, Italy and Switzerland.

Developing countries:
Bangladesh, China, India, Sri Lanka, Thailand, Pakistan, Indonesia, Taiwan, Malaysia, Korea, Hong Kong, Fiji, Papua New Guinea, Nigeria, South Africa, Brazil, Ecuador, Venezuela, Mexico, Philippines, Turkey, Spain, Portugal, and Singapore.

Data Definitions

RPAT – ratio of national patents granted per capita of the home country relative to Switzerland.

RHC – number of tertiary students over population relative to same for the US (1971, 1979, 1984) or Canada (1988).

RGNP – GNP per capita relative to the same for Sweden (1975), Switzerland (1979, 1988) or the US (1984).

XP – proportion of exports in primary commodities.

RDEMD – aggregate demand relative to aggregate demand in the US.

RIWPOP – stock of inward investment per capita.

RTI – exports plus imports over population.

Data Sources

National patent data for each country were taken from UNESCO *Statistical Yearbook*, 1991 and United Nations *Statistical Yearbook*, various issues

The number of students in the tertiary sector is taken from the UNESCO *Statistical Yearbook*, 1991.

Primary commodity data come from the *World Development Report*, various issues.

Private consumption data are taken in current prices from the IMF *International Financial Statistics Yearbook*, 1991.

GNP figures taken from the IMF *International Financial Statistics Yearbook*, 1991.

Population is taken from the IMF *International Financial Statistics Yearbook*, 1991.

Proportion of primary exports and primary imports is taken from *World Development Report*, various issues.

All FDI data are compiled from the *World Investment Directory*, plus additional national data sources. All FDI figures are current stock estimates on a historical cost basis. Where stock figures have been unavailable, they have been estimated using sum of flows from IMF data tapes. The use of this method as a proxy for stocks is discussed in Narula (1996, pp. 40–2) Exports and imports are based on data published in the IMF *International Financial Statistics Yearbook*, 1991.

All data from IMF sources and the *World Investment Directory* have been converted using nominal exchange rates from national currency to US dollars. Flow data are converted using annual average rates and stock data is converted with end of period figures.

NOTES

1. This is an extensive literature, see for instance Leamer (1980) and Wood (1994).
2. This has been formalized as the investment development path (see e.g. Dunning, 1981b; Narula, 1996; Dunning and Narula, 1994, 1996a).
3. See the Appendix for a list of countries, source, and exact definition of explanatory variables.
4. For a study considering the determinants of FDI over time see Narula and Wakelin (2001).
5. Patents have certain limitations as a measure of innovative activity, see Archibugi (1992) for a survey of the issues involved. A stock variable was not used as the number of patents granted changes only slowly over time.
6. Since the highest value in the sample was 99%, it was not necessary to make this variable relative.
7. Time dummies were also included in order to test for structural breaks across the four years included. As none of the time dummies was significant, they are not included in the final specification.
8. The number of observations *n* is higher for the second industrialised model as there are a greater number of missing data points for the patent data. The t-statistics given in brackets are calculated using heteroschedastic-robust standard errors.
9. The sign on the XP variable changes in the second model due to positive collinearity between the level of primary exports XP and the level of inward FDI per capita RIWPOP.
10. The results do not change using the whole sample, and with the industrialised countries alone, although the explanatory power of the latter is lower than when the whole sample is included.

10. Towards a theory of hegemon-led macro-clustering

Terutomo Ozawa

INTRODUCTION

In conjunction with studies on agglomeration economies in spatial clusters, sub-national regional clusters (microregions) have been the focus of research by many scholars (*inter alia*: Piore and Sabel, 1984; Porter, 1990; Krugman, 1991; Saxenian, 1994; Markusen, 1996; Ohmae, 1995; Nachum, 1999; Dunning, 2000a). Recognizing the role of multinational corporations as a potent instrument of globalization, some (Dunning, 2000b; Blomstrom, Globerman and Kokko, 2000; Eden and Monteils, 2000) examined FDI activities in 'macroregions,'[1] a concept used in Dunning (2000a), but little is said – and understood – of the dynamics of supranational macro-clusters as another form of agglomeration. Furthermore, microregions are usually treated as the creatures of historical accident, and their connectedness with macro-clustering remains unexplored.

This is rather surprising, given the fact that the EU, NAFTA, MERCOSUR and other regional arrangements, for example, are basically designed and created, at the policy level, as macro-clusters. Sure, they have already been analyzed as instances of economic integration, and some relevant theories – notably the theory of trade creation vs. diversion (Viner, 1950) and the theory of optimum currency area (Mundell, 1961) – have been advanced. But these theories are by nature *static* in analysis. True, usually mentioned are the 'dynamic gains' from expanded markets, such as raised efficiency due to increased competition, scale economies and stepped-up R&D, and a stronger bargaining power vis-a-vis the outside world. These are, however, only 'one-time gains' (Gray, 2002a) and merely the 'adjustment' effects of an enlarged economic unit, not the dynamic causes of macro-agglomeration *per se*.

In addition to artificially created (*de jure*) macro-regionalization, moreover, there have been those of the *de facto* type, which is truly dynamic in nature. East Asia's growth clustering, particularly in the pre-crisis period, is a case in point. It was once so phenomenal that the World Bank (1993) called it 'the East Asian Miracle'. East Asia has been recognized as one growth pole of the Triad (along with North America and the EU). But, this *de facto* macro-regional clustering has not yet been carefully theorized, although the so-called (now popularized) 'flying-geese (FG)' model originally conceived by Kaname Akamatsu in the 1930s and more recently expanded by Kojima (1958, 2000), Kojima and Ozawa (1984, 1985), and Ozawa (1992, 1996, 2000b) is now often invoked to ostensibly give theoretical underpinning. This model itself, however, is still to be elaborated on, especially in institutional and financial terms.[2]

Speaking of the FG model which, in essence, describes the phenomenon of a sequential process of tandem growth among closely interacting nations through leader–emulator relationships, the world first witnessed Pax-Britannica (PB)-led macro-clustering on the Atlantic Rim – and beyond – in the nineteenth century. In this respect, PB-led clustering was clearly the first instance of FG formation. In other words, Britain was originally the very first lead goose which ushered the rest of the world into the era of industrial capitalism. In fact, when Akamatsu was writing about the FG formation in the 1930s, he was actually observing Japan's industrial and trade development within the context of the global economic dynamics that prevailed as part and parcel of the PB-led wave of global industrial expansion, in which pre-war Japan itself participated as a novice latecomer goose. And the recent East Asian miracle was a manifestation of Pax-Americana (PA)-led supra-national clustering. Hence, an important distinction needs to be made between *de jure* macroregions (such as NAFTA and the EU) as spatially contiguous and officially formulated locational entities and *de facto* macro-clustering as a process of spreading growth largely through the market mechanism of trade and factor movement from a lead economy to emulator economies. A spatial logic mainly applies to the former, whereas an intertemporal logic mostly dictates the latter.

The purpose of this chapter is first, to conceptually explore the organizational, structural, and operational logic of macro-growth clustering (a hegemon-driven process of tandem growth), and second, to see if and how such macro-clustering is interrelated to micro-clusters. It is argued that although microregions are often depicted as 'historical accidents', they are not really the haphazard, random and discrete incidences of history but are the integral concomitants and facilitators of macro-clustering – first under the Pax Britannica and more recently under the Pax Americana,[3] and that PA-led clustering is basically the vicissitudinous continuation of PB-led macro-clustering (that is, a continuous process of Anglo-Saxon-led globalization). In this respect, once the FG paradigm is reinterpreted as an analytical construct in this larger historical context, it serves as a useful frame of reference.

THE LOGIC OF *DE-FACTO* MACRO-CLUSTERING

Let us consider the nature of hegemon-led *de facto* macro-clustering. This type of supra-national macro-clustering is by nature a much broader phenomenon in geographical coverage and involvement than its *de jure* counterpart. The latter type of macro-cluster formation like the EU and NAFTA is exclusive and restrictive in participation and formality-restrained. Membership qualifications are agreed upon and spelled out. And members tend to be more or less homogeneous economies operating at relatively similar levels of economic development, sharing in common economic policies and conditions, particularly when they aim at an advanced level of economic integration (e.g. a monetary union) as is the case with the EU. In contrast, NAFTA is a rudimentary phase of integration (free trade agreement without common policies) that can accommodate Mexico's membership, despite the fact that Mexico is so different from the US and Canada in factor endowments, per capita income, and technological sophistication. Furthermore, these *de jure* forms of integration are geographically contiguous and regionally confined. They are basically designed as 'closed systems' – at least initially.

In contrast, the *de facto* type of macro-clustering has no officially specified requirements for membership; any economy can 'free-ride' on the growth stimuli provided by a hegemonic (first-lead-goose) economy. It is a market-molded type of economic agglomeration (so far as international exchanges are concerned, though individual countries may be actively involved in *dirigiste* strategies), geographically expansive and intertemporally concatenated. The PB-led Atlantic Rim clustering in the 19th and early 20th centuries (prior to World War I) and the PA-led Pacific Rim clustering in the post-World War II period are both of the *de facto* 'open systems' type. In fact, there are many similarities between these two strands of macro-clustering. After all, the latter has been a vicissitudinous outcome of the former.

The PB-led growth agglomeration has been studied mostly by economic historians and usually presented in narratives. They are concerned with the rise of the West as an economic power. Among the most notable and influential are David Landes, *The Unbound Prometheus: Technological Change and Industrial Development in Western Europe from 1750 to the Present* (1969), and Nathan Rosenberg and L.E. Birdzell, Jr, *How the West Grew Rich: The Economic Transformation of the Industrial World* (1986). This chapter draws upon these pioneering studies but more upon others in constructing an evolutionary analysis of *de facto* macro-clustering.

How and why does a hegemon-led macro-clustering phenomenon occur? What are the key transmission mechanisms of growth stimuli, technology, and information from a hegemon economy to emulators? And what causes an eventual slowdown and even a breakup in the forces of macro-clustering?

Classical Economists

Actually, in the formative years of PB-led macro-clustering two famous classical economists began to muse on some of these questions (though they did not frame the issue in the same way as in this chapter). As is well known, David Hume (1754) was among the first who initially argued that British hegemony and prosperity would prove transitory because of the inexorable catch-up of other countries. He started out with his observation about 'a happy concurrence of causes in human affairs, which checks the growth of trade and riches, and hinders them from being confined entirely to one people'. He continued:

> Where one nation has gotten the start of another in trade, it is very difficult for the latter to regain the ground it has lost: because of the superior industry and skill of the former, and the greater stocks. But these advantages are compensated, in some measure, by *the low price of labour* in every nation which has not an extensive commerce, and *does not much abound in gold and silver. Manufactures, therefore, gradually shift their places, leaving those countries and provinces which they have already enriched, and flying to others, whither they are allured by the cheapness of provisions and labour; till they have enriched there also, and are again banished by the same causes* . . . [I]n general, we may observe, that the dearness of everything, from plenty of money, is a disadvantage, which attends an established commerce, and sets bounds to it in every country, by enabling the poorer states to undersell the richer in all foreign markets. (emphasis added, Hume, 1754/1985, pp. 283–4)

Thus, although the first movers tend to lock in advantages, low-cost labor, a relatively low price level (because of 'not much abound in gold and silver') in the catching-up economies would be sufficient enough in attracting manufacturing from the rich countries. Once such a catching-up country enriches itself from manufacturing, it too meets the same fate. Expounded here is clearly the idea of sequential transmigration of manufacturing activities from one country to another, the very idea embedded in the FG paradigm.

In addition, Hume (1742) argued that '*When the arts and sciences come to perfection in any state, from that moment they naturally, or rather necessarily decline, and seldom or never revive in that nation, where they formerly flourished*' (emphasis in original, Hume, 1742/1985, p. 135). The ineluctable decline of an advanced economy is thus caused by an internal decay in the arts and sciences, as well as by external challenges (low cost foreign competition). Elmslie (1995) calls such a climactic 'Hume's Theory of Endogenous Retrogradation'. Although Hume was concerned about the eventual loss of British competitiveness, however, he did not present a systematic explanation of how, in the first place, Britain began to grow and eventually became industrially dominant in the world economy. He was concerned mainly about Britain's eventual retrogradation.

In contrast, Adam Smith (1776) advanced an evolutionary theory of Britain's nascent rise to industrial power – that is, how Britain began to develop competitiveness in the early phase of industrialization. His analysis is particularly interesting, since it explains micro-clustering as the springboard for the emergence of hegemon-led macro-clustering. He was concerned with a sequential process of economic growth. Although Alfred Marshall (1920) is usually credited for introducing the notion of spatial agglomeration (via 'industrial districts'), Adam Smith (1776) had much earlier – indeed, as many as 144 years earlier than Marshall – conceptualized the growth of industrial clustering (Ozawa, 2000a). Smith first emphasized intersectoral growth complementarity between 'country' (agriculture) and 'town' (manufacturing) as the first-phase meso-level division of labor in British industrialization. As manufacturing develops around 'an inland country naturally fertile and easily cultivated' (which, however, is unable to export surplus 'corn' because of high inland transportation costs but which instead can provide surplus food and materials for local manufacturing), it starts to produce surplus 'artifices' which are exportable:

> The manufacturers first supply the neighbourhood, and afterwards, as their work improves and refines, more distant markets . . . *The corn, which could with difficulty have been carried abroad in its own shape (on account of the expence of land carriage, and inconveniency of river navigation), is in this manner virtually exported in that of the complete manufacture, and may easily be sent to the remotest corners of the world.* (Smith, 1776/1976, pp. 430–1)

This process of micro-regionalization thus involves what may be called 'surplus-resource transmogrification' – that is, surplus corn is transmogrified into manufactures as exportables in towns (i.e., micro-industrial clusters). And once these manufacturing clusters begin to export, productivity growth is further sparked and enhanced by trade itself (due to scale economies, learning, and agglomeration), as expounded in Smith's dictum: 'the division of labor is limited by the extent of the market'. It is, indeed, this dynamic micro-regionalization process that Smith attributed the rise of Leeds, Halifax, Sheffield, Birmingham, and Wolverhampton as England's dominant industrial clusters. Smith clearly saw how trade was both influenced by and in turn reinforced the process of geographical industrial agglomeration in Britain, the critical nexus between trade and geography (in fact, more than 200 years earlier than Porter and Krugman, who are often credited for brining geography into trade and growth theory).

Living through the dawn of the Industrial Revolution, furthermore, Smith recognized the source of British industrial expansion (the rise of the Pax Britannica). His use of a pin factory as a specific example of a new division of labor taking place among workers on the shop-floor is highly indicative of his insight into the revolutionary institutional and technological changes that were about to occur during the course of the Industrial Revolution.

According to Rosenberg and Birdzell, Jr. (1986), what characterized the Western world during the period of 1750–1880 in the wake of the Industrial Revolution, were (i) the organization of production from the artisan's shop to the factory, (ii) the use of steam and water power as energy sources in factory and transportation, and (iii) the substitution of iron and steel for wood in fabricating machinery, equipment, and tools, which 'changed the size, longevity, precision, and mechanical complexity of a wide range of products, from sewing machines to ships' (Rosenberg and Birdzell, Jr., 1986, pp. 145–6). Smith unfortunately did not live to see in detail the ultimate characteristics of the Industrial Revolution, but was clearly cognizant of the benefits of organizational and technological innovations to be fostered by the invisible hand.

In short, what Smith did was to conceptualize how microregions originated and thrived on international trade during the course of Britain's early-stage industrialization. Smith's dynamic model of industrial clustering, therefore, deals with an intertemporal sequential process of agglomeration – unlike Marshall's model which is focused on the compositional and functional structure of an industrial district.[4] Smith also emphasized how trade helped manufacturers upgrade the quality of manufactures from 'necessities' to 'conveniences' to 'elegancies' (all in his original words) – namely industrial upgrading from low value-added to higher value-added goods.

Combining Hume, Smith, and economic historians' views, we can construct a classicist 'cause-and-effect' sequence model, though crude and sketchy, of the rise and decline of PB-led macro-clustering from that lead country's point of view:

> Fertile inland regions → growth of 'towns' (manufacturing sector) → division of labor between agriculture and industry → organizational and technological innovations → surplus manufactures → exports → 'the division of labor is limited by the extent of the market' → economies of scale, learning, and agglomeration → further export competitiveness and dominance → accumulation of species → decline in price competitiveness → endogenous retrogradation → a shift of manufacturing to lower-wage and low-price countries abroad.

As a way of summarizing these classical economists' contributions, we can point out that they conceptualized the following four important driving mechanisms of macro-clustering: (i) structural (agriculture to industry) and sequential industrial ('necessities' to 'conveniences' to 'luxuries') upgrading, (ii) trade as a cause of dynamic increasing returns (trade-induced economies of scale, learning, and agglomeration), (iii) the tendency of currency appreciation for a lead economy relative to developing countries, and (iv) the tendency of self-retrogradation and hence the need for continuous technological progress (knowledge creation and intensification) in a lead economy.

Neoclassical Approach

Kevin O'Rourke and Jeffrey Williamson's *Globalization and History: The Evolution of a Nineteenth Century Atlantic Economy* (1999) is the first attempt to present a comprehensive analysis of PB-led macro-clustering in terms of a received neoclassical framework, the Heckscher-Ohlin-Samuelson factor-endowment theory. O'Rourke and Williamson's aim is to examine cliometrically if income (real wages) convergence occurred among major economies during the 1850–1914 period. They argue that the driving mechanisms of what they call 'globalization' (which is equivalent to the notion of macro-clustering) are (i) cross-border factor movements (labor migration and capital flows) and (ii) international trade, both of which were substantially liberated due to reductions in transportation and communications costs (railroads, steam ships, and the telegraph) and the hegemon's (Britain's) free trade stance. Put in terms of our lexicon, the more successful a catching-up country was in allowing labor immigration and capital inflows, the more effective it was in riding on the hegmon-led wave of macro-clustering in growth. This relates directly to the success of the US as a catching-up economy.

Harley (2000), however, rightly characterizes O'Rourke and Williamson's work as 'a neoclassical comparative static analysis . . . with an aura of precision and authority'. He instead proposes a more dynamic framework 'to model growth occurring endogenously' in terms of 'externalities, induced technological change, and induced capital formation (both human and physical)' (p. 929) and stresses 'the highly spatial pattern of nineteenth century America' (p. 930).

Indeed, Harley's argument is reminiscent of, and similar to, Adam Smith's dynamic approach to micro-regionalization as the starting point of PA-led macro-clustering. He explains the rise of the US as a rapidly catching-up economy in the late nineteenth-century:

> Iron and steam had wide applications, but eventually had their greatest impact in revolutionizing transportation, first on rivers and then with the railroad and the

ocean steamship. Cheap transportation came both from improved technology arising from purposeful learning and from economies of scale. Immediately after Robert Fulton's *Clement* first used steam power on the Hudson River in 1807, steamboats revolutionalized transportation in the American West. Transportation improvement and geographic expansion continued for a century, culminating with the 'closing of the American frontier' in 1890 and then settlement of the Canadian prairies. Improvement of transportation increased incentives for capital formation, industrial concentration, international specialization, and for labor and capital migration'. (Harley, 2000, p. 930)

Here, Harley's emphasis on 'the highly spatial nature' of America's nineteenth-century catch-up can be dovetailed with Krugman's (1991) study of the consolidation of the US 'manufacturing belt'; 'early in this century . . . the great bulk of US manufacturing was concentrated in a relatively small part of the Northeast and the eastern part of the Midwest – roughly speaking, within the approximate parallelogram Green Bay–St. Louis–Baltimore–Portland' (Krugman, 1991, p. 11).

No doubt, the Green Bay–St. Louis–Baltimore–Portland manufacturing belt (a vast microregion) was engendered as the key industrial anvil of industrial and geographical expansion throughout North America. But this evolutionary story is still incomplete. Once the national market was established and conquered via railroads and the telegrpah, however, large-scale American manufacturers then headed for overseas to seek out foreign markets:

> The most important destinations for American FDI were initially the United States' immediate neighbors, Mexico and Canada. The United Kingdom, which was culturally if not geographically close to the United States, was a popular destination (although continental tariffs often induced firms to locate there). . . . Then as now, MNCs helped spread new technologies internationally, especially those embodied in capital goods. The Singer sewing machine and the McCormick reaper were prominently involved in the early wave of American FDI in Europe. (O'Rourke and Williamson, 1999, p. 218)

In addition to the frontier settlement accompanied by investments in nation-wide transportation and communications, mining, manufacturing, and financial services, it needs to be emphasized that American firms led the development of mass-production technology epitomized by Ford's moving assembly-line production (1913) and Taylor's scientific management (time and motion study). This 'American system of manufacturing'[5] was born out of America's unique industrial environment characterized by 'mass market, cheap power and raw materials, and a malleable labor force' (Harley, 2000, p. 932). In particular, 'immigrants and their sons made up over 60 percent of America's machine operatives in 1910. These unskilled but ambitious individuals, already committed to change, found high-wage but demanding employment packages attractive (Harley, 2000, p. 932).

Gathering and weaving these discrete observations into a broad framework of analysis, we can now summarize the Harley–Krugman–O'Rourke–Williamson self-augmenting mechanism of North America's emergence as a new hegemon. The sequence involved is:

America's fertile frontiers → improved transportation and communications → labor and capital inflows → further expansion of the frontiers → capital formation in the manufacturing belt → more labor immigration → geographical market expansion (until the closing of the American frontier) → the American system of manufacturing → settlement of the Canadian prairies → overseas business expansion in search of foreign market (the emergence of American MNCs).

Thus this sequential development tells how the wave of PA-led macro-clustering began – based on America's fertile frontiers, the resultant US manufacturing belt (a powerful microregion in North America), and the technological revolution in mass production. We can further add the effects of World War II, completing a full roadmap to the birth of the Pax Americana as a newly risen wave of macro-clustering.

This dynamic pattern of macro-clustering has a familiar ring with Adam Smith's model of a resource-transmogrification cluster which is a function of the expansion of the market (namely 'the division of labor is limited by the extent of the market'), involving the rapid development of America's vast frontiers. In short, we have thus outlined the fertile frontier-based expasion model of a second lead goose, the US.

FEATURES OF PB- AND PA-LED MACRO-CLUSTERINGS

There are at least six important common features (though there are obviously many dissimilarities as well) between the two strands of hegemon-led macro-clustering.

Leader's stance   Both types of macro-clustering are based on a hierarchy of diverse economies in terms of degrees of technological advance and levels of per capita income. Each hegemonic economy (the first lead goose) initially even adopted a unilateral free-trade stance. This created the vast and readily available markets to which the emulating economies were able to export goods. The hegemons thus provided a crucial external market (demand) so that the follower countries could supplement their underdeveloped internal markets and earn foreign exchange (dominant currency). The only difference between Britain and the United States as a lead economy was that the former at least initially restricted technology out-flows to retain trade competitiveness at home, while the latter was much more willing to impart its technological and organizational knowledge overseas (as evidenced by America's various programs of technology transfer in the post-World War II period) – most importantly, because of a huge technological gap that existed at the end of war.

Layers of emulators   Both the PB and PA hierarchies had layers of challengers. For the PB, as Rostow (1990b) shows in terms of his stages theory of growth that Britain had a take-off over the 1783–1802 period, followed by 'take-off Class II (1830–50)' (e.g. US, France and Germany), then by 'take-off Class III (1870–1901)' (e.g. Sweden, Japan, Russia, Italy, Canada, and Australia), and by 'take-off Class IV (1933 onward)' (e.g. Argentina, Turkey, Brazil, Mexico, Iran). Although Rostow is concerned only with identifying when the take-off (and subsequently the drive to technological maturity and high mass consumption) has occurred in different countries, his classification of countries demonstrates the time lags involved among what he calls the 'four graduating classes'. It is also of interest to note that Japan was already in the third graduating class along with such other countries as Sweden and Italy under the PB-led macro-clustering in the pre-World War I period.

The PB hegemony ended by World War I, and the between-the-wars period witnessed a global stagnation. And the United States, a member of the second graduating class, whose economy dramatically expanded during World War II, emerged decisively as a new hegemon after the war. Thus, the PA-led clustering was clearly a continuation of the PB-led clustering. In turn, the PA-led Pacific Rim clustering has been a sequence of tandem growth: US→Japan→NIEs→ASEAN→China. That is to say, the FG pattern of tandem growth has been a regional manifestation of PA-led macro-clustering.

Emulators' catch-up policy – 'infant industry' protection   The PB-led clustering indicates that the emulating nations all used dynamic infant-industry protection (import substitution) policies. Interestingly, Friedrich List (who lived 1789–1846) greatly influenced both Germany and the United States (of the second graduating class or the second geese) in adopting protection as a means of building up national manufacturing industries in their efforts to catch up with Britain. Surprisingly enough, it is not widely known that List himself was actively involved in the early protectionist movement and the formulation of the early tariff policies of the United States where he was in exile from Germany in the United States from 1825 to 1830 to escape from a ten-month sentence he received for his liberal ideas too far advanced for the government at that time (Bell, 1953).

Japan as a second goose under the PA hierarchy similarly pursued a dynamic infant-industry protection strategy; so did South Korea and Taiwan (the third-ranking geese). On the other hand, China is currently engaged in a new form of protection, what may be called 'MNC-assisted growth' (Ozawa, 2000b), involving the participation of many foreign multinationals in local industrial development in its still protected markets.

It is worth noting that even Britain's rise to power itself in the wake of the Industrial Revolution may be interpreted as an outcome of import substitution involving Indian cotton cloth. Textile machinery was invented for the very purpose of manufacturing 'the cotton yarn that European hands were too clumsy to produce by methods long used in India' (Rostow, 1990a, p. 22).

Emulators' technological contributions A successful catch-up process is not a mere borrowing of advanced knowledge (technology and skills) from the hegemonic economy. It involves original knowledge creation, normally as improvements on – or alternatives to – existing knowledge. Among the most notable innovations made by the followers during the PB-based period were, as mentioned earlier, the interchangeability/standardization of parts and the assembly line mass production (Fordism/Taylorism) in the US. Later on, under the PA-led clustering, mass production in turn came to be replaced by flexible or lean production ('Toyotism') in Japan (Womack, Jones and Roos, 1990). Japan's consumer electronics industry also made a significant contribution to innovating and commercializing a slew of sleek and wondrous gadgets, devices and components (ranging from pocket-size transistor radios in the late 1950s to business-card-size calculators, the quartz watch, portable stereos, VCRs in the 1970s to LCDs and camcorders in the 1980s to CD players, digital cameras, and high-definition flat TVs in the 1990s). The simultaneous existence of the technologically capable second geese is critical in augmenting and further spreading the forces of macro-clustering initially set in motion by the lead goose. The role of the second geese as a technological augmenter cannot be overemphasized.

Trade pattern In both hierarchies, multilateral patterns of trade ensued. Britain (the first goose) and its close emulators, continental Europe and the US, focused on manufacturing, while the primary producing countries (mostly colonies) specialized in producing and providing raw materials to the industrial North. And a new international division of labor developed between Britain and other newly industrialized European countries and the US, in which Britain tended to specialize in the old industries (steel, ships, rails, and related goods) and services (especially international finance and insurance), and Europe and the US in the new industries (chemicals and electrical goods) (Landes, 1969).

Similarly, under the PA hierarchy the US and Japan – and later on, the Asian NIEs – have been supported by imports of industrial materials and fuels (oil and natural gas) from the Third World. In addition, a new division of labor developed between the US and East Asia, in which the former became ever more services-oriented (e.g., R&D, banking, finance, and insurance), while the latter specialized in manufacturing, both old and new. These patterns of multilateralism are the reflections of trade based on differences in the stages of growth and structural upgrading.

Currency stability   Both the PB-led and PA-led regimes produced a golden age of capitalism – chronologically speaking, 1820–1913 for the former and 1950–73 for the latter, respectively. During the PB-led golden age the GDPs and exports of constituent countries rose phenomenally; 2.2 (1820–70) to 2.5 percent (1870–1913) in growth rates and 4.0 percent (1820–70) and 3.9 percent (1870–1913) in export expansion. During the PA-led golden age, 4.9 percent in growth and 8.6 percent in export expansion for the PA (Maddison, 1982 as cited in Glyn *et al.*, 1990). Thus, global economic involvement (Gray, 1999), another way of describing a process of globalization, intensified. The golden-age growth of the PB was facilitated by the gold standard, and that of the PA first by the Bretton Woods system of fixed exchange rates – but later also by its ability to adapt to and manage flexible rates when this proved vital.

Disruptions in macro-clustering   The PB-led clustering was ended by World War I, while its PA-led counterpart has so far been interrupted by oil crises (in 1974 and 1978) and most recently by a series of financial crises, notably in Asia and Latin America. But the hegemonic power of the United States continues.

INTERACTIONS BETWEEN MICRO- AND MACRO-CLUSTERING

Notwithstanding the conventional wisdom that microregions are haphazard accidental outcomes of history, their origins and formations have been closely related to the different stages of growth and structural upgrading under the forces of hegemon-led macro-clustering. In fact, microregions have come into existence as facilitators of structural consolidation for each stage of growth. This relationship can be best demonstrated in terms of the industrial upgrading stages model of growth, which is a reformulated FG theory (Ozawa, 1992, 1996, 2000b and 2001b). This framework of analysis is a leading growth sector model a la Schumpeter (1934), in which a sequence of growth is punctuated by stages in each of which a certain industrial sector can be identified as the main engine of structural transformation – in sharp contrast to the neoclassical view of growth as a smooth incremental accumulation of capital.

The growth sequence has so far consisted of five different stages.[6] Although derived from the Japanese experience, these stages are exactly the ones through which the currently advanced countries have gone through over an extended period of time. The latecomers, however, have been able to catch up by climbing up these stages more quickly in a time-compressed fashion, as Japan and the Asian NIEs have done most recently, and China is in the midst of such a fast-track structural transformation. Within this framework, we can now consider how microregions fit into the path of hegemon-led industrial upgrading and economic growth. In each stage, a stage-specific type of microregion has come into existence, driven primarily by the market logic but frequently assisted by the government:

(i) *Stage I: 'Heckscher-Ohlin' factor-driven industries (labor-intensive goods and natural resources, such as minerals and oil)*: This stage represents the elementary start of industrialization. Resource-rich countries initially develop resource-exploitative clusters (centered on, for example, coal, iron ore, and oil). Labor-abundant developing countries give birth to the Marshallian type of clusters, especially the export processing zone clusters in low-cost labor-intensive manufacturing. And in Britain, historically speaking, the Smithian surplus-resource transmogrification clusters played the key role in developing export-oriented industrial areas (such as Sheffield and Leeds), enabling Britain to quickly move up to the next stage of heavy and chemical industrialization.

(ii) *Stage II: 'Non-differentiated Smithian' scale-driven industries (steel, basic chemicals, petrochemicals)*: The industrial complex clusters emerge around steel mills and petrochemical complexes, which are dominated by some large companies and served by a number of subcontractors and service providers. Postwar Japan built the so-called konbinato clusters in the coastal areas to develop heavy and chemical industrial complexes, capitalizing on low-cost ocean transportation for importing raw materials and shipping out bulky and heavy goods. In this stage of economic growth the state usually plays an active role as the promoter of heavy and chemical industries which are often regarded as strategic to national interests, since their products are closely related to armaments and defense.

(iii)   *Stage III: 'Differentiated Smithian' assembly-driven industries (air-craft, automobiles, and early-generation electric/electronics goods)*: These industries are vertically integrated and intensive in the use of parts, components, and accessories. The hub-and-spoke clusters (e.g. the Boeing town and the Toyota town) are the products of this stage of structural upgrading.

(iv)   *Stage IV: 'Schumpeterian' R&D-driven industries (latest generation electronics goods and biotech goods)*: The knowledge-leader-based clusters (such as Silicon Valley) and the science and technology park clusters (such as the Research Triangle in North Carolina and the Hsinchu Science Park in Taiwan) are the concomitants of this stage of growth. In fact, there are close inter-regional interactive relations between Silicon Valley and Hsinchu in the integrated corporate chains of value-added across the Pacific (Saxenian, 2000).

(v)   *Stage V: 'McLuhan' IT-driven industries (Internet-based industries)*: The IT-Net-based clusters (such as Bangalore in India, Bit Valley in Japan, and Cyber-Sheikdom in Dubai) have come into existence in the wake of the information and communications technology revolution in the 1990s.

All the microregions are thus the creatures of the forces of macro-clustering that have brought about the different stages of industrial upgrading, the stages that were created over time by the pioneering innovations originated in the lead-goose countries and emulated – and sometimes reinvigorated – by the follower-goose countries. In this evolutionary development, the market-coordinated type of microregions (e.g. Marshallian industrial districts) were first created, then followed by the hierarchically structured type (e.g. hub-and-spoke clusters), and more recently by the networking type (e.g. Silicon Valley) – each compatible for the evolution of growth stages. In this connection, it should be noted that the PB-led regime was responsible for initiating the first two stages (Heckscher-Ohlin and non-differentiated Smithian), whereas the PA-led regime for constructing the third, fourth, and fifth stages (differentiated Smithian, Schumpeterian, and McLuhan). Toward the end of the third stage, Japan momentarily nearly surged ahead of the United States in assembly-driven manufacturing due to the innovation of 'just-in-time' lean production as if it was about to lead another genre of hegemon-led macro-clustering (there was even a suggestion of the emerging Pax Japonica). But the United States decisively restored its hegemonic dominance once and for all by innovating McLuhan industries. And the rest of the world has again been trying to catch up with the United States in this latest phase of information technology-based structural transformation.

In the wake of such leader–emulator rivalry, therefore, collective involve-ment – government-led and core-firm-led alike – in establishing microre-gions has been on the rise, now that the benefits of micro-regionalization are increasingly recognized and consciously sought after at the policy level. In other words, the degree of consciousness in the construction of micro-regions seems to have risen, especially in emulator countries. In this regard, a further study on policies for capitalizing on the forces of macro-clustering is called for – parallel to a theory of microregional policy proposed in Gray and Dunning (2000).

FINAL WORDS

Microregions within a country have recently attracted attention among scholars and have been eagerly explored, both conceptually and empiri-cally. At the same time, the notion of macroregions has been introduced as a counterpart of microregions. Yet macroregions are not yet adequately explored conceptually as the dynamic phenomenon of economic agglom-eration. In this connection, a distinction needs to be made between two types of macro-agglomeration, *de jure* and *de facto*. This chapter intro-duced the new concept of hegemon-led *de facto* macro-clustering and explored the nature of two genres of such macro-clustering: PB-led and PA-led growth agglomerations.

The so-called FG model is directly aimed at explaining a process of macro-clustering mainly in the context of East Asian experiences. Japan is often depicted as Asia's lead goose, but such an FG formation itself has been a branched-out manifestation of PA-led macro-clustering. The latter in turn has been the most successful vicissitudinous extension of PB-led macro-clustering. Indeed, the present trend of globalization is nothing but the thrust of PA-driven growth agglomeration, while the once-observed rapid global integration at the end of the nineteenth century was the outcome of PB-led macro-clustering.

This chapter has made the first attempt to analyze the interconnected-ness between macro-clustering and the different types of stage-specific microregions. It is argued that the emergence of a specific type of microre-gions ('sticky places' in Markusen's celebrated phrase, 'sticky places in slip-pery space', 1996) should be interpreted as an essential part of higher-order hegemon-driven macro-clustering that occurs globally (in 'slippery space') at the supranational level – that is, microregions are both facilitators and concomitant outcomes of macro-clustering. This relationship is best illus-trated in terms of the reformulated FG paradigm of stages-based industrial upgrading.

NOTES

1. Dunning (2000b) examines how MNEs' FDI has been affected by recent events in the EU, while Eden and Monteils (2000) look at the impact of the formation and progress of NAFTA on the strategies of multinationals. Blomstrom, Goberman and Kokko (2000) study how FDI flows increase as a result of regional integration agreements.
2. Nevertheless, the FG model has so far been the only paradigm to explain hegemon-led macro-clustering. Its weakness is that the model is still confined to the real sector alone, with little analysis of the critical institutional, especially financial (money sector), aspect of FG growth. For the first attempt to correct this weakness, see Ozawa (2001b).
3. Even before the emergence of PB-led macro-clustering, micro-regionalization had occurred. This is because there existed many other hegemon-led clusters, for example, under the changing fortunes of Florentine, Venetian, Genoese, and Dutch hegemonies (Arrighi, 1994).
4. For a detailed analysis of Smith's conceptualization of industrial clustering, see Ozawa (2000a).
5. 'The idea of standardizing a product and its various parts originated in Sweden in the early eighteenth century and before 1800 had been tried at least once in France, Switzerland, and England. Through standardization, the parts of one product could be interchanged for the parts of a like product, facilitating manufacture and repair. The first permanently successful application of the idea in a nontrivial use was made in the American armament industry. At the turn of the nineteenth century, Eli Whitney and Simeon North almost simultaneously obtained contracts from the government to manufacture firearms by the interchangeable parts method. The two men worked independently, making different contributions to the field, and it is hard to say which of these geniuses had the more important influence on the evolution of what Europeans came in time to call 'the American System' (Robertson, 1955, p. 194).
6. How an economy moves from one stage to the next is explained in cause-and-effect relations in Ozawa (1992, 1996, 2001b). It is not a mere typology of stages.

11. Understanding the entry strategies of international franchisers with Dunning's envelope OLI paradigm

Yong Suhk Pak and Sam Beldona

INTRODUCTION

Mainstream scholars of international business (IB) have tended to neglect the question of the determinants of the choice of entry modes to distribute and sell their products in foreign markets, indeed, it could be said that, with certain exceptions such as of Root (1994) and Buckley and Casson (1998), the questions of foreign marketing and distribution have not been given the importance that these issues merit. One possible reason for this neglect is the relatively small amount of capital required for a sales organization compared with that required by production units (although this reason could be less convincing when defined in terms of value-added): this explanation would suggest that the question of which entry mode is adopted for local sales by foreign multinational corporations (MNCs) is of little consequence.

The activities of US firms using the franchising approach for foreign sales have grown steadily (McIntyre and Huszagh, 1995) so the problem of identifying the determinants of choice of entry mode deserves more attention. This chapter provides an empirical analysis of the choice of entry mode of MNCs, which rely on some version of a franchising mode, and addresses the determinants of the choice of mode in terms of the latest 'envelope' version of Dunning's eclectic paradigm (2000b).

Because firms that adopt a franchise system abroad will provide a special kind of goods and services which lend themselves to this mode of servicing markets, there is a natural tendency for believing that firms which utilize the franchise system at home will use the same system for penetrating foreign markets. However, there are many additional problems to be faced, such as geographical and cultural distance (Root, 1994) and agency problems (Contractor and Kundu, 1998), which may qualify the simple assumption. Firms need to incorporate both internal and external or foreign factors (such as local demand conditions, legal restrictions, and the active role of foreign applicants) in the selection of an entry mode (Pak, 2000). That said, it is reasonable to suppose that firms which adopt the franchise mode of servicing markets in their home country are likely to comprise the population of potential international franchisers.

The chapter first reviews the determinants of franchisers' choice of entry mode in terms of the latest version of Dunning's paradigm – the so-called envelope version (2000b). Then, the interaction between the determinants and two types of entry modes will be analyzed empirically.

OLI ADVANTAGES AS AN ENVELOPE PARADIGM: RESEARCH FRAMEWORK

Dunning's OLI paradigm (1977, 1993a, 1995) provides the analytical basis for nearly all studies of international production and foreign direct investment (FDI). To this point, the eclectic paradigm has not been utilized for analyses of the international franchising process. By virtue of its position as the core paradigm of IB, it can be expected to provide valuable insights into the franchising decision. Dunning (2000b) has reconfigured the OLI paradigm to embrace the 'asset-augmenting' aspects of FDI and MNC activity. For example, O-specific advantages have been divided into two categories – static and dynamic. Those advantages that are possessed by a firm and which generate income at a given point of time are defined as static. The proprietary factors which allow a firm to increase (or improve) its income-generating assets over time are defined as dynamic O advantages. In the empirical study below, the static O advantage is operationalized as deriving from the country of origin (or home country), while a dynamic O advantage is operationalized as the management of production knowledge to access new capabilities overseas.

Dunning and many others have stressed the importance of the spatial dimension, i.e. locational advantages, as it affects the competitiveness of the investing MNCs. In the modern globalized environment, it is important that firms continuously upgrade their knowledge capital, and one way of accomplishing this goal is to extend its operations to locations that offer asset-augmenting environments. Dunning (2000b) emphasizes the importance of entry into an established research and development (R&D) area as being the prime example of asset-augmenting investments (either through mergers or acquisitions), but the concept of dynamic O advantages can apply to all activities in foreign countries.

Geographic locations whose main attractions used to be seen either as sources of supply for primary products relying on mineral deposits or climate or as markets can be identified as static L advantages, and those regions in which agglomeration yields scope for asset-augmenting activities (in, say, R&D) constitute dynamic L advantages. Note that the sources of dynamic L advantages are well entrenched so that the advantage cannot be easily reproduced elsewhere. While individual firms may easily relocate knowledge and similar assets, assets with a public goods or collective characteristic cannot be easily moved (Markusen, 1996; Porter, 1998). The concentration of pharmaceutical research in New Jersey and its neighboring regions in southern New York and Connecticut is one example and Silicon Valley is another. Presence in such a region is seen as a dynamic L advantage although, as the examples suggest, it is necessary to identify sub-national regions as well as countries. A static L advantage is operationalized in the empirical study in terms of demand potential in foreign markets, while a dynamic L advantage is operationalized as the importance of foreign market as sources of learning.

Lastly, internalization (I) advantages explain (given a set of O and L specific advantages) why firms prefer to internalize their foreign value-adding activities within the hierarchy rather than to lease/license the rights to use their O advantages. The dynamic I advantage is identified by the increasing role of learning and knowledge-creating activities in the global economy as it continues to integrate more deeply. The static approach mainly concerns how to take advantage of the current assets, while a dynamic I advantage needs to explain why asset-augmenting activities have to be internalized. Accordingly, one variable for a dynamic I advantage is operationalized as the efforts to develop foreign markets.

TWO TYPES OF ENTRY MODE

The foreign market entry choices are dichotomized based on the degree of control of the foreign outlets, the level of resource commitment, and the opportunities to learn (Table 11.1). Many researchers have already set a ground rule between the relationships of equity commitment and the ability to control (Davison, 1982; Anderson and Gatignon, 1986; Root, 1994). The opportunity to learn is emphasized in our work. The resulting two types of entry mode are shown in Table 11.1. Table 11.2 shows the distribution of two types of entry modes of sample firms.

There were 72 sample firms. Among them only seven firms engaged in more than one type of the entry modes. The results are listed in Table 11.2, which shows that the majority of international franchisers preferred to enter overseas markets through contractual modes such as master franchising, area developer, direct franchising, and licensing (e.g. EM1); 81.9% of total sample firms entered foreign markets by making contracts with foreign

Table 11.1　Two types of foreign market entry mode of international franchisers

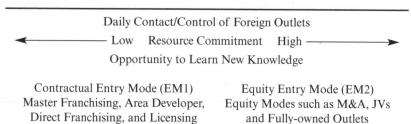

Daily Contact/Control of Foreign Outlets
◄──────── Low　Resource Commitment　High ──────────►
Opportunity to Learn New Knowledge

Contractual Entry Mode (EM1)	Equity Entry Mode (EM2)
Master Franchising, Area Developer,	Equity Modes such as M&A, JVs
Direct Franchising, and Licensing	and Fully-owned Outlets

Table 11.2　Distribution of two types of foreign market entry mode

	EM1	*EM2*	*Total*
Frequency	13	59	72
Percentage	81.9	18.1	100.0

Table 11.3　Cross-tabulation of entry types and nationality of samples

	US	*UK*	*Total*
Entry EM1	55	4	59
Percentage within nationality	91.7	33.3	83.19
Types EM2	5	8	13
Percentage within nationality	8.3	66.7	16.9
Total	60	12	72
Percentage of total count	83.3	16.7	100

business partners. Only 18.1% of the total entry cases were conducted through equity ownership modes such as merger and acquisition, joint ventures, and company-owned outlets. Since the samples consist of international franchisers from the US and the UK, one needs to check whether the origin of country plays a role in selecting an entry mode. Erramilli (1996) and Hennart and Larimo (1998) showed that national origin affects the subsidiaries' ownership strategy. Table 11.3 is a cross-tabulation between the two types of entry mode and the nationality (US vs. UK) of sample firms. It shows the preference of entry mode by firms with a different nationality.

Of the US entry cases, 91.7% concentrated on contractual modes (e.g., EM1), while 33.3% of the UK entry mode cases were through contracts. As a result, only 8.3% of the total US entry cases were via equity modes, while two third (66.7%) of the UK entry cases were committed by equity modes (e.g. EM2). In addition to the nationality, there are various factors affecting the selection of entry mode. The determinants are addressed by reviewing Dunning's OLI paradigm in the following section.

RESEARCH HYPOTHESES

In the following section we analyze the interface between the above-mentioned static and dynamic OLI advantages and selection of entry modes between the two types.

Nationality of the international franchisers   Country of origin should impact the selection of entry mode (Erramilli, 1996; Hennart and Larimo, 1998) due to the firm-specific advantages originating from the home country characteristics (Nachum and Rolle, 1999; Dunning, 1998, 2000b). Different home country conditions, which include economic and political features and serve as a global platform of international franchisers, may lead to different firm behaviors.

Based on the size of population, we can safely argue that US franchisers have been more actively engaged in international operations than UK firms. Consequently, they could have accumulated knowledge that institutionalizes the contract procedure of forming franchising relations overseas different from that of UK firms. Therefore we propose that:

H1: The selection of entry mode will vary by country of origin.

Change of production knowledge   Dunning's envelope OLI (2000b) contrasts with previous ones (1988b, 1993a, 1995) regarding its emphasis on knowledge gaining and augmentation of firm-specific assets. His argument is that firms expand into overseas markets not only to exploit but also to protect and to augment their O specific advantages. If we apply his argument to the franchising business, franchisers with dynamic ability of accessing and organizing production knowledge throughout the world are expected to change their production knowledge more frequently.

Then, between the transactional and equity entry modes, the latter seems appropriate to access, learn, and change production knowledge of franchisers. Therefore, a positive relationship is expected between the management of changing production knowledge and the selection of equity modes.

H2: The more a franchiser changes its production knowledge, the higher the probability of selecting equity modes to enter overseas markets.

Demand condition   In a booming market, a franchiser may expect to have many applicants who try to take advantage of potential demand. A high demand condition will subsequently generate large numbers of applicants and minimize the opportunistic behaviors of franchisees. As a result, a franchiser may wish to expand through franchisee-owned outlets.

On the other hand, high demand potential rationalizes the high commitment level of foreign production, while low and uncertain sales potential of the target market induces low commitment entry modes such as licensing (Root, 1994). This is a typical condition of Dunning's locational advantage. In a high potential market, a franchiser may wish to establish its franchising network quickly within the hierarchies.

Based on this reasoning we propose that:

> *H3: The more a franchiser recognizes the importance of demand potential overseas, the higher the probability of selecting equity modes.*

Foreign locations as a source of learning   In the study of international franchising, the importance of foreign locations as a source of learning has been rarely emphasized. We feel that this may be due to the conventional wisdom that franchisers have a repository of knowledge that is transferred to franchisees. That is a franchiser develops a business format franchising system and transfers the whole package of knowledge to franchisees. In reality, however, an international franchiser learns from international experience. For example, McDonald's has benefited from the distinctive market condition of foreign locations. The Dutch operation created a prefabricated modular store that can be moved over a weekend (Serwer, 1994). Satellite stores, or low overhead mini-McDonald's, which operate in hospitals, downtown business districts, and sports arenas in the US, were invented in high-rent Singapore. Therefore, equity ownership is preferred due to the tacit component of knowledge gaining when a company tries to learn. Therefore we propose that:

> *H4: The more a franchiser recognizes the importance of foreign locations as a source of learning, the higher the probability of selecting equity modes.*

Foreign market development   The effort to develop foreign markets is operationalized for the internalization sub-paradigm. International franchisers should have two options between the market and within its own organization to develop foreign markets. Master franchising and area developer entry modes seem to be the quickest ways to penetrate and develop a foreign market. Merger/acquisition is also another way of quickly penetrating a target market. M&A seems the best option for market development since the existing operation can smoothly pass on within the hierarchy under the control of a franchiser's daily involvement. In reality, however, it may not be a feasible option. It is harder to come across firms that are ready to sell their operations than to find qualified master franchising or area developers. Then, international franchisers may set up company-owned outlets, which should generate management costs of remote foreign operations.

Therefore, efforts to develop foreign markets entail both firm-specific and market-specific transaction costs. However, a company that tries to aggressively develop foreign markets, may consider less about the management costs than market transaction costs. Subsequently, in terms of minimizing transaction costs, international franchisers may choose to use equity modes to aggressively develop foreign markets. Based on this reasoning we propose that:

H5: The more a franchiser tries to develop foreign markets aggressively, the higher the probability of selecting equity modes.

In sum, the framework based on Dunning's 'envelope' OLI paradigm is shown in Figure 11.1, which shows the key determinants of foreign market entry modes of international franchisers. In order to include as many as possible international franchisers from diverse countries of origin, thirty-two

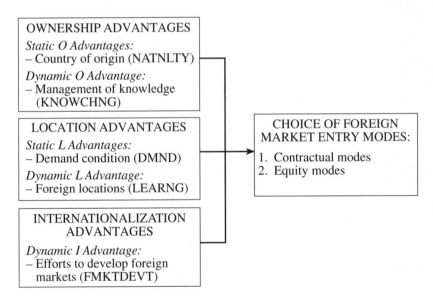

Figure 11.1   A dynamic OLI framework affecting the selection of foreign market entry modes of international franchiser

national franchise associations across the world were contacted by mail. Twenty-three associations wrote back. None of them were aware of their national firms operating overseas except the British Franchise Association, which had a list of thirty international UK franchisers. Since two had gone out of business, twenty-eight of them serve as the universe of this survey of UK international franchisers.

The US franchisers listed as the 'top 200 international franchisers' in *International Entrepreneur* magazine were individually contacted by phone for information about directors in charge of the international operations. Among them one hundred sixty franchisers were recognized as appropriate for this research. The rest were disqualified because the firms were controlled by the same management team under the different brand names, or were not engaged in international operations other than in Canada. Subsequently, a total of one hundred eighty-eight firms became the population of this research.

Dillman's (1978) methods were followed as closely as possible. The first mailing consisted of the questionnaire, a cover letter, and a business reply envelope to return the survey. Three weeks after the first mailing, a reminder post card was mailed to the respondents requesting that the survey be returned. Two weeks after the first reminder post card was mailed, a second mailing of questionnaires was done identical to the first one. Three weeks after the second questionnaire was mailed a second reminder card was mailed to the respondents. Two weeks after the second reminder cards were mailed a third questionnaire was mailed to the respondents requesting their participation. In all survey questionnaires were sent three times within an interval of ten weeks.

Eight surveys were returned uncompleted for several reasons: 1) a company policy of not responding to surveys; 2) the CEO to whom the survey was addressed was no longer with the firm; or 3) they considered themselves as non-international. In total, seventy-two useable responses were received for a response rate of 38.3%. A total of twelve UK and sixty US international franchisers responded, resulting in a response rate of 42.9% and 37.7% respectively from each survey population.

STATISTICAL METHODS

Binary Logistic Regression

For a binary response variable where EM1 represents contractual modes and EM2 represents equity modes, a binary logistic regression such as the following is appropriate (Mendenhall and Sincich, 1993):

$$\text{Logit } (P_i) = \text{Log } [P_i/1 - P_i] = \alpha + \beta X_i,$$

where $P_i = \text{Prob } (Y_i = Y_i | X_i)$ is the response probability to be modeled, α is the intercept parameter, β is the vector of slope parameters, and X_i is the vector of explanatory variables. Other researchers (Contractor and Kundu, 1998 studying international franchisers have also dichotomized the entry mode selections. To include all five explanatory variables in a regression model, a simple correlation table among the explanatory variables is prepared to inspect the multicollinearity bias (Table 11.4). Since there seems to be no serious violation of multicollinearity bias as shown in Table 11.4, we included all five variable to test the relations with the two entry mode types.

The binary logistic model (Table 11.5), with an overall Chi-square value of 46.979 at a .0001 significant level, indicates the null hypothesis that all coefficients are zero is rejected at a statistical significance of .0001 (Kleinbaum, 1994). Accordingly, the correct classification or concordance ratio is a fairly high 94.9% with this model (Table 11.6). For the explanation of variation, Nagelkerke (1991) proposed a modification of the Cox and Snell's R^2 so that the full explanation of variation (e.g. the R^2 of 1) could be achieved. For this model, 78.8% of the variation could be explained.

Among the five explanatory variables included in the logistic model, two revealed statistical significance. The variables include nationality of the firm ($p < .01$) and recognition of foreign locations as a source of learning at ($p < .005$). The signs of the two significant variables are as expected. Since contractual and equity modes were recorded as 0 and 1, respectively, and since nationality of the firms was recorded as 0 (UK) and 1 (US), the negative sign of country of origin (nationality) indicates that the UK firms are more likely to engage in equity entry modes. The large magnitude of the nationality coefficient signifies its influence in the regression. Since research on international franchisers has samples from the US, the different preference over the foreign market entry modes between international franchisers from the US and UK is detected for the first time in this research. Then, the positive sign of the learning variable explains that international franchisers paying attention to the importance of foreign locations as a source of learning will enter foreign markets via equity modes.

In sum, a static O advantage (e.g. nationality of the firm) and a dynamic L advantage (e.g. foreign locations as a source of learning) combined to explain US and UK international franchisers' entry modes. Therefore, it was found that US international franchisers prefer to enter foreign markets via contract modes, while the majority of the UK franchisers, entering foreign markets via equity modes, recognize the importance of learning overseas markets.

Extending the eclectic paradigm

Table 11.4   Correlations among explanatory variables

	1	2	3	4	5
1. NATNLTY	1.000	–	–	–	–
2. KNOWCHNG	.033	1.000	–	–	–
3. DMND	.068	.048	1.000	–	–
4. LEARNG	.337**	.169	.289*	1.000	–
5. FMKTDEVT	.019	.230	.157	.282*	1.000

Note: * and ** indicate significant at the 0.05 and 0.01 level (2-tailed) respectively.

Table 11.5   Binary logistic regression using a generalized LOGIT model

Variable	Parameter estimate (β)	Standard error	Wald Chi-square	Significance P > Chi-square
Intercept	−9.809	4.109	5.699	.000
NATNLTY	−3.967	1.545	6.589	**.010**
KNOWCHNG	.847	.533	2.527	.112
DMND	.017	.257	.005	.946
LEARNG	1.094	.391	7.838	**.005**
FMKTDEVT	.259	4.109	.579	.447

Table 11.6   Classification table and model summary

	Predicted		Percentage correct
	Contractual modes	Equity modes	
Observed Contractual mode	57	1	98.3
Equity modes	3	10	76.9
Overall percentage			94.4

−2 Log likelihood Chi-square: 20.622   With 5 d.f. $p = .000$
   Cox & Snell's $R^2 = .484$ Nagelkerke's $R^2 = .788$

DISCUSSION

The largest coefficient of nationality of firms indicates the different prefer-ence of entry mode selections between two national franchisers, the US and the UK. As shown in Table 11.3 the UK sample firms preferred equity modes of foreign market entry. The country of origin has been recognized as significant elsewhere, affecting FDI activities in the US (Grosse and Trevino, 1996; Hennart and Larimo, 1998) and foreign subsidiary owner-ship decisions (Erramilli, 1996). This finding is consistent with the test result of firms' preference to have control: firms that desire to have more control are likely to have more equity ownership in the domestic market and also in foreign markets than those with less desire to control. Despite rejection of the hypothesis of the management of production knowledge due to an insignificant p value (.112), the positive sign of its beta coefficient indicates that firms wish to have more control via the equity modes to manage their production knowledge.

The static L variable, foreign market demand condition (DMND), does not show statistical significance between firms with the different entry modes. Zietlow and Hennart (1996) could not find statistical significance for the role of market size differentiating between the usage of wholesale distributors and retailers, either. The second largest coefficient with statisti-cal significance was managerial perception regarding the significance of foreign locations as a source of learning. As hypothesized, the positive β coefficient indicates the positive relationship between the selection of equity modes and the recognition of foreign markets as a dynamic source of learning. Therefore, the UK international franchisers, who emphasize the significance of foreign locations for enhancing competitiveness, are most likely to select equity modes. It means that the US sample firms, on the contrary, pay little attention to worldwide learning and tend to strike contractual relations overseas. The only concern regarding research proce-dures is the sample size of firms with equity modes: there were thirteen firms, eight of which were from the UK. The majority of the US sample firms favored contractual modes. Given the exploratory nature of this study this lopsided representation of firms was hard to avoid. However, in line with other research conducted in non-franchising sectors, the country of origin is recognized as one of the key determinants affecting the selection of entry mode for international franchisers.

The franchising format enables franchisers to enjoy diversified sources of revenue by expanding into overseas markets without taking full respon-sibility for the operational results (Caves and Murphy, 1976). An exogenous franchiser can relatively lower the risk of foreign operation by signing con-tracts with local foreign franchisees, who can manage and/or take the full

responsibility for foreign outlets. Accordingly, most international franchisers enter overseas markets via a non-equity entry mode (Zietlow and
Hennart, 1996; US Department of Commerce, 1988). There, however, still
remain a few international franchisers who prefer to enter foreign markets
by investing financial and managerial assets. The overall percentage of this
group of international franchisers is much smaller than those who select
the contractual mode of foreign market entry. However, the underlying
strategic rationale of the former group needs to be highlighted because of
its implication for the future competitiveness of firms.

In his 'envelope' paradigm, Dunning (2000b) tried to embrace asset-
augmenting foreign direct investment. Dunning's eclectic paradigm served
both as an envelope of context-specific theories and a common analytical
framework for the understanding of foreign value-added activities. Since
contextual theories have mainly been applied to explain the selection of
entry mode in the field of international non-franchising research, this
chapter empirically tests Dunning's OLI paradigm. By embracing the asset-
augmenting international production of companies, the 'envelope' OLI
paradigm provides an opportunity to understand international franchisers
not only through the conventional view of market seekers but also through
the evolutionary view of knowledge learners. The traditional understanding of international franchisers trying to maximize rent extraction by
engaging in international operations needs to be complemented with a
dynamic view of firms building core competencies and knowledge by
matching their competitive advantages to global markets.

It was found that firms with different entry strategies have different global
strategic motivations and a different understanding of foreign locations and
partners as sources of dynamic learning. This research supports the theory
that hierarchies are considered more appropriate than price mechanisms in
terms of gaining new knowledge, and international franchisers with equity
modes are expected to have greater strategic motivation to learn or gain
competitiveness overseas. This research also supports the fact that country
of origin has special meaning in understanding firms' behavior.

CONCLUSION

Results of this study indicate that the most preferred mode of entry by the
majority of international franchisers, (most of whom are from the US), is
found to be contractual. The US government has observed that the majority of international franchisers have entered foreign markets by setting up
master franchisers (US Department of Commerce, 1988). It seems quite
natural that they prefer contractual modes since the intrinsic nature of the

franchising business is to form franchising relations by signing contracts with franchisees. Consequently, in the study of franchising, the efficiency of asset exploitation has been regarded as the core determinant affecting the choice of the organizational mode of franchisers.

The underpinning theoretical framework of Dunning's envelope OLI paradigm, which dichotomized the exploitation and asset-augmentation of OLI advantages, provided a solid framework for testing not only what the companies were trying to take advantage of but also the dynamic learning aspect of international franchising operations. Accordingly, the selection of foreign market entry mode could be regarded as a strategic approach to acquiring new knowledge, especially for UK franchisers. In sum, the influence of foreign locations on the competitiveness of multinational franchisers that take advantage of foreign capabilities could be a very fruitful research topic in the field of international franchising.

12. Asynchronous political and economic development and the Asian financial crisis: a preliminary analysis

Michael A. Santoro and Changsu Kim[1]

INTRODUCTION: TOWARD A BETTER PREDICTOR OF FINANCIAL CRISIS.

In the course of his distinguished career, our colleague, mentor, and friend John H. Dunning, left an indelible mark on virtually every aspect of international business studies. The subject of this chapter – the relationship between economic and political development and risk – is no exception to this rule. In his 1993 Geary Lecture to the Economic and Social Research Institute in Dublin, Professor Dunning offered the prescient observation that 'just like the emerging managerial structure of the twenty-first century firms, we need governments to be lean, flexible and anticipatory of change. The new paradigm of government should eschew such negative or emotive sounding words such as "command", "intervention", "regulation", and replace them with words such as "empower", "steer", "co-operative", "co-ordination" and "systemic"' (Dunning, 1993b).

As the twenty-first century begins, Professor Dunning's vision of soft government oversight of the economy is still markedly ahead its time, particularly among the developing nations of East Asia. Indeed, as we argue below, the heavy-handed direction of economic resources was one of the factors contributing to the financial crises besetting East Asia in 1997.

For private investors, the biggest shock of the financial crisis derived from the inability of the debt and equity markets to anticipate the crisis. Indeed, foreign capital continued to flow into East Asia as usual until just before the crisis commenced (Rahman, 1998). Until the crisis started in mid-1997, the Euromoney Country Risk Assessment ratings of the East Asian countries hardest hit by the crisis changed curiously little (*Euromoney*, 1996–98). Credit rating agencies such as Standard and Poor's (1996–98) and *Institutional Investor* (1996–98) also did not provide any indication of the impending crisis in their ratings of the sovereign debt of the East Asian countries.

The dismal failure of standard investment risk measures to presage the crisis calls into question the methodology and accuracy of currently prevailing forms of country risk assessment. A better screen for country risk would have helped to detect the financial crisis at an earlier stage and thereby ameliorated both its private and public impacts. In this chapter we examine the economic development history of East Asian countries in order to construct an alternative method of assessing country risk in general and the East Asian financial crisis in particular. We then present some very preliminary empirical findings about the viability of our alternative metric.

THE EAST ASIAN FINANCIAL CRISIS: LOOKING BACK AND LOOKING FORWARD.

In recent years numerous studies have established a positive association between economic and political development (e.g. Scott and Lodge, 1985; Przeworski, 1995; Barro, 1997). These studies all suggest that the congruence of economic and political development is a crucial factor. In order for a country to engage in sustainable economic development, economic growth must be accompanied by political development. Conversely, for political development to be sustainable, a certain level of economic development must generally be obtained.

We propose to illustrate the foregoing general propositions by considering economic openness along with political development as shown in Figure 12.1. In our metric, open economy countries have embraced free trade and investment, as well as active public securities markets. The political development dimension encompasses factors such as the structure and distribution of power within a society, the transparency of the legal environment, and the development of professional bureaucratic institutions to regulate macro-economic variables.

Viewed in these terms, the East Asian model of development is depicted in Figure 12.1. The model typically involves highly centralized, if not authoritarian, regimes that have fostered a market economy before experiencing political development. Ironically, the very factors that we suggest contributed to the crisis – heavy-handed government controls over investment and industrial policies – were the very factors that just a few years ago were being hailed as responsible for the economic rise of East Asia. Indeed, in the case of Malaysia, the imposition of these sorts of policies after the crisis has been credited by some with helping that country to recover from the crisis.

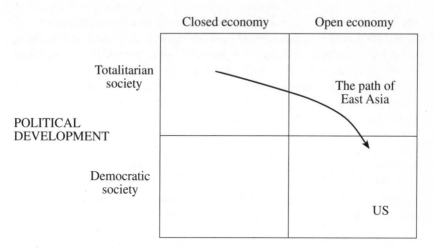

ECONOMIC
OPENNESS

Note: Economic openness concerns free trade and investment and public securities markets. Political development encompasses the structure and distribution of the power within a society, the transparency of the legal environment, and the development of professional bureaucratic institutions.

Figure 12.1   East Asian model of development

Despite enormous differences in local conditions and stages of development, the East Asian economies have embraced a common open industrialization development strategy thought to be responsible for their success (Altomonte *et al.*, 2000). Open industrialization, particularly the greater freedom of inward and outward flow of goods, services, and capital, has helped East Asian economies to enjoy dynamic growth and rapidly catch up with more developed economies. Other factors contributing to growth have been high savings and investment rates, emphasis on education and human capital, and flexible labor markets (Dunning and Narula, 1996a).

These open industrialization policies have, however, been leavened with a sizable dosage of central planning. East Asian governments tend to exercise significant control over investment flows within industrial sectors, often guiding capital to particular companies. As the East Asian economies were achieving rapid growth from a low stage of development, the ability of autocratic central governments, unfettered by political and institutional bureaucracies, to direct capital flows was viewed by many as a positive development factor. However, after these counties reached a certain stage of development, the absence of intermediary institutions and political checks and balances proved to be a liability, as heavy-handed government involvement in the economy often resulted in significant capital misallocations. Corruption and cronyism further exacerbated the problem. As a result, much of the capital that flowed into the developing economies of East Asia was either siphoned off by unscrupulous characters with government connections or squandered in worthless investments. The empty office towers one finds today in many large East Asian cities are a testimony to the market failures at least partially engendered by government controlled investment flows. The credit crunch thwarting the growth of otherwise viable firms was the flip side of the local crisis.

In our view, the success of East Asian economies in the future will depend on the quality and speed of *both* economic and political transformation. Economic liberalization must proceed at a pace commensurate with the institutional and regulatory capacities of a nation in order for economic development to be stable and sustainable (Tan, 1999). The iron hand of authoritarian governments is of little use in steering critical macro-economic factors in the open industrialization context. Paradoxical though this may seem, it is important to understand that effective management of open economies depends less on the magnitude of government power and more upon the manner in which power is exercised. As Professor Dunning noted in his 1993 Geary Lecture, 'there is a fundamental difference between the kind of government action necessary to help overcome endemic market failure and to facilitate the upgrading of resources and capabilities and that which seeks to replace or modify the behavior of firms in the belief that central planning can do a better job in advancing economic and social welfare than can markets' (Dunning, 1993b). Central planning utilizes hard government power and regulation. However, the challenges and opportunities of open industrialization depend upon the exercise of the gentle (not to be confused with loose) regulation Professor Dunning advocated in his Geary Lecture. We would argue further that the ability to sustain such cooperative and coordinating regulatory systems correlates with a certain level of political development.

ASSESSING THE SIGNIFICANCE OF UNEVEN POLITICAL AND ECONOMIC DEVELOPMENT

The end of the twentieth century witnessed a series of financial crises all over the world – Latin American countries (principally Mexico, Brazil and Argentina) through the 1980s and early 1990s, Japan in the late 1980s and the early 1990s, Russia since 1992 and the East Asian countries (most notably Thailand, Indonesia, Korea and Malaysia) in 1997. While it seems safe to suggest that the political architectures of the East Asian countries shaped the depth and character of the financial crisis there (Gehani, 1999), it is important to note that a variety of political experiences accompanied similar crises elsewhere.

The sequencing of political and economic reform seems one promising factor for understanding the relationship between political and economic development. However countries in the various regions suffering economic crises experienced political and economic transformations in various sequences and intensity. In the late twentieth century, a wave of democratic revolutions swept the world. At the same time, there was a strong move away from centrally planned economies and toward a system of relatively free markets. However, political development and economic liberalization have not necessarily marched forward in any particular order. For instance, China adopted economic liberalization before political liberalization while Russia took the opposite route.

Based on the variety of countries experiencing financial crisis, it would appear that no sequence of political and economic development immunizes a country against financial crises. Does this mean that the relationship between the relative paces of economic and political development plays no role in predicting economic instability? We think not. It is not, however, the order of political and economic development that helps to predict potential macro-economic problems in a particular country. Rather, the question one must ask is whether political and economic liberalization are proceeding at a roughly equal pace. It is unrealistic to expect that political liberalization will be sustained without economic development (Przeworski, 1995). Conversely, it is also unrealistic to expect that economic liberalization will be sustainable without political liberalization (Barro, 1997). Our working 'congruence hypothesis' is, therefore, that country risk should be measured according to the imbalance between economic and political development. The more unevenly political and economic liberalizations proceed (regardless of which proceeds more quickly), the greater the country risk score one should assign to that country.

THE ROLE OF UNEVEN POLITICAL AND ECONOMIC DEVELOPMENT IN THE FINANCIAL CRISES: A (VERY) PRELIMINARY ANALYSIS

To begin to determine whether our congruence hypothesis is a plausible one, we analyzed the country risk indicators of six East Asian and three Latin American countries that have been severely hit by a series of financial and currency crises. Japan experienced a collapse of a 'bubble economy' in the late 1980s and has yet to recover. The financial crisis in 1997 arguably affected five Asian countries most severely – Indonesia, Malaysia, Philippines, South Korea, and Thailand. Argentina, Brazil, and Mexico have been plagued by chronic financial and currency instability since the 1980s. Risk indicators for these nine countries, over the years from 1986 to 1995, were drawn from data gathered by the PRS Group – a private country risk research firm.

Country risk indicators are estimated by various objective and subjective components as shown in Table 12.1. To approximate a very rough and imperfect proxy for our congruence variable we employ the discrepancy (hereafter, GAP) between political and economic risk indicators.

Table 12.1   Criteria underlying country risk indicators

Indicators	Components of country risk
Political risk (13 subjective components)	Economic expectations vs. reality; Economic planning failures; Political leadership; External conflict; Corruption in government; Military in politics; Organized religion in politics; Law and order tradition; Racial and nationality tensions; Political terrorism; Civil war; Political party development; Quality of the bureaucracy
Economic Risk (6 objective components)	Inflation; Debt service as a percentage of exports of goods and services; International liquidity ratios; Foreign trade collection experience; Current account balance as a percentage of goods and services; Parallel foreign exchange rate market indicators
Financial risk (5 objective & subjective components)	Loan default or unfavourable loan restructuring; Delayed payment of suppliers' credits; Repudiation of contracts by governments; Losses from exchange controls; Expropriation of private investments

Source: Political Risk Service (PRS) Group.

The sequence plot in Figure 12.2 shows how different proxies yield different results for country risk. The standard financial risk indicator exhibits the decreasing pattern of risk over the relevant years while the GAP between political and economic risk indicators shows the increasing pattern of risk during the time period. This result suggests that a GAP variable could serve as a more accurate predictor – than at least one traditional country risk indicator – of financial crises in our nine sample countries.

Figure 12.3 exhibits the scatter plot of GDP growth and GAP. It shows the inverted-U shaped link between the GAP and GDP growth rate. Up

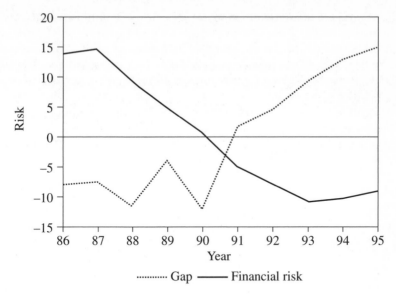

Notes:
(1) GAP value is estimated by subtracting economic risk from political risk.
(2) GAP and financial risk on the *y*-axis are the average value of nine countries.
(3) These average values are standardized for a comparison of GAP and financial risk; (+)
      means high risk and (−) means low risk.

Figure 12.2   Financial risk and GAP by year

until a certain point the GAP is positively related to GDP growth. Beyond
that point, the GAP is negatively related to GDP growth. This result
implies that centrally controlled growth strategy works well up until certain
point, but that beyond that point it functions negatively as an indicator of
economic growth.

CONCLUSION: WHITHER CHINA?

One way to interpret the financial crises in East Asia and in other regions of
the world in the latter half of the twentieth century is that they demonstrate
the necessity of political and economic development proceeding in tandem.
On the surface, China would seem to be a formidable counter-example to
our congruence thesis. China has continued to enjoy near double-digit
growth rates, even as its leaders eschew significant political reform. Despite
this asynchronous development foreign investment capital continues to
pour into China, reflecting the implicit judgment that the overall country

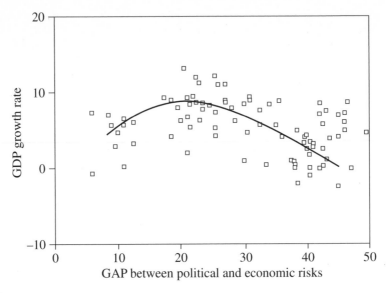

Notes:
(1) GAP value is estimated by subtracting economic risk from political risk.
(2) GAP is the average value of nine countries.

Figure 12.3   GDP growth versus GAP

risk of investing in China is low. It will be interesting to see whether China
will be able to sustain its economic development without political development 'catching up' or whether asynchronous development will ultimately
result in financial crisis, perhaps one initiating in the banking sector where
political controls have already resulted in significant capital misallocations.
Our hypothesis is that any incongruent sequencing of political and economic development is inherently unstable. The best strategy for countries to
take for a sustainable economic development is to avoid asynchronous political and economic development. For private firms, countries that do not
follow such a simultaneous path must be viewed as presenting greater investment risks than those that endeavor to develop political and economic institutions at the same pace as economic liberalization.

NOTES

1.   The authors gratefully acknowledge a research grant from the Aspen Institute's Initiative
     for Social Innovation in Business.

13. Multidimensional theorizing: some methodological comments about John Dunning's eclectic approach

J.-C. Spender

INTRODUCTION

This chapter treats the OLI framework as a three-dimensional analytic space laid out by the constructs underpinning Dunning's definitions of the O, L, and I assets. While the eclectic paradigm has not been presented as a structured space, it is revealing to approach it in this way. We begin by analyzing spatial presentations (matrices) common in the strategy field, move on to Bartlett and Ghoshal's theory of MNE activity (1989), and the analysis of spillovers. The use of a three-dimensional space to consider policy and managerial matters is illustrated in the Advanced Technology Program. We conclude that the OLI approach is powerful way of meeting the conceptual needs of business and government decision makers, rather than those of economic and business theoreticians with positivist tendencies.

BACKGROUND

I was lucky to arrive at Rutgers during John Dunning's time, to share some of his many PhD students, and to experience his academic leadership as he created the Rutgers CIBER. As its initial Director, I promptly let him down by taking a year off in Washington with the Department of Commerce. Then I quit Rutgers to become a Dean elsewhere and so generally did not do all I should have done to help our CIBER succeed, of which more in due course. So I feel lucky to be invited to take part in this *Festschrift* in his honor.

Both JHD and I served our academic apprenticeships in the UK. Though we never met there, and worked in different fields, I like to feel we both benefited from the broader methodological attitudes that prevailed there. We were pressed to think broadly – even arrogantly – about theory without being constrained, as are many PhD students in the US, to produce statistically significant findings. Maybe it was an L advantage that gave our modest God-given O assets some leverage as we struggled to internalize our discipline. Although I began with a behavioral theory of industrial location I soon found my way into 'corporate strategy'. Both of us were interested in firms, their management and competitive behavior. I suspect such illustrious compatriots as Marshall, Sargent Florence, EA Robinson, and Shackle influenced us both, and tempered any narrow focus on the specifics of the firm with attention to those of its industry. Putting distance between our micro-economic colleagues and ourselves, we both concluded that any meaningful analysis of the firm needed to be couched in the peculiarities of its industry – even though no one was convincing about what that meant. Attempting to bracket different levels of analysis – firm, component, and industry – we chose methodologies that invited criticisms that continue to this day. But the fruitfulness of JHD's choice is obvious in his long line of successful students and colleagues who have found research value and even careers in the eclectic paradigm.

I am no expert in International Business so I shall restrict my comments to JHD's choice of method and resulting conceptual model. While its richness creates many problems for those educated into narrower ways, I believe the evident achievements of the eclectic approach illustrate well the subtle possibilities and travails of multidimensional theorizing.

THEORY OR FRAMEWORK? AND IS THERE A DIFFERENCE?

Kuhn's (1970) great contribution was to provide historical leverage to raise concerns about the ways even the most widely accepted scientific enquiries were framed. In the natural sciences these frames – approaches or paradigms – seem secure. Kuhn helped us realize these frames are not as stable as most of us were taught to believe. In no sense could we be completely sure (post Kuhn) that our descriptions of nature captured 'reality'.

Social scientists had long recognized, at least since Marx, that we start our analyses from patterns of assumptions, axioms. Those of social science are very insecure. As social beings we are never able to see social things 'as they truly are'. We can never fully abstract ourselves from the phenomena observed. We are captive to our axiomatic conceptual structures – which Marx believed were grounded in the class structure. As in Ancient Greece, much of what social scientists do is to probe and challenge current axioms using two very different methods. First, we use empirical evidence to test the truth content of the current theoretical paradigm. This process is somewhat passive, for irrespective of whether we believe in falsification or in verification it does not lead to new axioms. Second, we apply a rather different kind of creativity to conjure up new axioms. Plenty of creativity is required when developing a more powerful test of current theory, so I do not suggest that one kind of research is more creative or of a higher order than the other. They seem complementary and I would argue that scientific progress follows their rigorously controlled interaction.

JHD has often spoken of the eclectic approach as a method rather than as a predictive theory. I want to press the distinction between theory testing and framing, in part because I am probably more enamored of the dialectical model of enquiry sketched above than is he, but also because I want to point up some consequences of the difference. It is worth noting that the history of the social sciences – among which we must count the kind of economics that interests FDI researchers – treats those who develop new frameworks better than those whose talent lies in using them to gather data and test theories. As with the Constitution, the framers are remembered better than those whose job it was to make it work.

Novel framings arise when we make two – or more – concepts 'interact'. Concepts are axiomatic, the taken-for-granted point of departure. As empirical scientists, we hope they are empirically useful. The resulting interactions all fall into a 'universe of discourse'. This sounds lofty but is really quite simple (Spender, 1979, p. 394). To illustrate: most organizational theorists remember Ansoff's (1965) matrix, which neatly defined the meaning he attached to the term 'diversification'. There are products old and new, and markets old and new. Only when firms produce new products for new markets are they diversifying. As the Lockheed Aircraft Corporation's 'diversification manager', Ansoff cautioned against diversification – too risky. Peters and Waterman (1982), using the same 'universe of discourse' and with the collapse of LTV and the diversification bubble behind them, offered the same advice, urging firms to 'stick to basics'. Thus once Ansoff had framed the strategic discourse, Peters and Waterman, and many strategy PhDs, were able to test the proposition that diversification away from the firm's established knowledge base would likely result in disaster.

Chandler (1962) had earlier created a rather different discourse for strategists. For him the defining concepts were market engagement and corporate structure. His proposition was that engagement in several different markets required the firm to adopt a divisionalized structure. Simple market engagements called for simpler structures. In the divisionalized firm the knowledge necessary to operate in the different lines of business (industries) would be located close to its point of application. It would be structurally separated from the financial and legal knowledge used to build the collection of heterogeneous divisions. While diversification would increase

the heterogeneity, Chandler was not especially concerned with the problems it might produce, for top management should be able to encompass it
with their coherent set of legal and financial skills. They ran the corporation, not its industry-specific divisions.

I offer these oversimplifications of two of the strategy field's principal
framers to illustrate (a) that testable theory is inevitably lodged within a
specific universe of discourse, (b) that universe is often created by the interaction of two sets of variables adopted as axiomatic, and (c) it is sharply
delimited by the axioms adopted. The result, at its most elementary, is the
familiar two-by-two matrix, an interaction of two binary variables. The
BCG (Boston Consulting Group) strategic matrix of dogs, stars, milch-
cows, and question-marks, that interacted market share and market
growth, is another that was hugely popular.

Many who accept their discipline's choice of concepts and variables
uncritically get very impatient with this kind of discussion. That is the
point, of course, for the academic world is indeed divided between those
who are uncritical of the frames they inherit and those who struggle to
replace them. Again I see neither kind of intellectual activity as inherently
superior to the other. Both, so long as they are allowed to interact freely,
are part of the dynamic of human knowledge. But from the simplifications
offered above we can see a third important characteristic. Each universe of
discourse defines its own population of events – or, to put it another way –
each frame captures a different set of empirical phenomena. Actually there
is some deceit here, for we often presume that empirical phenomena have
an identity independent of any frame and, as I suggested above, they do
not. What really happens is that we have 'lay' or pre-scientific notions of
events, which are incompletely defined. As we use our measurement
systems to fit these events into a frame and gather population statistics and
experimental samples, they become sufficiently defined to be brought into
rigorous scientific discourse.

THE ECLECTIC APPROACH

The OLI model began when JHD chose to interact the resources that a firm
was able to move to a different country (O) against those that could not be
so moved (L), whilst also assuming a theory of the firm as an apparatus for
integrating these types of resource (factors of production). This provided
an uncontroversial framing for his hypothesis that some non-national firms
seemed able to import strategically significant resources not available to the
national firms and so overcome the other penalties of foreign-ness. Had he
followed the presentation style then common in the strategy field, JHD

would have drawn a matrix of mobile and immobile resources, binary in the sense of their being strategically significant or not. In the event he moved on to puzzle why the firms owning these strategic and mobile resources integrated them into their operations rather than trading them in the open market. That led to the possibility that some firms found strategic superiority in their 'internalization' (I) capabilities, as well as in their mobile and immobile strategic factors of production. Thus organizational capabilities are interacted with resource mobility and strategic significance. We sense a rich and conceptually complex universe of discourse.

As we consider JHD's frame, it clearly restricts the phenomena to be analyzed to between-nation operations since mobility is defined – at least initially – in terms of crossing national borders. The frame implies a theory of international trade, but one that may have little comparability with other international trade theories whose axioms – and phenomena captured – are quite different. It is worth noting that JHD has answered Kojima's (1982) critique by asserting that their theories are incommensurate (2001, p. 14). He makes similar points about Rugman's (1997) work on risk diversification.

THE THREE-DIMENSIONAL FRAMING

As one moves from a two-dimensional analysis into a three-dimensional one, there is a huge increase in complexity. The bad news is that not everyone has a taste for this kind of complexity. Some react viscerally and with impatience. The good news is that more of the real world may be framed, for the world is clearly a place whose richness demands we apply a staggeringly heterogeneous range of concepts. Frames adapted to deal with abstract phenomena can be simple, and this undoubtedly gives them greater rigor. But it seems appropriate to construct complex frames to grasp complex phenomena like international trade.

A second question is about the intended beneficiary of this intellectual labor. The social sciences may or may not be about developing powerful theories of social phenomena that can stand shoulder to shoulder with the theories of the natural sciences, but they are certainly about providing those who operate in and on society with more powerful insights. International trade theory – even in its present nascent state – is already vitally important to business and government. It is clearly going to be even more important in the future. And in these arenas decisions are seldom made with scientific precision. Far too many matters must be borne in mind. There is no framework that can take account of them all.

This implies two rather different notions of the power of a theory. The philosophy of science teaches us that the fundamental test of a theory's truth content is its predictive power. But a theory's ability to grasp (frame) and provide insight into complex everyday managerial concerns is a different type of power –of equal importance. International trade is complex and those involved in it seem ready to use whatever useful tools fall to hand.

The three-dimensional OLI approach can be illuminated by contrasting it with the two-dimensional international business frame offered by Bartlett and Ghoshal (2000a) (see Figure 13.1). They interact the concepts of global integration (GI) and local responsiveness (LR) to define firms as 'international', 'multinational', 'global', or 'transnational'.

	Low *LR*	*High* *LR*
Low *GI*	International	Multinational
High *GI*	Global	Transnational

Figure 13.1   The Bartlett and Ghoshal matrix

This matrix has given many managers good insight into their firms and the dynamic challenges they face. The definitions may be of some value in themselves but the matrix gets more interesting as an exploration of differences between the quadrants and therefore of the firms located within them. For Bartlett and Ghoshal (2000a, p. 255) the different types of firm reflect differences in strategic orientation and resource disposition. While there are some commonalities, the international firm exploits home-base assets. The multinational meets local needs. The global firm exploits economies of scale. The transnational firm finds ways of exploiting all of these strategies. Some firms find themselves attached to particular quadrants by the physical constraints of their factors of production. The cement business, Bartlett and Ghoshal tell us, is international for it gains no strategic advantage from either greater LR or GI. Consumer electronics – with voltages corrected – are the archetypal 'global' products, while packaged foods – even McDonald's hamburgers – need to be re-fashioned to respond to local conditions and tastes. Transnational firms, such as ABB, are often both knowledge- and capital-intensive and learn to exploit the inherent flexibility that derives from the mobility of these resources.

In addition to providing a system for categorizing extra-domestic firms, the matrix provides a universe of discourse within which Bartlett and Ghoshal can consider the evolutionary paths through the matrix – from international to global to transnational – or equally from international to multinational to transnational. Their point is that wherever the inherently mobile firm is located in their space, increasing global competition will drive it to become more transnational, steadily growing in complexity and sophistication. Strategic and competitive advantage accrues to those able to organize their operations so that they increase both GI and LR – quite a managerial challenge. And they can argue that if these firms do not evolve, they will be raided from elsewhere by those that do.

But while the matrix carries some implications for organizational structure and internalization capabilities it is not dealing directly with the distinction between mobile and immobile strategic resources. JHD's framing does deal with this – and since management's actions include both the design and administration of corporate structures, and the allocation and transfer of resources, one might argue that JHD's framing is likely to provide senior management with more relevant insights than Bartlett and Ghoshal's framing – even though their framing is simpler and much easier to explain. Likewise JHD's framing may be more useful to government and regulators. They are not concerned with firms' organizational structures; on the other hand their legislative levers enable them to control directly the cross-border movement of resources.

THE HETEROGENEITY OF THE OLI SPACE

The matrices mentioned above – Ansoff's, Chandler's, BCG's, and Bartlett and Ghoshal's – are useful in several ways. First, they offer researchers a typology, a way of categorizing and defining the admissible phenomena. A binary matrix framed by variables A and B allows only four statements: A/B, A/~B,~A/B, ~A/~B. Each is associated with an observation, which is thereby categorized.

Second, a matrix can help us probe why some areas of its space are not only inhospitable – such as Ansoff's diversification – but also non-viable, such as BCG's dogs. If we make an analogy to physical chemistry, we can think of the universe of discourse as setting out a complex 'phase space'. We can plot how water changes its physical state under various combinations of temperature and pressure. While water's phase space is 'continuous', for it is always solid ice, liquid water, or gaseous steam, in sub-atomic physics we know that particles cannot occupy all energy states. Their phase-space has discontinuities that are highly significant and lead us to quantum theory. Third, an international business matrix may offer insights into the possibilities and problems of moving around the space, of transforming a firm from one category, such as an MNE, into another, such as a 'global' enterprise.

I am not aware of anyone yet researching the heterogeneity of the OLI space but it would seem useful to know, for instance, if some combinations of O (mobile) strategic assets and L (immobile) strategic assets cannot be compensated for by an infinite amount of I (internalization) capabilities. This would mean that some parts of the OLI space are 'blacked out' and non-viable. The reader will gather that I see this as an interesting research project.

Considering the 'independence' of the framing axioms can help map the space. This is an important matter. If the axioms are completely collinear, then the space collapses. Some will deal with the ideas being considered here as terms within a regression equation. Given some assumptions about the comparability of the data points, statistical tests can reveal collinearity much better than a wordy discussion about 'phase spaces'. I appreciate this, but the real issue is that regression and multivariate approaches presume the continuity of the variables in ways a geometric or graphical approach need not – and an examination of the discontinuities and incompatibilities in the axiomatically created space can be crucial to the development of more powerful strategic insights.

JHD has taken considerable criticism on the matter of his axioms' independence (2001). In some senses his responses focus on the dynamics through which immobile resources become mobile, and vice versa. He also suggests that the most immobile resources are those that comprise the host nation's strategically relevant infrastructure. This raises the interesting possibility of a theory of the production of a nation's infrastructure, making a distinction between 'home grown', 'imported', and 'grown as a result of FDI'. A theory of much subtlety, it would deal with putting infrastructure in place through firms' activity in the host country, rather than simply importing such facilities and having them put in place by overseas suppliers. I am reminded of concerns about 'screwdriver' plants that contribute little to the host infrastructure and simply exploit local assets such as cheap labor.

SPILLOVERS – AN EXAMPLE OF THREE-DIMENSIONAL ANALYSIS

Recognizing that the axes of these matrices are not fully independent leads to the idea of 'spillovers' from the properties of one axis to another. In Ansoff's matrix new products eventually create new – and old – markets. In the Bartlett and Ghoshal matrix the firm's ability to raise LR becomes generic and eventually enables a different kind of GI. Thus a dynamic version of JHD's framework could focus directly on these interactive dependencies. Understanding more about them could be of great value to managers and legislators as they plan beyond the present time period.

The heterogeneity of the space is one measure of its research value. A space without discontinuities, blacked-out regions, trajectories, and so forth is scarcely worth researching. JHD has suggested that the heterogeneity of the OLI space is a complex dependent on the industry being analyzed and the host nation's infrastructure of assets, attitudes, policy and history. That is clearly true. So the value of the OLI analysis will likely vary widely, contingent on the particulars and context of the nation and industry being considered. Hence I would argue that one of the richest areas for future OLI research is the examination of the spillovers that can be considered – such as those from created assets, whether mobile or not, and the infrastructure of the host country.

When I left Rutgers and the Directorship of the CIBER to work for the US Department of Commerce, it was because I had been invited to help analyze the spillovers resulting from the public funding of US private sector technology research. The program, the Advanced Technology Program (ATP), was politically sensitive and many eminent economists and public policy theorists – to say nothing of powerful senators – were dead set against this use of the tax-payers' money. It was labeled 'corporate welfare' even though the public funding merely 'matched' the recipients' own private funding. In spite of many attempts to shut the program down, it survives and since its inception in 1991 has invested some \$3 billion of matching funds in some 600 projects (http://www.atp.nist.gov). There is little doubt that it has more than fulfilled its mission.

The underlying agenda was to understand the program in ways that would allow it to be (a) managed more closely, (b) explained to non-participants, and (c) evaluated in cost/benefit terms. The conceptual task was to bring its several fundamentally different kinds of activity – scientific research, product development, commercialization, and generating the public benefits – into a single frame in order to analyze their interaction.

The prevailing analysis was based on the notion of market failure, specifically the unwillingness of private sector research-intensive companies to develop methods and technologies for which they saw only the most distant possibilities of profit for themselves (Tassey, 1992). ATP's process – without going into its details – is to invite research proposals and assess the likelihood of public benefits, including profits for others, if the project succeeds. If these benefits are judged significant, the proposers are invited to provide a business plan. ATP evaluates whether the proposers have the resources to develop the technology, product or service, and the ability to bring it to market. The assumption is that spillovers then occur and the public benefits. Awards can be given to large companies as well as to individual researchers and entrepreneurs, though past awards to IBM, GM, Ford, and Chrysler drew particularly hostile political attention.

The reader may well be skeptical. In ATP's defense I have to say that the possibility of public benefits always depends on the specifics and details. For example, one area of ATP's involvement is in software programming tools. These tools can be enormously expensive to produce but if made widely available, might have a significant impact on US software productivity. This is a matter of rising strategic and economic importance, for we now see both India and China competing with the US to become the principal producers of software. Currently US quality and productivity gives us an edge over their lower labor costs in most areas of the market. In spite of this, the history of attempting to commercialize such tools is depressing and most companies feel there is insufficient market to encourage them to invest in their development. But if the cost of the tools is partially covered by ATP and the prices lowered, then the resulting volume might be considerable. In this sense ATP might 'pump-prime' the market much as high profit defense contracts have primed many high-tech markets in the past, which technology then 'trickled down' or 'spilled over' into the private sector to the considerable benefit of the nation.

A group of the nation's leading industrial economics researchers was assembled to help monitor ATP's activities. They were funded to produce position papers about the program, do relevant conceptual and empirical research, attend conferences, and so forth. Immediately it was appreciated that the key to the possibilities of a proposal succeeding lay in understanding the spillovers from the private firm's commercial activity into the public domain. Spillovers are poorly understood, so the economists debated at great length how to advance the state of their art. There was some research at the national level, comparing the technology support programs in Europe, Israel, and Canada. There was some research about the aggregated effects of national policies. But there was little that could illuminate industry or firm level phenomena.

As a non-economist, I was left to think about these matters in rather different ways and eventually developed the three-dimensional space shown below (1997). Its purpose was to explore possible relationships between the three types of activity – technical research and product development, commercialization, and producing public benefits – while assuming that they were largely independent. In particular I wanted to explore whether all parts of the analytic space created were equally viable or, if there were discontinuities, where they might be located.

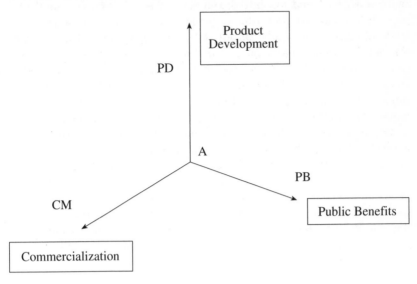

Figure 13.2   The ATP analytic space

Using this space (Figures 13.2 and 13.3) I could argue that ATP was chartered to seek and then help manage proposals to move through this space from the origin (A) to some destination point (Q) which captured the project's expected public benefit (PB) component as well as its corresponding PD (product development) and CM (commercialization) components. There seemed to be a logical sequence, suggesting some parts of the space are blacked out. Product development necessarily precedes both commercialization and public benefits. While product development might create technical and scientific knowledge of benefit to the public – so long as is it not closely held by the awardee through trade secrets, patents, etc. – this kind of spillover was not that most expected. Indeed one of the ongoing policy questions was whether the frequent involvement with universities and the need of their researchers to publish was consistent with or contrary to the program's objectives. The ATP policy was to focus on the public benefits that would follow commercialization. It is important to note that while ATP retained residual 'national need' rights to all knowledge or products produced, the government did not require the awardees to pay a royalty or give up equity. The ATP funds thus leveraged the awardee's own funds at zero cost.

The most expected path was that which would follow the trajectory ATPQ. This raises interesting policy, economic and managerial problems. First, the spillovers occur at the points T and P. While one might imagine that knowledge could spill into the public domain while moving up the PD axis (from scientific publication) or while moving along the CM axis (from trade and professional publication), or by both as employees leave the firm, the awardees were not asked to ensure that happened. Rather the proposals were restricted to those likely to produce public benefits after commercialization. In this sense, the PD and CM variables are binary – complete or not – and of no great policy concern. Secondly, there are some interesting issues around consumer surplus or pricing the resulting product or service so that it is of substantially greater value to the purchaser than the price charged. This is often a demarcating characteristic of tools, i.e. methods of creating value rather than simply satisfying market needs.

Perhaps of greater relevance, the diagram illuminates some of the managerial and accounting problems encountered by ATP. It is well known that one of the challenges facing technology companies is the transition from 'knowledge generation' to revenue generation. The switch of trajectory at point T shows this is a spillover problem – and because it entails a switch

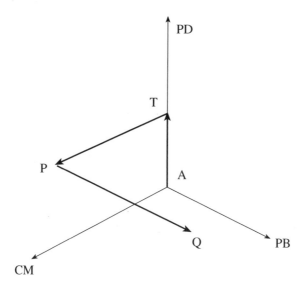

Figure 13.3   The project trajectory through ATP space

of concepts, is not a straightforward project management problem. To evaluate and manage that part of the trajectory requires an understanding of how to resolve and integrate two very different kinds of activity. There has been a considerable amount of research into the problems of transferring technology from the laboratory into production. It is neither conclusive nor worth citing. The spatial approach shows it as a quite different task from that of managing either the production of the technology or the development of marketable goods and services. Among the messages for ATP is the one that they need people with special skills if they are to monitor the awardees effectively.

Even more challenging is understanding the spillovers occurring at point P, where the result of commercialization is not simple customer satisfaction but more widespread public benefits. Economists have traditionally focused on the direct measurable public benefits such as job creation, enlargement of the tax base, and other ways in which the firm's needs and activities lead to 'economic multipliers'. ATP was chartered to look beyond these, in particular to provide a means of preventing a version of the 'short-termism' so widely criticized in corporate America – resulting from stock market demands to produce short-term returns for investors – depleting the stock of technologies which, long term, has provided the US with its current competitive edge. Recalling Hardin's comments about over-grazing the commons, there is a major policy concern that the US pool of public technological knowledge is being drained, and ATP was seen as a publicly funded mechanism to add to it. Finally the diagram suggested the methods for evaluating progress needed to be matched carefully to the particular types of activity being tracked.

The orthogonal tracks AT, TP, and PQ imply that while they connect at discrete points T and P, they are otherwise independent activities. The notion of spillovers is that something, maybe some form of economic asset, passes from one kind of activity to another that is largely independent. Simon (1962), among other social scientists, has explored the idea of the decomposability of social systems. One way to analyze spillovers is to determine the boundaries and processes of the social systems of which the activities AT, TP, and PQ are part. We already appreciate that the processes of technological discovery are different, and must be differently managed, from the processes of taking a product to market. More mysterious are the processes of public goods. Clearly the spillovers at P are a function of the receptiveness or 'absorptive capacity' of the 'public' social processes they impact as well as of the quality and quantitiy of the economic assets being transferred from the process TP. Consumer surplus depends on the consumers' system of use and consumption.

From a methodological point of view we can see that creating a three-dimensional analytic space facilitated discussion in ways that would have been much more difficult without it. It certainly cannot substitute for a rigorous statistical or regression analysis of the variables and outcome measures, and it might not please those used to a more quantitative approach. But the policy and management issues are well illuminated for those whose direct responsibilities lie in these areas. We need to appreciate that the needs of managers, policy-makers and legislators may not be the same as those of academics, and that the methods used to deal with matters that are both interesting to academics and or national importance may need to be different too.

FINAL REMARKS

The overall thrust of my comments is that methodologies need to be matched to needs, and in many nationally important matters the needs of non-academics loom large. JHD's choice of field, and choice of method, reveals his commitment to do more than simply publish – though his record in this respect is truly astonishing. It is also to do work that has value and impact on matters of national significance. Far too much of what passes for academic activity in business schools lies gathering dust unread, unreferenced and unremembered. My hunch is that the impact of the OLI framework will continue to grow simply because the methodology chosen suits the needs of the business and government managers who have to make decisions about allocating and transferring assets between nations.

JHD and a generation of colleagues and students are now exploring, articulating and refining the OLI model. I would argue that there would be tremendous value in metrication of the space he spelt out – even in basic binary terms. As experience grows these metrics can be ordinalized and more rigorous quantitative research begun.

Considerable effort is going into evolving dynamic models such as that implied by the investment development path (IDP). I see this as researching the viable trajectories through the OLI space, trying to get a sense of the relative priorities of the dimensions, and discovering the space's discontinuities and blacked-out regions. As this work continues profound questions about the interplay between foreign firms, domestic firms, the local infrastructure providers, and the host country legislators will emerge.

But at the same time JHD himself continues to press forward and be more eclectic than ever – to extend the three-dimensional paradigm into four or more dimensions. His recent interest in non-equity alliances is an attack on the simplicity of the distinctions on which the OLI model was grounded. Non-equity alliances imply splitting the internalization (I) dimension into operational level capabilities and strategic level capabilities in ways reminiscent of the divisional and head office separations in Chandler's model. Likewise the exploration of R assets attacks the notions of ownership and, therefore, of O assets in the earlier literature. Through alliances and 'relations' firms increasingly have access to O assets everywhere without having to own them.

Who knows? This second *Festschrift* could well be followed by a third in ten years or so celebrating JHD's success in evolving the OLI model into a theory of international trade policy making, or maybe, given the rising capabilities of neural networks, a WTO-based simulation of the whole world's trade. Clearly, the OLI space presents us with a world of work to be done, and JHD's achievements so far provide us with powerful tools that will continue to yield much public benefit all over the globe.

14. Location determinants of foreign MNCs investing at the sub-national level: the role of State government

Bindu Vyas

INTRODUCTION

The structure of the world economy today is clearly very different from that of two decades ago. The liberalization of markets within and between national economies accompanied by dramatic technological advances in bio-technology, electronics and telecommunications have created greater scope for multinational corporations to integrate the world economy through hierarchical strategic management of foreign affiliates. Multinational corporations (MNCs) seek advantages over uninational competitors by virtue of the greater geographic range of their activities.

The impact of these new forms of enterprise has received substantial attention at the national level but very few studies have addressed sub-national levels of host countries. While the reasons for inbound foreign direct investment (FDI) in the United States are well established, the problem of the location of affiliates at the sub-national level remains inadequately researched (Bagchi-Sen and Wheeler, 1989).

The purpose of this chapter is to examine the determinants and effects of inbound FDI on the economy of the Commonwealth of Pennsylvania.[1] The chapter uses historical data to examine the distribution of inward FDI in Pennsylvania as revealed by country of origin, mode of entry, magnitude of investment, growth, sectoral distribution. In the process, the chapter generates some comparisons between the industrial structure of FDI in Pennsylvania with that of the United States and other important states.

The second section brings together the existing contextual theories of the determinants of sub-national location and the existing empirical research. The third creates a general framework for diagnosing current policies towards inward FDI of state governments with particular emphasis on Pennsylvania and the fourth assesses their success. The final section offers such conclusions as can currently be drawn on the pattern of sub-national allocation within a geographically large country.

INWARD FOREIGN DIRECT INVESTMENT AT THE STATE LEVEL: THEORY AND EMPIRICISM

Theory

While the evolution of the global economy has increased the potential mobility of some factors of production, it has made immobile factors potentially more important (Markusen, 1996). Modern MNCs need to be both globally integrated and locally responsive. The most successful MNCs are those that find new ways to minimize spatial transaction costs and to reap the advantages of their global asset portfolio while, at the same time, gaining access to complementary immobile assets.

The different cultures and motives of individual firms and the variety of opportunities available in each sub-division make it nearly impossible to derive a general location theory for FDI related activities (Bagchi-Sen and Wheeler, 1989; Dunning, 2000a). Methodologically, the problem requires a paradigm in which variables can be identified as having different effects in sub-national regions, by country of origin and industry. An important aspect of the problem identified by Hymer's breakthrough study (1976), is that the 'cost of being foreign or unfamiliar with host-country practices' wanes with the maturity of the affiliate. Therefore MNCs which are already established in a location can expand with greater assurance (with a smaller coefficient of uncertainty) than can an MNC which is investing in the country or sub-national region for the first time.[2] By the same token, the latter have no roots so that the location of their investments will be more sensitive to the perceived attractiveness of a sub-national unit's resources, capabilities and policies.[3]

Dunning (1998) notes the evolution of locational determinants for affiliates as created assets increase in importance relative to 'natural resources'. Early FDI emphasized 'market-seeking' investments but modern locational decisions depends very much upon efficiency-seeking and strategic asset-seeking investments.

Although MNCs are constrained in their locational decisions by a whole set of exogenous and endogenous variables, many options exist as to where MNC activities can and may be located (Dunning, 1993a).[4] But realistic statistics on this subject have become available only since the late 1970s, and it is hard to draw generalized conclusions because the evidence is still growing and changing. In addition, research on reasons for location decision making remains in the formative stage (Bagchi-Sen and Wheeler, 1989). Dunning supported this argument, but also suggested that the location specific variables affecting FDI decision making in the 1990s were generally very different to those in the 1970s (Dunning, 1998).[5]

Within the framework of different motives for FDI (i.e. resource seeking, market seeking, efficiency seeking, or strategic asset seeking), the variables influencing location choice by MNCs in 1990s were mainly efficiency seeking and strategic asset seeking. The impact of created assets (technology, experience, organizational structure, and management competitiveness) is significant in our understanding of the extent and direction of FDI in the global economy. Unlike natural assets, many firm specific created assets are locationally mobile. This mobility is in contrast to the spatial immobility of many natural assets. Increasingly location specific assets have themselves become created assets (such as infrastructure and firm clusters). Created assets may be both firm and location specific. The resultant characteristics of created assets primarily reflect technological and environmental change, but the organizational entities, such as domestic firms, MNCs, governments and international agencies may also affect the availability and locational impact of both mobile and immobile resources and capabilities.

According to Mudambi (1998), multinational investment is significantly time dependent, and may be motivated by a firm's experience of a particular location. The learning qualities offered by a particular location is a created asset (Dunning, 1993a) that help firms gain substantial first mover advantages. Therefore, a firm with greater experience of a particular location is more likely to invest there than one with lesser experience. For the same reason, an investment agency is short-sighted if it seeks to attract new investors at the expense of those which are already located within its jurisdiction.

Economic theory predicts that a company investing in production facilities will choose the location that both allows them to respond to demand in local (national) or adjacent markets, and is also cost effective. Research has suggested that the costs of doing business and controlling foreign operations are likely to be lower in familiar markets. Familiar markets are defined as those that are culturally similar to those in the home country, or in foreign markets in which the company has previous experience (Benito, Gabriel and Gripsrud, 1992). Ethnic connections can also provide a measure of cultural similarity and low psychic distance.

Within the theory of corporate networks and location choice a partial explanation of the spatial distribution of corporate investment is provided by a city-system approach (Pred, 1977). Accordingly decision makers can only choose from alternatives of which they become aware through either an information search or unintentional information acquisition, any decision-making individual or group possessing specialized information at a given location is more likely to have actively sought or accidentally obtained it from some contacts or places rather than others and the most readily accessible specialized information is almost certain to be spatially biased; most probably in the sense that it is obtained from near the decision-making unit's existing partners and or related contacts e.g. suppliers and customers.

According to Geldner,[6] at national level, a gravity measure is useful in identifying the extent to which the cross border trade undertaken by MNCs (parent companies and their affiliates) is linked with their home economies. Later, empirical research at sub-national level, by Friedman, Gerlowski and Silberman (1989), and Woodward (1992) included a gravity measure of market, market potential and per capita income of State location respectively.

The theory of economic geography and FDI location implies that in some industries, MNCs are found to be geographically concentrated within countries (Dunning, 1997c). Evidence from previous research suggests that MNCs are attracted to clusters of economic activity in their own and in closely related industries and activities (Nachum, 2000). But flexible specialization is fundamental to geographic concentration, and this is especially so in the case of small firms that produce small batches in rapidly changing process and product configurations, and which are knit together by sub-contracting and other comparative ventures. Rather than internalizing intermediate product markets, their success is based on their ability to access these products from other firms; and then to coordinate these with their own core competencies. Hence the collective ability of firms in the same location to upgrade their collective capabilities and advantages is an important component of contemporary theorizing by economic geographers. One limitation of such a model is that it deals with small and medium-sized firms with high levels of specialization and limited ties with the outside world.[7] Hence the model can only provide a partial explanation for the choice of investment location by large integrated MNCs.[8] In particular the recent restructuring of the governance of MNCs – brought about inter alia by the liberalization of cross border markets – has changed the extent and nature of their external linkages, and in so doing, has affected the locational portfolio of their assets.

Incentives and FDI Location

Immobile assets, including traditional location-bound natural resources as well as sub-national economic clusters, have become increasingly important determinants of locational choice over the last two decades (Dunning, 1998). As these assets within sub-national units exist and are immobile, government policies and regulations are relevant and important. Many government policies and regulations are in fact are region-specific liabilities or assets. Governments can and do strongly influence such activities both indirectly through their macroeconomic and macro-organizational policies and their attitude towards business, and directly through selected taxes and incentives, controls and promotions (Gray and Dunning, 2000).

Governments recognize that positive externalities or spillovers can result from economies of scale, the creation of new knowledge that is widely diffused, and upgrading the skills of workers and individual investments can lead to sequential investment (UNCTAD, 1995). Government investment incentives involve benefits and costs to the regional economies that grant them (Gray and Dunning, 2000). They can distort the production structures, favor large over small foreign firms, and impose financial and administrative costs on the community. Hence the costs for the regional government offering incentives should not be more than the expected value of the private and social benefits (UNCTAD, 1996). It is not sufficient for a State government to give incentives to attract FDI; it is also important to execute the appropriate incentive measures effectively. Also the incentives offered need to be based on a complete understanding of their effects and not just to match incentives offered by other regional authorities.

According to Mudambi (1999), different types of support structures[9] will have different consequences for the national or regional governments as well as for the multinational investors.[10] Investment agencies and governments need to take into consideration the financial conditions and the risk aversion of multinational investors in structuring their financial packages. The combination of financial packages, incentives and support schemes may be used to reduce the risk borne by the MNC, the private lender and the State. The firm specific characteristics are strongly related to the type of investment support obtained; hence inward investment agencies may benefit from creating and sustaining more suitably tailored support packages.

Likewise research into the determinants of FDI at the sub-national level can benefit from a more client-specific approach to investment incentives. Culling from the existing literature the components that are most relevant, what emerges is a hybrid theory of location determinants summarized in Figure 14.1 that takes into account several factors that distinguish one State from another. Clearly these include fiscal policies that affect costs for prospective foreign investors. They also embrace human capital and technology investments in education, both at the secondary and tertiary levels. State investments in transportation infrastructure also need to be considered as a determinant of FDI location, not only for the movement of

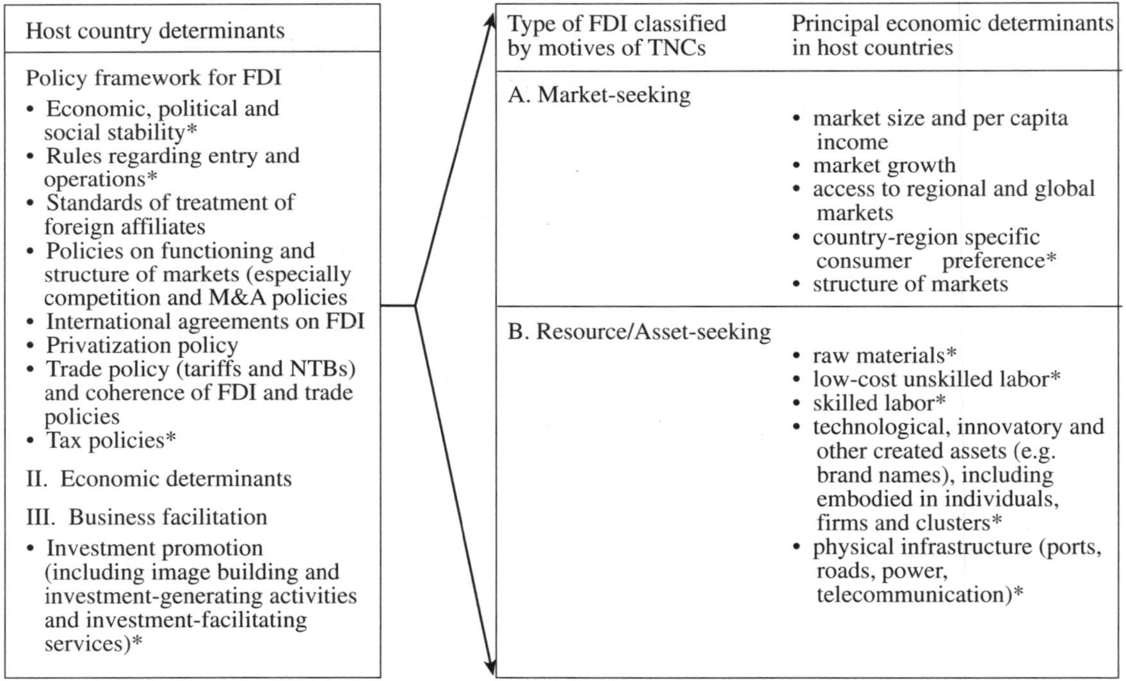

Host country determinants

Policy framework for FDI
- Economic, political and social stability*
- Rules regarding entry and operations*
- Standards of treatment of foreign affiliates
- Policies on functioning and structure of markets (especially competition and M&A policies
- International agreements on FDI
- Privatization policy
- Trade policy (tariffs and NTBs) and coherence of FDI and trade policies
- Tax policies*

II. Economic determinants

III. Business facilitation
- Investment promotion (including image building and investment-generating activities and investment-facilitating services)*

Type of FDI classified by motives of TNCs	Principal economic determinants in host countries
A. Market-seeking	• market size and per capita income • market growth • access to regional and global markets • country-region specific consumer preference* • structure of markets
B. Resource/Asset-seeking	• raw materials* • low-cost unskilled labor* • skilled labor* • technological, innovatory and other created assets (e.g. brand names), including embodied in individuals, firms and clusters* • physical infrastructure (ports, roads, power, telecommunication)*

Note: * These determinants particularly relate to regions and/or policies of regional authorities. Adapted from Table IV.I (p. 91) in UNCTAD (1998).

Figure 14.1   Host country and sub-national determinants of FDI

202

goods, but also for that of managers from work to home and to leisure activities, particularly those that will maintain cultural ties with their home country.

Empirical Research

Classifying the location of FDI by way of State boundaries is bound to be somewhat arbitrary as many intra-State distances are greater than interState distances (Wallace, 2000). However, although State boundaries may not provide a distinct break in terms of the spatial proximity of the economic activities of MNCs, they do indicate natural breaks for some of the factors that affect the choice of investment location (e.g. taxes, labor laws, education systems, and industrial and monetary incentives). Regions and States within nations exist, and are important because they are governed by administrations whose policies affect the movement of goods, resources and capabilities. In addition official US data on the spatial distribution of economic activity are usually compiled at a State level. Thus, there is a strong rationale for monitoring FDI on a State basis, and for considering the actions and policies of State governments as they relate to inbound FDI.

Nearly every one of the eleven empirical studies, undertaken between 1989–2000, that have analyzed the factors that most influence FDI in the US, identified several factors over which State governments have at least some influence, if not direct control. Not surprisingly, the level of rate of taxation – in the guise of corporate, sales, right to work, unitary, or overall rate forms – showed a significant inverse relationship in most of the studies (Coughlin *et al.*, 1991; Woodward, 1992; Ulgado, 1996; Shaver, 1998; and Vyas, 2000). Local labor laws also showed an inverse relationship with FDI (Cleeve, 1997). Conversely, government support for FDI, in the form of local investment incentives (Sokoya and Tillery, 1992 and World Bank, 1989), financial assistance, attitudes towards inbound FDI (Cleeve, 1997), the quality of information provided by investment agencies (Vyas, 2000), the representation of a State office in a foreign country or city (Woodward, 1992), public policies, and labor subsidies (Wallace, 1998), showed a significant positive relationship with a foreign affiliate locating in a particular area.

State governments also can influence several other factors that foreign investors consider as important locational attractions (UNCTAD, 1998). These include housing and educational facilities (Vyas, 2000), income per capita, and infrastructure (Coughlin *et al.*, 1991; Woodward, 1992, Shaver, 1998), all of which have a direct relationship with FDI. Other conditions, which State governments can affect through fiscal and educational policies, including local wage rates (Shaver, 1998), the degree of social deprivation, and the level of unemployment (Woodward, 1992; Shaver, 1998) all of which showed a significant inverse relationship with FDI.

As both this encapsulated summary of empirical research and the preceding review of the theoretical literature have shown, sub-national governmental units can and do play an important role in determining where within a country a foreign firm will locate its affiliates. In order to flesh out what that role is, the following section considers the specific case of the Commonwealth of Pennsylvania, and offers a glimpse at the policies and practices of its government.

POLICIES OF GOVERNMENT OF PENNSYLVANIA TO ATTRACT FOREIGN DIRECT INVESTMENT

As part of a larger effort to increase exports from the State, the Commonwealth of Pennsylvania is actively attempting to attract direct investment from foreign MNCs (Vyas and Rose, 2000). In pursuing this objective it has established trade offices in a number of locations around the world, referred to as the LINK program. In 1996, Governor Ridge announced plans to increase the number of foreign trade offices operated by the State Department of Commerce including those in Singapore and Mexico City. The Governor himself has joined trade missions to several foreign countries, including Chile and Mexico. He has continually asked the legislature for larger export promotion budgets. In 1996, the Ridge administration hired Richard Marcks, former president of Hershey International as director of international business development. Currently the State Department of Community and Economic Development provides a direct outreach to foreign direct investors, through the Office of International Business Development (OIBD).

Another intriguing and apparently successful initiative to attract new business activities involves the designation of honorary consulars, particularly in the Pittsburgh area, who voluntarily host visitors and/or delegations from their home or adopted countries, and connect them with business and government leaders in the State (Thuermer, 1998). The success may be due to the fact that this strategy is coupled with a favorable cost of living status of Western Pennsylvania's largest city. In fact, a 1997 survey by the Swiss based Corporate Resources Group ranked Pittsburgh as one of the best-valued international business centers in the United States. Of the 145 major world markets, Pittsburgh ranked 124th in terms of the cost of living. John Thornburgh, President of Penn's Southwest Association, Downtown, cited four factors which explain why Pittsburgh has much to offer for this low price: accessibility to major US markets; high productivity of Pittsburgh's workers; extensive transportation options – airport, highways and riverways; and the personal roots of many business professionals, especially attorneys and engineers (Mukherjee, 1997). These may be important components of the Pennsylvania-specific location decision making of MNCs.

CURRENT PROFILE OF FOREIGN DIRECT INVESTMENT IN PENNSYLVANIA

Figure 14.2 gives a good visual representation of the geographic distribution of foreign owned establishments within Pennsylvania (Dun and Bradstreet, 2000). Currently Pittsburgh and its adjacent counties, and Philadelphia and its adjacent counties attract the largest number of foreign establishments. This is a similar profile of inbound FDI transactions to that of the 1989–94 period. Philadelphia enjoyed the largest dollar value of new FDI from 1989 through 1994, followed by Montgomery and Cumberland counties. Allegheny and Westmoreland counties received the next highest levels (Vyas and Rose, 2000).

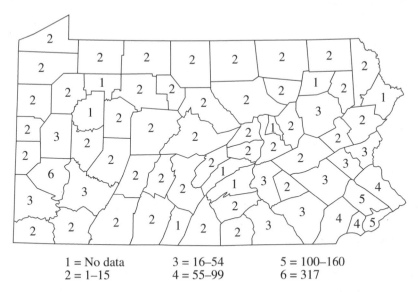

| 1 = No data | 3 = 16–54 | 5 = 100–160 |
| 2 = 1–15 | 4 = 55–99 | 6 = 317 |

Source: Map generated by Thomas Sawyer of the Northeast Pennsylvania Marketing and Planning (MAP) Center at King's College.

Figure 14.2   Foreign companies in Pennsylvania by county, 2000

Table 14.1   A profile of FDI in Pennsylvania, 1997

Profile				Per cent	Rank **
1	Number of affiliates of which first three are	Numbers	1149		8
	1. Japan		212	18.5	
	2. United Kingdom		198	17.2	
	3. Germany		159	13.8	
2	Gross assets of affiliates of which first three are	US$ million	25671		9
	1. United Kingdom		5786	22.5	
	2. France		4584	17.9	
	3. Germany		4556	17.7	
3	Employment of affiliates of which first three are	No. '000s	225		6
	1. United Kingdom		51.4	22.8	
	2. Germany		34.6	15.4	
	3. France		27.8	12.4	
3a	Manufacturing empl. of affiliates of which first three are	No. '000s	104.7		5
	1. United Kingdom		26.8	25.6	
	2. Germany		18.3	17.5	
	3. France		14.9	14.2	
4	Commercial property of affiliates of which first three are	US$ million	3257		14
	1. United Kingdom		548	16.8	
	2. Japan		473	14.5	
	3. Australia		406	12.5	

Note: ** The rank is the standing of the State *vis-à-vis* the other States of the US.

Source: BEA, Department of Commerce, 1997 Benchmark Survey.

Transaction data, as well as establishment data summarized in Tables 14.1, 14.2 and 14.3, suggest that Pennsylvania is perceived as a desirable location for the manufacturing affiliates of foreign firms. While manufacturing accounted for only 45.6 per cent of new FDI transactions between 1989 and 1994 in the US as a whole, in Pennsylvania they accounted for 67.2 per cent of such transactions. With a ranking of six out of 50 for employment by foreign-owned firms, Pennsylvania ranks fifth in the

Table 14.2   Inbound FDI in Pennsylvania and the US, 1997

		Pennsylvania	All US
1 Average gross assets	US$ million	22.34	98.61
Gross assets / number of affiliates			
2 Average no. of employees	Numbers	196	588
Employees / number of affiliates			
3 Per employee assets	US$ '000s	114.09	167.73
Gross assets / employees			
4 Ratio of mfg to total employment	%	46.5	40.3
Mfg employees/Total employees			
Of which first three are 1. United Kingdom	%	52.1	41.3
2. Germany	%	52.9	43.0
3. France	%	53.6	43.1
5 Ratio of commercial property to total assets	%	12.7	19.9
Commercial property/total assets			
of which first is United Kingdom	%	9.5	10.8

Source: BEA, Department of Commerce 1997 Benchmark Survey.

country for the manufacturing employment of foreign affiliates. The home countries of MNCs with the largest number of employees in manufacturing subsidiaries in Pennsylvania are Britain, Germany, and France (BEA, 1997).

These three European countries also source the largest number of affiliates from foreign countries operating in Pennsylvania, closely followed by Canada and Japan. Between 1997 and 2000, the number of foreign affiliates operating in Pennsylvania has increased by 25.9 per cent. This growth has been accompanied by an increase in employment of 92.7 per cent (BEA, 1997 and Dun and Bradstreet, 2000).

The research on the economic geography of FDI and its determinants, the locational strategies of MNCs, and the international and sub-national allocation of value-added activity is fragmented, and needs to be updated to take account of the advent of the knowledge intensive globalizing economy (Dunning, 1998). This chapter has sought to provide a review of the theoretical and empirical research on the location of MNC activity in order to explain decisions at the sub-national level.

Future research based on primary data collection through a questionnaire survey of the foreign-owned firms operating in Pennsylvania may be useful for evaluating not only the determinants considered important for making an initial location decision, but also those for sustaining an active presence in the State. Relatively little scholarly research has been

Table 14.3   FDI in Pennsylvania by country of origin, 2000

3.1 Breakdown based on country of origin

Region / country	Number of affiliates	Per cent	Rank
European countries			
Austria	11	0.8	17
Belgium	16	1.1	15
Denmark	18	1.2	13
United Kingdom	347	24.0	1
Finland	13	0.9	16
France	133	9.2	3
Germany	324	22.4	2
Italy	29	2.0	10
Netherlands	77	5.3	6
Norway	10	0.7	18
Sweden	39	2.7	9
Switzerland	53	3.7	7
Other European countries	17	1.2	14
(Iceland, Israel, Luxembourg,			
Liechtenstein, Netherlands			
Antilles, Ireland N. Ireland, Spain)			
Total European countries	**1087**	**75.2**	
Japan	128	8.6	5
Other countries			
Australia	10	0.7	18
Bermuda	21	1.5	12
Canada	132	9.1	4
Others	45	3.1	8
(Hong Kong, Israel, Singapore,			
Saudi Arabia UAE and			
Undefined 35)			
Developing countries	23	1.6	11
(India, Mexico, Malaysia, S. Korea,			
Taiwan, Argentina, Bahamas, Brazil,			
Chile)			
TOTAL	**1446**	**100.0**	

Note: Multi subsidiaries/affiliates of same parent are individually counted.

Table 14.3 (continued)

3.2 Other data (2000)

2a	Total number of employees in affiliates	No. thousands	433.64
2b	Total sales of the affiliates	US $ billion	1517.60
2c	Sales/employee of the affiliates (b/a)	US $ million/employee	3.50
2d	Growth in number of affiliates over 1997	%t	25.9
2e	Growth in employment over 1997 by affiliates	%t	92.7

Source: 1997 data from BEA Benchmark Survey is compared to year 2000 figures, calculated by authors from Dun and Bradstreet (2000).

undertaken on the variables influencing the sustainability of inward FDI, or its relevance for sub-national policy makers. For one such effort in respect of FDI in North East of England see EAG (2001). Previous experience with a questionnaire survey of foreign firms in the USA suggests that, to ensure a good response rate, the sponsorship of the survey by a key person or organization engaged in international operations or by an official state agency may be very useful (Vyas, 2000).

Another dimension of this study that has not yet been fully explored is the impact of FDI on the State economy, particularly at a county or business district level. Therefore, subsequent research will need to involve the collection of income and employment data before and after the time period under consideration to examine the effectiveness of FDI in supporting the local economy.

As this chapter concerns FDI in the State of Pennsylvania, it is relevant to all types of organizations and government agencies operating in the State, which are able to influence the economic, and investment climate. Policy implications of this research can be useful to the organizations from an operational perspective, and to sub-national governments as they seek to attract, retain and raise the productivity of inbound FDI in the State. The research would also be useful to the economic community in other US States who may be looking for comprehensive explanations of FDI location decision-making. Such research might also be extended to consider the factors lending to the sustainability and upgrading of the quality of FDI at a State level.

Indeed it would be worth investigating annual transaction and establishment data (Department of Commerce) for the 1990s to verify the impact of global political and economic changes on inbound FDI at both a national and a State level. Such changes might include the impact of NAFTA and the deeper economic integration of the European Economic Community.

CONCLUSIONS

Since a case can be made that the pattern of MNC locational decision making in Pennsylvania does not reflect that for the overall United States as whole, it could be argued that there must be particular attributes of Pennsylvania that attract (or detract) inbound foreign investors. Attributes particular to Pennsylvania, such as government incentives, market structure, and corporate networks in the northeastern United States, proximity to New York and New Jersey and other economies of agglomeration, help to attract FDI in Pennsylvania. The present evaluation of theoretical and empirical material enables us to identify the important factors affecting location choice, giving particular attention to the role of efforts by State government. Both directly, through tax and investment incentive policies, and indirectly through investments in education and infrastructure, as well as by their efforts to reduce unemployment and poverty, State governments can take actions that will encourage foreign investors to locate within their borders. Moreover, State efforts can help to create or maintain conditions that will encourage affiliates of foreign companies to maintain their operations within the State.

NOTES

1. This chapter derives from ongoing research on the analysis of sub-national patterns of FDI within the United States.
2. There is a potential problem in empirical work deriving from the overlap between cultural similarity of the home and host economies and the greater understanding of the host by virtue of experience in the country (Benito *et al.*, 1992).
3. This has self-evident implications for the importance of attracting new investors in any assessment of sub-national policies.
4. The OLI paradigm, the determinants of MNC activity and detailed explanation of the location-specific variables are given in Dunning (1993a, table 4.1 p. 81).
5. Dunning in table 1 of his 1998 paper sets out the main differences between 1970s and 1990s location specific variables
6. Based on the above hypotheses Marian Geldner (1986, p. 104) has suggested that: 'this argument holds well when applied within the domain of international trade where the role of established linkages in shaping their intra-firm division of labor and corresponding pattern of foreign trade TNCs can minimize the political and economic risks of their operations and disadvantages of psychic distance with simultaneous maximization of the benefits from the established information networks and flows.'
7. Nachum (2000) provides a detailed account of the evolving contribution of research in economic geography to our understanding of MNC activity.
8. The greater part of FDI is undertaken by MNCs which are large and have wide geographic coverage. As MNCs operate in two or more countries, they are potentially embedded in two or more localities, and the external ties of MNCs are supplemented by internal ties with a whole network of affiliates spread across the globe.
9. According to Mudambi (1999), basic investment support schemes include, grants, infrastructural development, tax concessions, loans and loan guarantees, and interest subsidies.

10. Principal –agent relationships are important as the MNC investor attempts to put together a package. The main agents of the investment are the government, the inward investment agency, the MNC investor, and the private lender. For a detailed explanation of principal–agent models refer to Mudambi (1999).

15. The OLI paradigm – an effective framework for assessing global strategic leadership

Lorna H. Wallace and Marguerite Schneider

The modern world economy has become increasingly deeply integrated or globalized (Gray and Wallace, 1996; Kobrin, 1995; Wallace, 1998) requiring today's multinational enterprise (MNE) to be simultaneously globally integrated and locally responsive through its network of operations (Hume, 1993). The high level of both integration and responsiveness reflects that leading global competitors have found new mechanisms for harnessing mobile resources and gaining access to immobile ones, while minimizing the transaction costs of both (Gray, 1996; Hume, 1993; Stopford, 1995; Storper, 1995; Wallace, 1998). These developments have led to the growth of 'alliance capitalism' (Gerlach, 1992), characterized by burgeoning inter-firm cooperative activity – a hybrid mode of governance.

We suggest that changes in the world economy associated with the new age of 'alliance capitalism' have presented an increasingly challenging land-scape to those who are most influential in determining the direction of MNEs, the strategic leaders that comprise their top management teams. The process of globalization has made leader effectiveness more difficult to achieve. As the importance of MNE transactions grows, so too does the analysis of the effectiveness of strategic leadership with the MNE.

There has been a long-standing association in the management literature of leadership with change and adaptation to the environment.[1] Our chapter further explores this association, and increases its relevance to international business, by focusing on the relationship between globalization and organizational strategic leadership. Our use of Dunning's eclectic para-digm (EP) as the framework for a model of this relationship provides new insight into global strategic leadership, and helps to further demonstrate and extend the applicability of the paradigm within this new age of capitalism (Dunning, 1995).[2]

The chapter views MNEs as complex open organizational systems that influence, and are influenced by, their environments; whose parts are interdependent; and in which order tends to emerge despite counter-tendencies toward non-linearity and chaos (Anderson, 1999; Lewin, 1999). By using Dunning's EP (1993a) we seek to develop an *eclectic model of global leadership*. Within the context of the OLI paradigm, we describe how globalization has in effect raised the bar or standard for organizational leaders, rendering leader effectiveness to be more difficult to achieve. Indeed, the new global business environment calls for a leader who has the aptitude, skills, experience and training to be effective across a range of diverse, contradictory and inter-linked environments.

We first present a brief summary of the literature on global strategic leadership and then integrate that literature with the EP as the framework for the eclectic model of global leadership. The argument is essentially that explicit recognition of the dimensions of the OLI paradigm provides insight into effective global leadership in that the specific shareholder attributes identified by Mitchell *et al.* (1997) and the leadership attributes advanced by leader complexity theory (Hooijberg *et al.*, 1997), moderate leader effectiveness.

MNE STRATEGIC MANAGEMENT AND THE OWNERSHIP-SPECIFIC ADVANTAGE OF STRATEGIC LEADERSHIP

> Strategic management is essentially concerned with the ways in which managers act to achieve their long-term objectives in conditions of market failure. It embraces decisions about how resources are acquired, created and utilized, the way in which markets are identified and served and how transactions relating to these decisions are organized. It is concerned with the ways in which firms with different mixtures of physical human and financial assets deploy these strengths between countries with very different cultures, institutional structures and economic systems. Like the 'how' and 'where' to produce, these various strategic strands must be integrated and it is the extent to which an MNE is successful in this task that is increasingly determining its ability to sustain or advance its competitive position in global markets. (Dunning, 1993a, pp. 93–4)

In addition, Dunning notes that global strategy concerns the various strategic strands of a complex web of cross-border transactions and that it is 'the totality of this strategy rather than its individual component parts that is likely to determine the competitive success of MNE hierarchies' (Dunning, 1993a, p. 93). Crucial to success is the ability to generate, sustain and exploit the firm's proprietary ownership advantages. Recognition of the importance of firm-specific proprietary advantages is found in the foundations on which the EP was built and implies that MNEs operate in imperfect markets in which ownership assets are a distinctive difference among competitors.

Based upon the behavioral research tradition of Cyert and March (1963), Aharoni (1966) argued that the decision to invest abroad essentially involves three critical elements: uncertainty, information and commitment. Uncertainty is involved because managers tend to overestimate the amount of risk involved in foreign ventures. Information is therefore acquired about the potential for foreign involvement, often by a person who may become a 'champion' for the international venture thus supplying the commitment. Unless all three elements occur, it is unlikely that foreign involvement will take place. Aharoni's theorizing indicates the critical nature of leadership to the opportunities and dangers of FDI.[3]

Ownership advantages (O) are specific competitive enhancing attributes of firms. They include proprietary technological know-how;[4] R&D capacity; the reservoir of experienced and internationally mobile workers and well-trained managers with industry-specific human capital; and trademarks and known brand names. Dunning (1993a) suggests that proprietary knowledge is a temporary O advantage but an efficiently functioning research operation could make that a long-lasting advantage. O advantages were operationalized as 'net' O advantages (Dunning and McQueen, 1981) where firms were found to be able to enter a foreign market if they have some set of advantages over other firms such as the O-specific advantage of effective global strategic leadership.

As the world economy has become more globalized, the nature and character of O advantages has evolved. The original significance of the country of MNE ownership has diminished, replaced by the increasing importance of both its management and its degree of multinationality. Three kinds of O advantages have evolved: some are related to monopoly power; others to the possession of valuable resources and capabilities; and the third kind to the competencies of management in developing valuable resources and capabilities (Dunning, 2000b). MNE management has become a more critical factor through its ability to develop assets or resources into core competencies, the sub-set of resources that are unique, of value, non-imitable and non-substitutable (Barney, 1995), and are thus of great strategic value. Likewise, management contributes by coordinating the use of these resources across countries and modes of transacting, in order to exploit their contribution to the firm. The emphasis is now on the dynamic management process of accessing, organizing, and integrating knowledge-intensive resources within and across firms (Dunning, 2000b).

Although the constructs of management and organizational leadership may well not be wholly distinct or orthogonal, we follow the fairly standard demarcation between the two made in the literature. Management is the process of engagement in relatively ongoing or routine activities, while organizational leadership is the process of engaging in change above the level necessary for compliance with routine direction (Katz and Kahn, 1966; Selznick, 1957; Zaleznik, 1992). While commitment to routine and commitment to change are both necessary for organizational success (Collins and Porras, 1994), an increasingly volatile and unpredictable environment has come to place greater emphasis on leadership *vis-à-vis* management (Schneider, 2002). The leadership process is dynamic with current decisions dependent upon the actual/inherited portfolio of assets at the decision time (Gray, 1996).

The identification and value of specific OLI parameters will influence individual MNE leaders in any particular production decision. Each will vary according to the motives underlying the production (Dunning, 1988) and according to managerial perception and attitude (towards, for example, risk taking). Leadership strategies are likely to differ depending upon the nature of the investment (i.e. resource-, market-, efficiency-, or strategic asset-seeking) and the motivation (e.g., to acquire new competitive advantages) (Dunning, 1993c). This implies that effective global strategic leadership is, to a certain extent, the integration of O, L, and I over time. A firm's OLI configuration influences the firm's strategic response. Each firm must consider the combination of its O advantages with those of its competitors, in order to gain sustainable competitive advantage. Leadership decision-making juggles all of the variables in the OLI paradigm with the motivations for FDI from which MNEs look to implement effective strategy across their value chains.

O advantages largely take the form of the privileged possession of intangible assets, including but not limited to leadership, as well as advantages that arise as a result of the common governance of cross-border value-added activities. Effective leadership, particularly among those at the strategic apex of the MNE, is an O advantage that is important in its own regard. But we put forth that leadership is a particularly critical advantage in that it influences the development and use of other O advantages, or core competencies, as well as the MNE's ability to exploit L and I specific advantages.

The quality of an MNE's strategic leader is clearly only one of many variables influencing organizational effectiveness and their discretion or latitude of action is limited (Hambrick and Finkelstein, 1987). But despite the presence of other variables, there is support for a positive relationship between strategic leader effectiveness and organizational effectiveness (Cannella and Monroe, 1997; Day and Lord, 1988). Accordingly, MNE performance is viewed as an appropriate dependent variable of strategic leadership (Finkelstein and Hambrick, 1996; Hart and Quinn, 1993). In our eclectic model of strategic leadership, the effective usage of quality O advantages such as effective leadership increases the wealth creating capacity of the MNE, and hence the value of its assets.[5]

LOCATION FACTORS AND STRATEGIC LEADERSHIP

Much theorizing regarding the MNE in international business focuses on the complexity of these organizations and their environments, in part due to the multiple geographic or spatial environments in which they operate and the internal complexity this promotes (e.g. Bartlett and Ghoshal, 1990; Dunning, 1977; Lundan, Chapter 7 in this volume). Early conceptualizations of complexity view it as the presence of multiple, inter-linked components (Thompson, 1967). While a complex system has more variables and interactions than does a simple system, there was still thought to be a good degree of predictability regarding a complex system, assuming that it was sufficiently understood. More recent conceptualizations of complex systems transcend this view. It is now thought that, as opposed to structured or highly predictable systems, or random or unpredictable systems, a complex non-linear system can be partly understood or predicted, but only with great difficulty, due to the chaos inherent in the system. Small changes to one or two parameters can drastically change the whole system, which is very different from the sum of its parts (Anderson, 1999).

Here, we explore how globalization increases the complexity that strategic leaders face, addressed in terms of L advantages reflected in the MNE's multiple institutionalized environments. Leadership is best thought of broadly, in terms of relationships with the organization's stakeholders (Blair and Rivera, 1992; Hooijberg and Schneider, 2001), those groups or individuals who can affect, or are affected by, the achievement of the organization's objectives (Freeman, 1984). A conceptualization of leadership in terms of stakeholder relationships is particularly appropriate for the MNE's top management team whose positions involve interaction with, and accountability to, a broad range of stakeholders[6] (Jacobs and Lewis, 1992). Globalization results in a series of inter-related national environments, each with its own stakeholders and institutionalized values regarding stakeholder groups. In this section, we illustrate both some of the many differences across, and the dynamic and at times unpredictable quality associated with, the institutionalized environments facing global strategic leaders. This illustration is accomplished by focusing on a sample of three of the MNE's primary stakeholder groups.

Government

The business–government interface within market-based systems has been found to fluctuate in terms of strength of the executive leader and the leader's political party platform, the influence of special interest groups and prestige of employment in the public sector (Hillman and Keim, 1995).[7] Business–government relationships may be favourable, varying from co-involvement in determining industrial policy though a more *laissez faire* approach that may include influence via the lobbying process. Relationships may also be unfavourable and indeed might be hostile.

Government policy may influence MNE performance indirectly, by affecting the competitiveness of national industries. Specifically, government policies related to tariffs, exchange rates, taxes, and innovation may enable host-based firms to become more efficient, or may subsidize their activities, thereby increasing their amount of free cash flow available to finance industry-determined mandatory investment expenditures. While MNEs clearly have limited ability to capitalize on host-based national competitive advantages, in some cases the MNE may be able to transmit some host-country advantages to its home country (Milberg and Gray, 1992).

Global strategic leaders must develop a keen sensitivity to the tremendous variance in governments across national contexts and the foreseen probability of change through elections or crisis. Business–government relations are better conceptualized not on a case-by-case basis within each local country, but rather from a complex systems perspective in which favourable relations with one government might hurt relations with other stakeholder groups both within the local country and across the MNE's broader domain. In addition, supra-government institutions such as the UN and the WTO further increase the complexity facing strategic leaders. Their sovereignty is not always clear, nor can the reaction they will generate from other stakeholders be reliably predicted. The increased presence of supra-government organizations renders further support for a complex perspective of business–government relations.

Owners

Despite the global trend toward privatization, there is still a significant degree of government ownership of industry in some countries (Gedajlovic, 1993; Pedersen and Thomsen, 1997). Further, the legitimacy of owners varies significantly among countries.[8]

Ownership concentration also varies, with greater owner concentration associated with greater power (Mintzberg, 1983), one of the key stakeholder attributes.[9] The expected role of ownership fluctuates by country.[10] Increased ownership concentration, brought about by institutional investment, is associated with increased market volatility and price swings in equity markets (Norris, 1996; Schwartz, 1991; Wyatt, 1997).

MNEs, characterized as networks engaged in a dynamic web of production and sales functions across various countries (Bartlett and Ghoshal,

1990), increasingly encounter cross-border complexity in their ownership.[11] We put forth that owner expectations within a country affect not only local firms, but also expectations of MNEs operating within the country, further increasing the complexity facing the MNEs' global strategic leaders.

Labour Unions

Labour unions are one of many non-governmental organizations that have emerged as influential players in global trends. Although recent trends suggest a decline in the power and influence of labour unions, their impact cannot be discounted; instead, it varies by country (Brunner, 1999) and can be significant.[12] A global leader must understand the historical development of labour union ideology in each of the countries where the MNE conducts business and develop insight into its current and potential future ideology. Additionally, the leader must assess the potential power and influence of the involved labour unions in the MNE's markets. The effects of trade agreements and other linkages across countries, such as the EU and NAFTA must also be considered.

From the above discussion illustrating significant variation across institutionalized environments regarding three of the MNE's primary stakeholder groups, we propose an extended application of the EP into an eclectic model of global strategic leadership. Knowledge of the organization's stakeholders and the L advantages of affiliates accrue to MNEs with existing FDI in a country.

INTERNALIZATION FACTORS AND STRATEGIC LEADERSHIP

Just as strategic leadership is affected by, and affects, those L-specific advantages that are reflected in the MNE's institutionalized environments, strategic leadership is also affected by, and affects Internalization-specific advantages. The significant costs and risks associated with globalization have encouraged, if not required, many MNEs to engage in activities for the sharing of costs, risks, and returns. Many organizations are choosing to engage in cooperative strategic alliances (Contractor and Lorange, 1988; Jorde and Teece, 1989; Kanter, 1990; Ring and Van de Ven, 1994) that enable MNEs to share risks often beyond the capacity of the individual alliance members (Kogut, 1988). Indeed, Dunning has acknowledged that O advantages may arise from the conclusion of successful cooperative strategic alliances with other firms and by the harnessing and coordination of resources and capabilities throughout the world (Dunning, 1995).

Outsourcing[13] reflects the view of the firm as a series of internal markets that contract with each other and with external markets based on efficiency and other criteria (Halal, 1994). The ability of the MNE to strategically and successfully manage its outsourcing activities is an O advantage specific to the firm, enabling it to choose various combinations of alternative governance structures rather than to internalize each and every function within a single organization.

We propose that globalization increases the complexity global strategic leaders face, as it brings forth strategically significant hybrid stakeholders emerging from the hybrid governance structures (Hennart, 1993; Williamson, 1991) of strategic alliances and outsourcing. While globalization is about larger markets, it is also about the variance in country environments and governance structures and 'the ability to profit through the system-wide management of this variance' (Kogut, 1989, p. 388).[14] Thus, from the above discussion illustrating greater reliance on new governance structures, we offer that analysis of the relationship between Internalization-specific advantages that are associated with the MNE's governance and global strategic leadership can be furthered through the use of the EP.

STAKEHOLDER ATTRIBUTES, LEADER ATTRIBUTES AND LEADER EFFECTIVENESS

Stakeholders

Stakeholders – whether those within an institutionalized environment or those in the more narrowly defined 'hybrid' category involved in strategic alliances – have various and sometimes conflicting expectations of the firm. As the firm's strategic leaders are at the nexus of its stakeholder relationships (Hill and Jones, 1992) their effectiveness rests in part upon the assessment of stakeholders' respective capabilities to influence and affect, and be influenced and affected by, the firm. Leaders need to discern '. . . who and what really count' (Mitchell *et al.*, 1997), which is a significant intellectual challenge given the web of stakeholders and their relationships within the MNE network (Harrison and St. John, 1996; Savage *et al.*, 1991).

Leadership effectiveness requires the ability to make keen assessments regarding the relative legitimacy, power and urgency of stakeholders (Mitchell *et al.*, 1997).[15] The effectiveness of leadership regarding MNE stakeholder groups is an O advantage. We propose that the legitimacy, power and urgency of the MNE's relevant stakeholders will moderate the relationships among L, I and leadership effectiveness (O) in the eclectic model of global strategic leadership.

Leader Complexity

Three aspects of leader complexity – cognitive, behavioural and social complexity – distinguish those who tend to be effective leaders.[16] Accordingly, these three aspects of leader complexity, along with stakeholder salience, influence the relationships between L, I and effective global strategic leadership (O).

Cognitive complexity

Cognitive complexity is the ability to think in a multidimensional, abstract manner and synthesize information at various levels of abstraction (Jacques, 1986). It has two dimensions: differentiation and integration (Boal and Whitehead, 1992). Within the organizational domain, cognitive complexity has been posited as requisite for strategic leaders (Jacobs and Lewis, 1992).

Behavioural complexity

Cognitive complexity is necessary but insufficient for leader effectiveness. Effective leaders will also be behaviourally complex, tending to '. . . act out a cognitively complex strategy by playing multiple even competing roles, in a highly integrated and complementary way' (Hoojiberg and Quinn, 1992: p. 164). Accordingly, more effective leaders will evidence a wider repertoire of roles than less effective leaders.[17] Behavioural complexity has been positioned as a leadership competency that may lead to sustainable global competitive advantage (Petrick *et al.*, 1999).

Social complexity

Social complexity, a leader's ability to apply interpersonal skills in a socially appropriate manner, reflects the leader's social perceptiveness and response flexibility (Zaccaro *et al.*, 1991). It has been proposed that leaders who are more socially complex have more developed and complex knowledge structures regarding people and situations, understand critical social organizational problems and develop more adaptive responses to the problems than do non-leaders (Zaccaro *et al.*, 1991). Two dimensions of social complexity are social differentiation and integration.[18] Based on the above discussion, we offer that leader complexity influences global strategic leader effectiveness.

IMPLICATIONS AND SUGGESTIONS FOR FURTHER RESEARCH

The original EP of international production (Dunning, 1977) is still relevant today, approximately twenty-five years after its conception, even though its three dimensions (O, L and I) are necessarily much more interdependent in the modern context (Gray, 1996). In this chapter we have extended the EP to include the interrelationship between leadership as an O variable with some Location and Internalization variables. Due to the dynamic changes in the global economy and because multinational OLI configurations vary and are in constant flux, the EP is used to analyse and capture the dynamic interdependencies among the components.

The resource-based view, with its emphasis on core competencies, has become a major influence within the field of strategy (Barney, 1986, 1991; Peteraf, 1993; Wernerfelt, 1984). This impact is in part because the resource-based view addresses the critical implicit assumption in strategy of firm heterogeneity (Mahoney and Pandian, 1992). Specifically, if MNEs within an industry face a similar array of L and I specific advantages in their institutionalized environments and governance structures, why do some succeed, others under-perform, and yet others fail? While the resource-based view has contributed by focusing on clarifying the conditions for firm heterogeneity, we find that Dunning had earlier insight into the issue in his EP. First, Dunning highlighted the importance of organization as an Ownership-specific advantage specific to the firm, which had been largely neglected in the international business literature. Second, he brought forth that it is not merely O advantages that lead to success or failure; instead, it is the interaction of endogenous variables with exogenous variables that present the firm's full range of possible actions upon which its performance is based.

Effective global strategic leadership is a particularly critical O advantage, or core competency. Thus far, research indicates that successful global leaders have much international experience and cross-cultural empathy, strong relational skills and understanding of the leadership processes of inspiring and motivating, value diversity and tolerate ambiguity (Kets de Vries and Florent-Treacy, 1999). More specific to the issue of effectiveness, it has been found that an MNE's competitive position depends upon the ability of its strategic leadership to build dynamic core competencies, develop human capital, effectively use new technologies, engage in valuable strategies and develop a flexible organization (Hitt *et al.*, 1998).

Effective global leadership is a net O advantage that the MNE has *vis-à-vis* other firms in serving particular markets. The greater the effectiveness of a global leader (an O-specific advantage) the more incentive the MNE has to exploit this advantage itself. We put forth that failed attempts at globalization, resulting in organizational retrenchment, may in part reflect strategic leaders' insensitivity to the OLI complexities that globalization brings.

Further analysis, refinement and testing of effective global strategic leadership within the framework of the Dunning's EP will contribute by serving to enhance our understanding of the successful strategy-making process within an MNE. For example, we suggest that greater strategic leader cognitive complexity will be associated with greater ability to interpret the environment and hence with greater leader effectiveness. It is offered that behavioural complexity will be related to successful strategy implementation. Hypotheses could be developed for the testing of specific relationships among the delineated aspects of environmental complexity, stakeholder and leader attributes, and the various outcomes of the MNE strategy-making process.

The EP encompasses many partial theories. We believe that the current OLI framework for analysis of international production, stemming from the research of Dunning (1977, 1993a, 1995, 1997a) is an excellent and appropriate tool to aid global strategic leadership research. The EP is a juxtaposition of not only national but also strategic characteristics with the ownership advantages specific to firms. The eclectic model of global strategic leadership that is suggested in this chapter is a further extension of Dunning's research, particularly appropriate to the new age of alliance capitalism.

NOTES

1. As is indicated by the seminal definition of leadership as '. . . influential increment over and above mechanical compliance with routine direction of the organization' (Katz and Kahn, 1966, p. 302).
2. Readers of this Festschrift are assumed to have a good knowledge of Dunning's eclectic paradigm.
3. Aharoni's analysis applies more closely to initial foreign involvement or to first ventures in an individual country or region.
4. Which can, unless the lead is maintained by adequate investment and success in R&D, be eroded.
5. See 'A critical assessment of the eclectic theory of the multinational enterprise', M. Itaki, (1991), *Journal of International Business Studies*, 22, 445–60.
6. Stakeholders are classified here as: *internal*, including employees, managers and board members; *external*, including owners, suppliers and competitors; and *hybrid*, consisting of stakeholders involved with the MNE in its hybrid governance. Stakeholders have also been classified into primary groups who are critical to the organization's survival, and secondary groups who are not essential to survival but may cause significant damage to the organization, such as special interest groups (Clarkson, 1995).
7. In particular, the French tradition of the *grande ecoles* and the power of the Japanese ministries have been noted to create idiosyncratic linkages and patterns of influence (Charkham, 1994).
8. In the US, shareholders tend to be accepted as the primary stakeholder group; indeed,

it is viewed that the firm's legitimacy rests upon its obligation to owners (Easterbrook and Fischel, 1991; Jensen and Meckling, 1976). In other countries, owners are viewed as one of several primary stakeholder groups so that their claims on the firm are either on equal ground, or subordinate to, the claims of other stakeholders such as employees or society-at-large.

9. In the US, ownership has become more concentrated due to the growth of institutional investors such as mutual funds and pension plans (Useem, 1996). But US concentration is much less than that of many other countries such as Germany (Demb and Richey, 1994; Woods, 1996). In lesser-developed countries, stock markets remain under-developed, with ownership largely continuing to be among families rather than diffused among individuals or concentrated among powerful financial institutions.

10. In Germany and Japan, owners tend to adopt a long-term, relational or 'patient capital' perspective (Porter, 1992) and through this perspective are able to influence the strategy of firms that are owned. In the US, owners in general remain skeptical regarding their role in influencing corporations (Useem *et al.*, 1993).

11. For example, 12% of the institutional market for US equity is held by non-US owners (Securities Industry Association, 1999) and many American institutional investors have diversified their portfolios by expanding investment into other markets (Zorn, 1997).

12. The Japanese civil service is an example of a strong union despite unfavourable legal rules governing labour relations (Simard, 1999). In Canada, the labour sector is a fairly strong political force although this power is limited by various factors including the diverse nature of Canadian federalism (Lynk, 2000). Currently, within western European trade unionism, some of the older ideological frames of reference – class struggle, social Catholicism – have declined in influence and have been replaced with new ones, including feminism and environmental concerns. This re-framing may increase the legitimacy of unions as it tends to enhance their relevance and attractiveness to today's workforce, and reflects a generalized ideological transformation away from a highly oppositional stance towards capitalism (Howell, 1998; Pasture *et al.*, 1996). While UK law has been changed to reduce union power and influence, unions have come to facilitate the introduction of organizational change by assisting corporate leaders in communicating with the work force (Gallie *et al.*, 1996; Wood, 1998). European labour unions sometimes adopt strategies borrowed from the boardroom, hence the intertwined relationship between unions and effective leadership in much of Europe (Valencia, 2000).

13. Outsourcing refers to the firm's reliance on external sources for value-chain activities that were previously internalized (see I-specific advantage of the eclectic paradigm Dunning, 1977; Lei and Hitt, 1995; Quinn and Hilmer, 1994).

14. See Boddewyn (1983) whose disinvestment research highlights the sensitive MNE exit strategy issue.

15. Mitchell *et al.* (1997) developed the classification system of legitimacy, power, and urgency for identification of stakeholder salience. Legitimacy is the perception that the actions of a stakeholder are desirable or appropriate. A stakeholder has power to the extent s/he develops an image of access to coercive, utilitarian or normative power, and utilizes this image to impose his/her will. Urgency reflects the perception of time sensitivity and the criticality or importance of a stakeholder claim.

16. The leaderplex model of Hoojiberg *et al.*, (1997) encompasses individual attributes, and their interactive effects, which are proposed to be related to the leader's effectiveness in dealing with complexity.

17. This has been supported in empirical testing. See Denison *et al.* (1995); Hart and Quinn (1993).

18. Social differentiation is the ability to discriminate aspects of a social situation, including the capacity to differentiate emotions in oneself and others. Social integration is the capacity to synthesize the components of a social situation that leads to increased understanding of it and accomplishment of instrumental objectives (Hoojiberg *et al.*, 1997).

16. The eclectic paradigm and the evolution of the United States public utility industries, 1875–2000

Cliff Wymbs

INTRODUCTION

Just as they did at the turn of the century, public utilities (telecommunications, electric, gas and water) today provide the basic infrastructure necessary for economic growth in both developing and developed countries. Over the past seventy years, government has regulated these industries and has maintained an uneasy balance of social, economic and political objectives. This government control, coupled with an inward industry focus, has made this a neglected area of research for international business scholars.

Trends associated with globalization of business, smaller government mandates and dramatic technological changes have been key factors in precipitating fundamental change and a worldwide growth of foreign investment in the public utility industries. This chapter provides a longitudinal view of both investment into the United States public utility sector and investments by United States public utility companies around the world. The dynamic interaction among large firms, markets and governments both in the home and host country markets provides valuable insight into understanding the rationale of public utility FDI.

The industries studied have historically been characterized as natural monopolies, i.e., their long run cost structures make competition inefficient, and provide basic consumer and business services that are billed at usage sensitive (e.g. per minute) rates. Traditionally, local, state and federal government regulatory agencies, rather than unimpeded market forces, have exerted significant control over firm behavior and geographic expansion in these industries. However, neither regulation nor industry dynamics are homogeneous across these industries. Water utilities provide a basic staple of life and have produced and distributed the product in much the same way for the past 125 years. The electric utility industry led the second industrial revolution that occurred at the turn of the twentieth century. Telecommunications, like electricity, was founded through a technological breakthrough just before the turn of the twentieth century, and is now leading the information revolution sweeping the global business landscape. Gas utilities, unlike traditional, vertically integrated electric utilities, operate production companies separate from distribution companies. Each of these services has common components, i.e., production, transmission and distribution, but different economies of production and governance are associated with each. Also, their ownership structures and foreign investments have varied a great deal. The analysis identifies where industry and firm specific factors dominate development, and where environmental and market factors dictate common cross-industry trends.

The framework developed was sufficiently general to explain the evolution of foreign investment by regulated utilities for four separate industries (though electric and telecommunications are discussed in more detail) over a 125 year period, and specific enough to incorporate this path dependent information into the firm-level partnering and project-level domestic and foreign investment decisions. The analysis is demarcated into four approximately 25 to 30 year phases: innovation/foreign expansion – (1875–1905); growth/increased government – (1905–35); economic turmoil/international isolation – (1935–65); globalization/liberalization – (1965–2000). Each of these eras began and ended with a period of fundamental change when social, economic and political forces were out of phase with one another (see Table 16.1).

Table 16.1   Industry innovation

Phase 1	Phase 2	Phase 3	Phase 4
Innovation/ foreign expansion	Growth/ increased government	Economic disaster/ international isolation	Globalization/ liberalization
1875–1905	1905–1935	1935–1965	1965–2000

ANALYTIC FRAMEWORK

The examination of the emergence and development of the multinational enterprises in the public utility industries has covered significant changes in economic, political and technological environments as well as different motives prompting firms to undertake market seeking (demand oriented), resource seeking (supply oriented), efficiency seeking (sequential) and strategic asset acquiring foreign direct investment (protect and augment proprietary advantages). The framework used to study this behavior is the eclectic paradigm that describes three conditions necessary for a firm to engage in foreign direct investment:

1. The firm's foreign value adding activities must possess net competitive advantage or ownership specific (O) advantage vis-a-vis firms in other nationalities in serving particular markets. These ownership advantages can take two forms: (a) the exclusive or privileged access to specific intangible assets and (b) the ability to govern these assets where the enterprise is multi-activity and geographically disperse.
2. Assuming condition (1) is satisfied, it must be more beneficial to the enterprise possessing these advantages to use them itself rather than to sell or lease them or their rights to a foreign firm. These are called market internalization (I) advantages.
3. Assuming conditions (1) and (2) are satisfied, it must be profitable for the enterprise to utilize these advantages outside the home market, thereby conferring a location (L) advantage on the countries possessing them over those who do not (Dunning, 1993a, p. 79).

Each of the OLI dimensions is analyzed for the four industry evolution phases.

LITERATURE REVIEW

The OLI eclectic paradigm draws extensively from a variety of theories, i.e., institutional structure, dynamic period of adjustment and closure theory, firm, FDI and dynamic FDI that are interwoven to create a tightly knit industry evolution analysis. An explanation of each is required before the OLI analysis is performed.

Institutional structure theory North (1981) defined institutions as the humanly devised constraints that structure political, economic and social interaction. Throughout history, institutions have been devised to create order and reduce uncertainty and, when they are combined with standard constraints of economics, have determined transaction and production costs and, ultimately, corporate profits. The change in power of the institutional players in the public utility industries has had a direct effect on the industries' structures. This has been particularly true during periods of economic uncertainty, such as in Phase 3 (1935–65), when the overall society has looked to government to recreate economic order; however, during periods of economic prosperity, such as in Phase 4 (1965–2000), society has wanted less government and a more competitive environment. Ruigrok and Tulder (1995) asserted that there is no one best industrial restructuring strategy or policy, but rather restructuring concepts, internationalization strategies and trade policies that are the result of economic, political and social interaction, i.e., struggles among bargaining processes. Ruigrok and Tulder's center of gravity concept applies in each of the four phases.

Dynamic change theories Schumpeter (1934) stated that technological progress would lead to instability in production and exchange and encourage more influential government. Perez (1985) identified a series of time specific clusters of radical innovation that were a manifestation of harmonious or disharmonious behavior of the total socio-economic and institutional system. Pavitt (1987) and Cantwell (1989) focused on the dynamic components of 'asset accumulation and restructuring'. Freeman and Perez (1988) looked at the prevalence of technological change and concluded that in the late 1980s the global economy was undergoing a third industrial revolution, almost one hundred years after the second in the late 1800s. Technology change theories help explain the creation of the electric and telecommunication industries in Phase 1 (1875–1905), their rapid global expansion in Phase 2 (1905–35) and their proliferation in Phase 4. Gersick's (1991) theories of change can be applied to these periods of industry discontinuities. Their 'punctuated' equilibrium analysis focused on the dynamics associated with, and the causes of, disequilibrium. They asserted that patterns of organizational evolution are characterized by periods of convergence punctuated by frame-breaking change leading to the convergence period. Industry discontinuities are characterized by sharp changes in the legal, political or technical conditions that shift the basis of competition.

Closure theory Cawson *et al.* (1990) asserted that firms used one of three closure strategies to achieve a dominant position in the market, within which is included the system of government–industry relationships. The first is closure by securing a dominant position vis-à-vis other competitors, which is the most market oriented. The second strategy is closure by associative action where producers define their collective interest as lying in the avoidance of competition. The third strategy is closure by the State where an economic organization attempts to consolidate its monopoly position by invoking the authority of the State, instead of winning in the marketplace. This theory introduces the dynamic interrelationship between the political and economic dimensions associated with regulated industries and a life cycle dimension that helps explain the evolution among the first three phases of the framework.

Firm theories   The evolutionary theory of the firm discussed by Nelson and Winter (1982) and Teece, Pisano and Shuen (1997) concerned itself more with the process by which firms evolve competitive advantage over time, i.e., how they organize their resources to achieve long term profits. This is similar to the resource-based view in that it is a dynamic theory but focuses more on successful processes or routines of the firm. Because the number of foreign investments in the utility sector have been growing rapidly and because each investment experience represents a unique set of incremental knowledge to the firm, the application of a dynamic resource-based theory of the firm appears to be a promising approach to explain outward foreign investment and partnering behaviors of United States utility firms.

Foreign direct investment theory   Hymer (1960), using an industrial organizational approach, asserted that for a firm to own and control foreign value adding facilities it must possess innovative cost, marketing or financial advantage specific to its ownership which would outweigh doing business in a foreign country. Buckley and Casson (1985) identified situations in which firms chose to internalize cross-border transactions in intermediate products rather than to use the market. This theory is used to explain horizontal and vertical integration of the foreign operations of firms. Dunning's (1993a) eclectic paradigm includes both internalization theory and ownership advantage and offers a general framework for determining the extent and pattern of both foreign-owned production by a country's own enterprises and domestic production owned by foreign enterprises. The paradigm differentiates between ownership advantages associated with property rights and/or intangible assets and the advantages of common governances. It cites internalization incentives related to the avoidance of search and/or negotiating costs and locational advantages associated with the spatial distribution of natural and created resource endowments and markets. Foreign investment is one important input to a firm's value-added chain of business activities. Wesson (1993) drew an interesting distinction between ownership advantages that are 'asset exploiting' and those that are 'asset augmenting'. Ownership advantage that is asset exploiting involves firms extracting monopoly profits from foreign markets by using their exclusive or privileged access to specific intangible assets, e.g., technology, management skills, usually created in the home market. With asset augmenting ownership advantage, the foreign investment upgrades the asset base of both the recipient country and sending countries' firms.

Dynamic foreign direct investment theories   Several partial theories of the firm introduce an important longitudinal dimension previously missing from Hymer's (1960) industrial organization view of FDI. Dunning and Narula's (1997) investment development path analysis identified several stages a country may pass through. As a country moves through these phases the OLI configuration faces outward and inward investment changes. Knickerbocker's (1973) 'follow my leader' addressed sequential behaviors of MNE oligopolies. The oligopoly theories are required to partially explain strategic behaviors not directly driven by short-term profit considerations.

APPLICATION OF THE ECLECTIC PARADIGM

The purpose of the remainder of this section is to evaluate the specific OLI variables that have affected different types of public utility investment by United States MNEs, and to determine how these variables change over time.

Ownership-specific Advantages (1875–2000)

Many of the ownership-specific advantages of the 1875–1905 period related specifically to the possession and exploitation of market power identified by Bain (1956) and Hymer (1960). Superior competitive positions in the electric and telecommunications industries were achieved through inventions of Bell and Edison and the protection of these monopoly rights through the US patent system. As with the start of a new techno-economic paradigm (Freeman, 1987), many different related inventions and innovations took place until a particular set of standards coalesced. Because of the technological nature of these sectors and the patent system, first movers proved very important for Westinghouse and General Electric in the electric industry and Bell in the telephone. In an attempt to rapidly deploy these framebreaking services throughout the developed world, large US and European firms cross-licensed technologies and focused on deployment in their home markets during this period.

The second phase's (1906–35) ownership advantages focused mainly on continuous innovation (Nelson and Winter, 1982) related to the previous period inventions. However, increasingly important were transactional ownership advantages (Dunning and Narula, 1997), where participants in these oligopoly industries developed extensive international networks of business relationships. These ventures were both asset exploiting (receiving monopoly returns on proprietary resources) and asset augmenting (learning about country operating practices to fuel further country and regional expansion) (Wesson, 1993). Due to geographic proximity and US government influence, most foreign investment by US firms was in Central and South America (Wymbs, 1999).

Breakthroughs in long distance radio technology and increased strength in natural gas transport made possible further international expansion of these services. Consistent with the findings of Prahalad and Doz (1987), competitive advantage associated with enterprise management also played a critical part in international expansion. One example was General Swope of Western Electric, who had previous experience in the Far East, and who provided critical leadership in organizing AT&T's activities in China and the Far East. However, the best examples of the importance of focused leadership as a competitive advantage were the creation of ITT (telephone) and American Foreign Power (electricity) which chose to have only international operating assets (Wymbs, 1999). (ITT bought AT&T international assets in 1922, while AFP was created as a fully separate subsidiary of General Electric during the same period.)

In the third phase (1936–65), governments changed the rules of the game (North, 1981) and turned previous ownership advantages into liabilities. Developing countries adopted inflationary macroeconomic policies and severely limited repatriation of dividends, while communist countries expropriated assets. Developed countries looked to exercise tighter domestic control over their critical infrastructure services. Many chose nationalization and created large government monopolies to run entire sectors. Bottom-line, the 1935–65 period eliminated the majority of ownership transactional advantages accumulated by firms during the first 60 years of the public utility sectors. Firms that maintained a domestic focus experienced gains commensurate with overall economic growth of the period and had sufficient internally generated cash flow to fund new technology investment. These firms were in a good position to manage the political process because they provided a critical service, knew more about the service than the government officials regulating them, and employed a large number of people (voters) in a concentrated geographic area.

Toward the end of this period communication satellite technology and nuclear technology were developed. The former made certain forms of communication distance insensitive and effectively shrank the economic world. The latter had great initial promise, but proved to be a failed technology due to environmental concerns and ultimately resulted in increased pressure by government agencies to deregulate the industry.

The fourth phase (1965–2000) began with technological advances at least partially funded by United States government research efforts attributable to the Cold War. Military funding helped the development of jet turbine engines, which have become the key components of smaller, more efficient power plants, and of secure telecommunications technology such as fiber optics. The Arab oil embargos in the 1970s created renewed interest in domestic energy sources. To spur exploration and output in the industry, natural gas was deregulated. Because the three distinct components of this industry, i.e., generation, transmission and distribution, were very similar to the electric industry components, it served as a template for future electricity deregulation (Phillips, 1993). Also because of a pro-competitive posture by regulatory agencies and a somewhat adversarial relationship between the United States industries and regulators, production costs were closely monitored and overall the United States public utility sectors of electric and telecommunications were efficient when measured against global standards (Cawson *et al.*, 1990). This reputation proved to be an extremely valuable competitive advantage when these companies chose to compete internationally.

INTERNALIZATION INCENTIVE ADVANTAGES (1875–2000)

Between 1875 and 1905 ownership advantage determined how firms were able to compete, but not why they chose to exploit these advantages in foreign markets rather than to sell or lease them to indigenous firms. The choice of foreign direct investment by the firm implies some market failure, e.g., structural and/or transactional (Dunning and Narula, 1997). As Stopford and Turner (1985) pointed out, few UK companies before WWII chose the licensing option due to lack of enforceable patent legislation. US utilities had similar fears and internalized operations where possible, cross-licensed technology from firms in geographically remote developed countries, and chose joint ventures when governments required, particularly in developing countries.

The period between 1906 and 1936 represented the rapid growth phase of the Kondratiev electric technology wave and American firms were leading the way. This era was characterized by the emergence of giant firms. Cartels and mergers with monopoly and oligopoly industries became the norm rather than the exception (Freeman and Perez, 1988). A rising US stock market plus a concentrated banking and finance-capital market facilitated funding of foreign expansion by United States utilities (Freeman and Perez, 1988). Also, the separation of communication from the physical transport of goods and the implementation of scientific management techniques aided the creation of hierarchical organizations that required large oligopoly players (Dickens, 1998).

The abuses of holding companies in the electric industry and the general economic distress of the Depression caused the third phase (1935–65) to be a period of structural market failures to be remedied by government legislation and regulation (Phillips, 1993). Geographically fragmented electric, water and gas industries and a highly regulated near monopoly telecommunications system resulted.

The fourth phase (1966–2000) was highlighted by the US government's uneasiness with the then current public utility industry structures and a sense that competition would lead to lower prices and an overall more efficient domestic market (Faulhaber, 1987). Eventually with the divestiture of the Bell operating companies in 1984, the organizational structure of the industry was radically changed. The divested Regional Bell Operating Countries (RBOCs) and AT&T quickly created overseas organizations to take advantage of new operating freedoms offered in the court settlement. After initially stumbling into international ventures with a lack of clear corporate vision, the RBOCs and AT&T eventually moved along the learning curve and sought out significant market seeking international ventures with profit in mind, e.g., the purchase of a large part of the Mexican telephone network, a significant stake in Germany's digital cellular service and the purchase of New Zealand Telephone (Smith, 1993).

In response to increasing prices and industry inefficiencies, the government in 1992 passed the Energy Policy Act that permitted electric utilities to form separate subsidiaries and compete as independent power producers in the United States and foreign markets. Also, electric utilities were allowed to own stock in foreign utility companies (Phillips, 1993). Thus began the re-internationalization of the electric industry after 60 years. Market seeking investment was the first type of investment, usually with local partners; however, in the latter part of the period, strategic asset seeking investment spurred on by 'tit-for-tat' oligopoly behavior followed (Knickerbocker, 1973). On average, these separate subsidiaries, operating in international markets, were much more risk-seeking than their staid parent companies, thereby creating a culture conflict friction (Adler, 1997).

Location-specific Advantages 1875–2000

In the late 1800s, the eastern corridor between Boston and New York and, eventually, the loci of central New Jersey became the Mecca for innovation in both the electric and the closely aligned telecommunication industry. Inventions in this localized knowledge hub (Scott, 1996) would set the stage for the electric based techno-market paradigm. Because the benefits of the new technology were apparent, it quickly spread throughout Europe, aided by cross-licensing agreements between European and US firms (Wilkins, 1974).

In the second phase, 1906–35, the technology reached around the world. United States telecommunication and electric utilities' market seeking FDI expanded into Asia and then focused geographically on Latin and South America (Lewis, 1938). Throughout the Latin American region, governments privatized their highly inefficient operations, with American companies acquiring ownership. However, not all location decisions were driven by the net present value of foreign projects. In an attempt to appease government regulators, AT&T agreed to divest its international operations to ITT in exchange for being granted a domestic monopoly. ITT continued massive investment in Latin America during the 1920s. Due to agglomerative economies, the hub of research activity remained in the southern New York and northern New Jersey area (Enright, 1991).

In Phase 3, 1936–65, government legislative initiatives, poor world market conditions, and increased country nationalism all led to an inward focus by domestic public utilities. The utilities that had a foreign focus, e.g., ITT and AFP, were left alone to negotiate with foreign governments and faired quite badly. World War II led to an increased US government research focus in the communications and computer areas that would lead to technology innovation in the next period. The hub of research activity for these industries continued to be in the southern New York and northern New Jersey area.

In Phase 4 (1965–2000) the US and the UK, through Reagan and Thatcher policies, were the first two countries to dramatically liberalize their public utility sectors. The belief was that competition spurred innovation, increased efficiency and eventually reduced consumer prices. Most developed countries followed and privatized their infrastructure networks and liberalized foreign investment policies for their previously domestic focused monopolies (Cawson *et al.*, 1990). In culturally similar countries, like Australia, the United Kingdom and New Zealand, United States utilities used strategic asset acquiring behavior as the market entry vehicle, while partnerships were used in other developed countries (Adler, 1997). Developing countries looking to participate in the rapidly increasing global economy realized that basic infrastructure was a necessary condition to obtaining other inward foreign investment (Lall, 1992). In the 1990s, large US public utility firms, usually acting through consortiums to minimize risk, actively participated in developing countries' infrastructure upgrades around the world, e.g., East Asia, Eastern Europe, South America.

CONCLUSION

In this chapter we have used the eclectic paradigm as a theoretical framework for examining the growth of the public utility industries since their inception in the late 1800s. The modality of investment by multinational enterprises, their geographical orientation, their foreign investment and how these have changed over the last 125 years, have been portrayed in terms of the changing nature of the OLI variables and the interaction among them.

This longitudinal view of industry evolution permits the reader to observe how different economic, political and social forces emerge over time as the most important drivers of industry change. The OLI paradigm provides the structure to systematically view these changes, and their punctuated periods of eruption, in the context of existing theory and market forces.

References

Abramovitz, Moses (1986), 'Catching up, forging ahead and falling behind', *Journal of Economic History*, **46** (2), 385–406.

Abramovitz, Moses (1993), 'The search for the sources of growth: Areas of ignorance, old and new', *The Journal of Economic History*, **53** (2), June, 217–43.

Abramovitz, Moses (1995), 'The origins of the postwar catch-up and convergence boom', in Jan Fagerberg, Bart Verspagen and Nick von Tunzelmann (eds), *The Dynamics of Technology, Trade and Growth*, Aldershot, UK and Brookfield, US, Edward Elgar.

Adler, Nancy (1997), *International Dimensions of Organizational Behavior*, Cincinnati, Ohio, South-Western College Publishing.

Aerospace Industries Association of America (1997), *Aerospace Facts and Figures*, 1997/98. Washington, DC, AIA.

Agarwal, Sanjeev and Sridhar Ramaswami (1992), 'Choice of foreign market entry mode: Impact of ownership, location and internationalization factors', *Journal of International Business Studies*, **23** (3), 1–28.

Aguilar, Linda M. (1996a), 'Foreign direct investment in the U.S. and Midwest', *Chicago Fed Letter*, no. 105 (May), Federal Reserve Bank of Chicago.

Aguilar, Linda M. (1996b), 'Foreign direct investment and the Great Lakes region, 1987–91', *Assessing the Midwest Economy*, no. GL-3, (18 September), Federal Reserve Bank of Chicago.

Aharoni, Y. (1966), *The Foreign Investment Decision Process*, Boston, Harvard Graduate School of Business Administration, Division of Research.

Aiken, Leona S. and Stephen G. West (1991), *Multiple Regression: Testing and Interpreting Results*, Newbury Park, CA, Sage Publications.

Allen, Linda and Christos Pantzalis (1996), 'Valuation of the operating flexibility of multinational enterprises', *Journal of International Business Studies*, **27** (4), 633–53.

Altomonte, C., R. Bolwijn and H. Peter Gray (2000), 'Open industrialization as a development strategy: The example of East Asia', in K. Fatemi (ed.), *The New World Order: Internationalizatism, Regionalism and the Multinational Corporations*, Amsterdam, Pergammon, 109–23.

Amable, B. and B. Verspagen (1995), 'The role of technology in market share dynamics', *Applied Economics*, **27**, 197–204.

Anderson, Erin and Hubert Gatignon (1986), 'Modes of foreign entry: A transaction cost analysis and propositions', *Journal of International Business Studies*, Fall, 1–26.

Anderson, P. (1999), 'Complexity theory and organization science', *Organization Science*, **10** (3), 216–32.

Ansoff, Igor (1965), *Corporate Strategy*, New York, McGraw-Hill.

Archibugi, D. (1992), 'Patenting as an indicator of technological innovation: A review', *Science and Public Policy*, **19** (6), 357–68.

Arrighi, Giovanni (1994), *The Long Twentieth Century: Money, Power, and Origin of Our Times*, London, Verso.

Arthur, Brian W. (1994), *Increasing Returns and Path Dependence in the Economy*, Ann Arbor, University of Michigan Press.

Bagchi-Sen, Sharmistha and James O. Wheeler (1989), 'A spatial and temporal model of foreign direct investment in the United States', *Economic Geography*, **65** (113).

Bain, Joseph S. (1956), *Barriers to New Competition*, Cambridge, MA, Harvard University Press.

Banerji, Kunal and Rakesh Sambharya (1996), 'Vertical keiretsu and international market entry: The case of the Japanese automobile ancillary industry', *Journal of International Business Studies*, 89–114.

Barney, J. (1986), 'Strategic factor markets: Expectations, luck, and business strategy', *Management Science*, **32** (10), 1232–41.

Barney, J. (1991), 'Firm resources and sustained competitive advantage', *Journal of Management*, **17** (1), 99–120.

Barney, J. (1995), 'Looking inside for competitive advantage', *Academy of Management Executive*, **9** (4), 49–61.

Barro, R.J. (1997), *Determinants of Economic Growth*, Cambridge, MA, The MIT Press.

Barro, R.J. and Xavier Sala-I-Martin (1995), *Economic Growth*, New York, McGraw-Hill.

Bartlett, C.A. and S. Ghoshal (1989), *Managing Across Borders: The Transnational Solution*, Boston, MA, Harvard Business School Press.

Bartlett, C.A. and S. Ghoshal (eds) (2000a), *Transnational Management*, 3rd edn, Boston, MA, Irwin McGraw-Hill.

Bartlett, C.A. and S. Ghoshal (2000b), 'Going global: Lessons from late movers', *Harvard Business Review*, **78** (2): 132–42.

(BEA) Bureau of Economic Analysis (1997), *Foreign Direct Investment Establishments in the U.S. Benchmark Survey 1997*, Washington, DC, Department of Commerce.

Beck, Ulrich (1998), *Democracy without Enemies*, Cambridge, Polity Press.

Bell, John F. (1953), *A History of Economic Thought*, New York: Ronald Press.

Benito, Gabriel, Gripsrud (1992), 'The expansion of foreign direct Investments: Discrete rational location choices or a cultural learning process?', *International Business Studies*, **23** (3), 461–76.

Berger, Philip and Eli Ofek (1996), 'Bustup takeovers of value-destroying diversified firms', *Journal of Finance*, **51**, 1175–200.

Bhagat, Sanjai, Andrei Schleifer and Robert Vishny (1990), 'Hostile takeovers in the 1980s: The return to corporate specialization', *Brookings Papers on Economic Activity*, 1–85.

Blair, J.D. and J.B. Rivera (1992), 'A stakeholder management perspective on strategic leadership', in R.L. Phillips and J.G. Hunt (eds), *Strategic Leadership: A Multiorganizational-level Perspective*, Westport, CN, Quorum Books, 81–98.

Blomstrom, Magnus, Steven Globerman and Ari Kokko (2000), 'Regional Integration and foreign direct investment', in John H. Dunning (ed.), *Regions, Globalization, and the knowledge-based Economy*, Oxford, Oxford University Press.

Bluestone, Barry and Bennett Harrison (1982), *The Deindustrialization of America: Plant Closings, Community Abandonment, and the Dismantling of Basic Industry*, New York, Basic Books.

Boal, K.B. and C.J. Whitehead (1992), 'A critique and extension of the stratified systems theory perspective', in R.L. Phillips and J.G. Hunt (eds), *Strategic Leadership: A Multiorganizational-level Perspective*, Westport, CT, Quorum Books, 237–54.

Boddewyn, J.J. (1983), ' Foreign divestment theory. Is it the reverse of FDI theory?' *Weltwirtshaftilches Archive*, **119**, 345–55.

Brealey, Richard and Stewart Myers (1991), *Principles of Corporate Finance*, 4th edn, New York, McGraw-Hill.

Brewer, Thomas (1993), 'Government policies, market imperfections, and foreign direct investments, *Journal of International Business Studies*, 101–20.

Brickley, James A. (1999), 'Incentive conflicts and contractual restraints: Evidence from franchising', *Journal of Law and Economics*, **42**, 745–74.

Brouthers, Keith D., Lance E. Brouthers and Steve Werner (1996), 'Dunning's eclectic theory and the small firm: The impact of ownership and locational advantages on the choice of entry modes in the computer software industry', *International Business Review*, **5** (4), 377–94.

Brouthers, Lance E., Keith D. Brouthers and Steve Werner (1999), 'Is Dunning's eclectic framework descriptive or normative? *Journal of International Business Studies*, **30** (4), 831–44.

Brunner, B. (ed.) (1999), *Time Almanac 2000*, Boston, MA.

Buckley, Peter J., and Mark C. Casson (1976), '*The Future of Multinational Enterprise*, New York, Holmes and Meier.

Buckley, Peter J. and Mark C. Casson (1985), *The Economic Theory of the Multinational Enterprise*, London, Macmillan.

Buckley, Peter J. and Mark C. Casson (1992), *Multinational Enterprises in the World Economy: Essays in Honour of John Dunning*, Aldershot: Edward Elgar.

Buckley, Peter J. and Mark C. Casson (1998), 'Models of the multinational enterprise', *Journal of International Business*, **29** (1), 21–44.

Bulmer-Thomas, Victor (1994), 'The economic history of Latin America since independence', *Cambridge Latin American Studies*, **77**, December.

Button, Kenneth (1998), 'Infrastructure investment, endogenous growth and economic convergence', *The Annals of Regional Science*, **32**, 145–62.

Calvo, Guillermo, Leonardo Leiderman and Carmen Reinhart (1992), 'Capital inflows and real exchange rate appreciation in Latin America', International Monetary Fund Working Paper.

Cannella, A.A. Jr and M.J. Monroe (1997), 'Contrasting perspectives on strategic leaders: Toward a more realistic view of top managers', *Journal of Management*, **23**, 213–38.

Cantwell, J. (1987), 'The reorganization of European industries after integration: Selected evidence on the role of multinational enterprise activities', *Journal of Common Market Studies*, **26** (2), December, 25–48.

Cantwell, J. (1989), *Technological Innovation and Multinational Corporations*, Oxford, Basil Blackwell.

Cantwell, J. (1991), 'The theory of technological competence and its application to international production', in D. McFetridge (ed.), *Foreign Investment, Technology and Economic Growth*, Calgary, University of Calgary Press.

Cantwell, J. and R. Narula (2001), 'The eclectic paradigm in the global economy', *International Journal of the Economics of Business*, **8**, 155–72.

Casson, Mark C. and S.M. Lundan (1999), 'Explaining international differences in economic institutions: A critique of the "national business system" as an analytical tool', *International Studies of Management and Organization*, **29** (2), 25–42.

Castells, Manuel and Pekka Himanen (2001), *Suomen Tietoyhteiskunta-malli*, Helsinki, WSOY.

Caves, Richard E. and William F. Murphy II (1976), 'Franchising: Firms, markets, and intangible assets', *Southern Economic Journal*, **42**, 572–86.

Cawson, A., K. Morgan, D. Webber, P. Holmes, and A. Steven (1990), *Hostile Brothers*, New York, Clarendon Press/Oxford University Press.

Chandler, Alfred D. (1962), *Strategy and Structure*, Cambridge, MA, MIT Press.

Charkham, J. (1994), *Keeping Good Company: A Study of Corporate Governance in Five Countries*, Oxford, Clarendon Press.

Chen Homin and Tain-Jy Chen (1998), 'Network linkages and location choice in foreign direct investment', *Journal of International Business Studies*, **29** (3) 445–68.

Chesnais, F. (1992), 'National systems of innovation, foreign direct investment and the operations of multinational enterprises', in B.A. Lundvall (ed.), *National Systems of Innovation*, London, Pinter Publishers.

Chesnais, F. (1995), 'Some relationships between foreign direct investment, technology, trade and competitiveness', in J. Hagedoorn (ed.), *Technical Change and the World Economy*, Aldershot, UK and Brookfield, US, Edward Elgar.

Christensen, Clayton M. (1997), *The Innovator's Dilemma: When New Technologies Cause Great Firms to Fail*, Boston, Harvard Business School Press.

Chuhan, Putnam, Stijn Claessens and Nlandu Mamingi (1993), 'Equity and bond flows to Latin American and Asia: The role of global and country factors', World Bank Policy Research Paper, no. 1160.

Claessens, Stijn, M. Dooley and A. Warner (1995). 'Portfolio capital flows: Hot or cold?', *The World Bank Economic Review*, **9** (1) 153–74.

Clarkson, M.B.E. (1995), 'A stakeholder framework for analysing and evaluating corporate social performance', *Academy of Management Review*, **20** (1), 92–117.

Cleeve, Emmanuel (1997), 'Multinational enterprises from the third world: Location characteristics in the UK', *Discussion Paper in Economics and Economic History*, Manchester, Manchester Metropolitan University.

Clegg, J. (1987), *Multinational Enterprises and World Competition*, London, Macmillan Press.

Collins, J.C. and J.I. Porras (1994), *Built to Last*, New York, Harper Business.

Comment, Robert, and Gregg Jarrell (1995), 'Corporate focus and stock returns', *Journal of Financial Economics*, **37**, 67–87.

Contractor, F.J. and Lorange, P. (eds) (1988), *Corporate Strategies in International Business*, Lexington, MA, Lexington Books.

Contractor, Farok J. and Sumit K. Kundu, (1998), 'Franchising versus company-run operations: Modal choice in the global hotel sector', *Journal of International Marketing*, **6** (2), 28–53

Cooke, P. and K. Morgan (1998), *The Associational Economy: Firms, Regions, and Innovation*, Oxford, Oxford University Press.

Cosset, J.-C. and J. Roy (1991), 'The determinants of country risk ratings', *Journal of International Business Studies*, **22**, 135–42.

Coughlin, Cletus C. and Eran Segev (1997), 'Location determinants of new foreign-owned manufacturing plants', Federal Reserve Bank of St. Louis Working Papers. no. 97-018B, September.

Coughlin, Cletus C., J.V. Tetza and V. Arromdee (1991), 'State characteristics and the location of foreign direct investment within the United States', *Review of Economics and Statistics*, **73**, 675–83.

Cowling, Keith and Roger Sugden (1987), *Transnational Monopoly Capitalism*, New York, St. Martin's Press.

Culem, C. (1988), 'The locational determinants of direct investments among industrialized countries', *European Economic Review*, **32**, 885–904.

Cyert, R.M. and J.G. March (1963), *A Behavioral Theory of the Firm*, New York, Prentice Hall.

Davison, William H. (1982), *Global Strategic Management*, New York, John Wiley and Sons.

Dawar, Niraj and Tony Frost (1999), 'Competing with giants: Survival strategies for local companies in emerging markets', *Harvard Business Review*, March–April, 119–29.

Day, D.V. and R.G. Lord (1988), 'Executive leadership and organizational performance: Suggestions for a new theory and methodology', *Journal of Management*, **14**, 453–64.

Demb, A. and B. Richey (1994), 'Defining responsible ownership', *European Management Journal*, **12** (3), 287–97.

Denis, David, Diane Denis and Atulya Sarin (1997), 'Agency problems, equity ownership and corporate diversification', *The Journal of Finance*, **52** (2), 135–60.

Denison, D.R., R. Hoojiberg and R.E. Quinn (1995), 'Paradox and performance: Toward a theory of behavioral complexity in management leadership', *Organization Science*, **6** (5), 524–40.

Department of Community and Economic Development (2000), 'Foreign Direct Investment', http: //www.dced.State.pa.us, May.

Dickens, Peter (1998), *Global Shift.* New York, The Guilford Press.

Dillman, Don A. (1978), *Mail and Telephone Surveys: The Total Design Method*, New York, Wiley.

Dilyard, John R. (1999), 'The determination of foreign private investment in developing countries', dissertation, Rutgers University, NJ.

Dilyard, John R. (2001), 'Foreign direct and foreign portfolio investment: Two sides of the same coin?', *Global Economy Quarterly* (forthcoming).

Dilyard, John R. and H. Peter Gray (2000), 'Increasing the contributions of FDI and foreign portfolio investment to sustainable development, Paper presented at UNCTAD conference on Finance for Sustainable Development: Recent Domestic and International Policy Measures, Nairobi, Kenya, December.

Dooley, Michael, E. Fernandez-Arias, K. Kletzer (1996), 'Is the debt crisis history? Recent private capital inflows to developing countries', *The World Bank Economic Review*, **10** (1), 27–50.

Dosi, G. (1984), *Technical Change and Industrial Transformation*, London, Macmillan.

Dosi, G. (1988), 'Sources, procedures and microeconomic effects of innovation', *Journal of Economic Literature*, **XXVI**, 1120–71.

Dosi, G., K. Pavitt and L. Soete (1990), *The Economics of Technical Change and International Trade*, Brighton, Harvester Wheatsheaf.

Dow, James and Gary Gorton (1997), 'Stock market efficiency and economic efficiency: Is there a connection?', *The Journal of Finance*, **52** (3), 1087–130.

Dowdy, John. (1997), 'Winners and losers in the arms industry downturn', *Foreign Policy*, Summer, 88–101.

Dun and Bradstreet (2000), *America's Corporate Families and International Affiliates*, Vol. III, Parsippany, NJ, Dun and Bradstreet.

Dunning, J.H. (1970), *Studies in International Investment*, London, Allen and Unwin.

Dunning, J.H. (1977), 'Trade, location of economic activity and multinational enterprise: A search for an eclectic approach', in B. Ohlin, P.O. Hellelborn, and P.J. Wijkman (eds). *The International Allocation of Economic Activity*, London, Macmillan.

Dunning, J.H. (1981a), *International Production and the Multinational Enterprise*, London, Allen and Unwin.

Dunning, J.H. (1981b), 'Explaining the international position of countries: towards a dynamic or developmental approach', *Weltwirtshaftliches Archiv*, **117**, 30–64.

Dunning, J.H. (1986), 'The investment cycle revisited', *Weltwirtschaftliches Archiv*, **122**, 667–77.

Dunning, J.H. (1987), 'The investment development cycle and third world multinationals', in K. Khan (ed.), *Multinationals of the South*, London, Francis Pinter.

Dunning, J.H. (1988a), *Multinationals, Technology and Competitiveness*, London, Allen and Unwin.

Dunning, J.H. (1988b), *Explaining International Production*, London, Unwin Hyman.

Dunning, J.H. (1992a), 'The competitive advantage of countries and the activities of transnational corporations', *Transnational Corporations*, **1**, February, 35–168.

Dunning, J.H. (1992b), 'The global economy, domestic governance, strategies and transnational corporations: interactions and policy implications', *Transnational Corporations*, **1**, December, 7–45.

Dunning, J.H. (1992c), 'Governments, markets, and multinational enterprises: some emerging issues', *International Trade Journal*, Fall, 1–14.

Dunning, J.H. (1993a), *Multinational Enterprises and the Global Economy*, Wokingham, England, Addison-Wesley Publishing.

Dunning, J.H. (1993b), *Globalization: The Challenge for National Economic Regimes*, 24th Geary Lecture, Dublin, The Economic and Social Research Institute.

Dunning, J.H. (1993c), *The Globalization of Business*, London and New York, Routledge.

Dunning, J.H. (1994a), 'Globalization, economic restructuring and development', *The Raul Prebisch Lectures*, Geneva, United Nations Conference on Trade and Development.

Dunning, J.H. (1994b), 'The role of FDI in a globalizing economy', paper presented on An Investment Regime for APEC, Washington, DC.

Dunning, J.H. (1995), 'The global economy and regimes of national and supranational governance', *Business and Contemporary World*, **7** (1), 124–36.

Dunning, J.H. (1995), 'Reappraising the eclectic paradigm in an age of alliance capitalism', *Journal of International Business Studies*, **26** (3), 461–501.

Dunning, J.H. (1997a), 'The changing geography of FDI', in K. Kumar (ed.), *Internationalization, Foreign Direct Investment and Technology Transfer: Impact and Prospects for Developing Countries*, New York and London, Routledge.

Dunning, J.H. (1997b), 'The European internal market programme and inbound foreign direct investment', *Journal of Common Market Studies*, **35** (1), 1–30.

Dunning, J.H. (1997c), 'A business analytic approach to government and globalization', in J.H. Dunning (ed.), *Governments, Globalization, and International Business*, Oxford and New York, Oxford University Press.

Dunning, J.H. (1998), 'Location and the multinational enterprise: A neglected factor?', *Journal of International Business Studies*, **29** (1), 45–66.

Dunning, J.H. (ed.) (1999), *Governments, Globalization and International Business*, Oxford, Oxford University Press (paperback edition).

Dunning, J.H. (ed.) (2000a), *Regions, Globalization, and the Knowledge-based Economy*, Oxford, Oxford University Press.

Dunning, J.H. (2000b), 'The eclectic paradigm as an envelope for economic and business theories of MNE activity', *International Business Review*, **9**, 163–90.

Dunning, J.H. (2000c), 'Regions, globalization, and the knowledge economy,' in J. Dunning (ed.), *Regions, Globalization, and the Knowledge-based Economy*, Oxford, Oxford University Press, 7–41.

Dunning, J.H. (2001), 'The eclectic (OLI) paradigm of international production: Past, present, and future', *International Journal of Economics and Business*, **8**, 156–73.

Dunning, J.H. and John R. Dilyard (1999), 'Towards a general paradigm of foreign direct and foreign portfolio investment', *Transnational Corporations*, **8**, April.

Dunning, J.H. and S.M. Lundan (1998), 'The geographical sources of competitiveness of firms: An econometric analysis', *International Business Review*, **7** (2): 115–33.

Dunning, J.H. and M. McQueen (1981), *Transnational Corporations in International Tourism*, New York, UNCTAD.

Dunning, J.H. and R. Narula (1994), ''Transpacific direct investment and the investment development path: The record assessed', *Essays in International Business*, **10**, May.

Dunning, J.H. and R. Narula (1996a), *Foreign Direct Investment and Governments*, London, Routledge.

Dunning, J.H. and R. Narula (1996b), 'The investment development path revisited: Some emerging issues', in J.H. Dunning and R. Narula (eds), *Foreign Direct Investment and Governments: Catalysts for Economic Restructuring*, London, Routledge.

Dunning, J.H. and R. Narula (1996c), *FDI and Governments*. New York, Routledge.

Dunning, J.H. and R. Narula (1997), *FDI and Governments*, New York, Routledge.

Dunning, J.H. and C. Wymbs (1999), 'The geographical sourcing of technology-based assets by multinational enterprises', in D. Archibugi, J. Howells and J. Michie (eds), *Innovation Policy in a Global Economy*, Cambridge, Cambridge University Press.

Dunning, J.H., E. Bannerman and S.M. Lundan (1998), *Competitiveness and industrial policy in Northern Ireland*, Belfast, Northern Ireland Economic Council.

Dunning, J.H., C. Kim and J. Lin (2001), 'Incorporating trade into the investment development path', in R. Narula (ed.), *International Trade, Investment in a Globalising World*, New York, Pergamon.

Dymski, Gary, Gerald Epstein and Robert Pollin (1993), *Transforming the U.S. Financial System: Equity and Efficiency for the Twenty First Century*, New York, M.E. Sharpe.

Easterbrook, F.H. and D.R. Fischel (1991), *The Economic Nature of Corporate Law*, Cambridge, MA, Harvard University Press.

ECLAC (1998–2001), *Foreign Investment in Latin America and the*

Caribbean. Santiago, Chile, UN Center for Latin America and the Caribbean, annual editions.

Economist Advisory Group (EAG) (2001), *A Bird in the Hand: The Northeast's Installed Base of Inward Investors*, London, EAG.

Eden, Lorraine and Antoine Monteils (2000), 'Regional integration: NAFTA and the reconfiguration of North American industry,' in Dunning (2000b), 170–220.

Elmslie, Bruce Truitt (1995), 'Retrospectives: The convergence debate between David Hume and Josiah Tucker,' *Journal of Economic Perspectives*, **9** (4), Fall, 207–16.

Enright, M.J. (1991), *Geographic Concentration and Industrial Organization*, Cambridge, MA, PhD dissertation, Harvard University.

Enright, M.J. (1998), 'Regional clusters and firm strategy', in A. Chandler, D. Solvello and P. Hagstrom P. (eds), *The Dynamic Firm: The Role of Technology, Strategy, Organization and Regions*, Oxford, Oxford University Press, 315–42.

Enright, M.J. (1999), 'The globalisation of competition and localisation of competitive advantage', in N. Hood and S. Young (eds), *The Globalisation of Multinational Enterprise Activity*, London, Macmillan.

Erramilli, M. Krishna (1996), 'Nationality and subsidiary ownership patterns in multinational corporations', *Journal of International Business Studies*, **27** (2), 225–48.

Euromoney, Country risk ratings, various issues, 1996–98.

Fagerberg, J. (1988), 'International competitiveness', *Economic Journal*, **98**, 355–74.

Faulhaber, Gerald (1987), *Telecommunications in Turmoil*, Cambridge, MA, Ballinger Publishing Company.

Fernandez-Arias, Eduardo (1994), 'The new wave of private capital inflows: Push or pull?', World Bank Policy Research Working Paper no. 1312, Washington, DC.

Fernandez-Arias, Eduardo and Peter J. Montiel (1995). 'The surge in capital inflows to developing countries: Prospects and policy response', World Bank Policy Research Working Paper no. 1473, Washington, DC.

Fernandez-Arias, Eduardo and Peter J. Montiel (1996). 'The surge in capital inflows to developing countries: An analytical overview'. *The World Bank Economic Review*, **10** (1), 51–77.

Festinger, Leon (1957), *A Theory of Cognitive Dissonance*, Evanston, Row, Peterson and Company.

Finkelstein, S. and D.C. Hambrick (1996), *Strategic Leadership: Top Executives and Their Effects on Organizations*, St. Paul, MN, West Publishing Company.

Fladmoe-Lindquist, Karin and Laurent L. Jacque (1995), 'Control modes in international service operations: The propensity to franchise', *Management Science*, **41** (7), 1238–49.

Flamm, Kenneth (1999), 'Redesigning the defense industrial base', in Ann Markusen and Sean Costigan (eds), *Arming the Future: A Defense Industry for the 21st Century*, New York, Council on Foreign Relations.

Freeman, C. (1982), *The Economics of Industrial Innovation*, 2nd edn, London, Francis Pinter.

Freeman, C. (1987), 'The challenge of new technologies', in OECD, *Interdependence and Cooperation in Tomorrow's World*, Paris, OECD, 123–53.

Freeman, C. (1995), 'History, co-evolution and economic growth', IIASA Working Paper 95–76, September.

Freeman, C. and Carlota Perez (1988), 'Structural crises and adjustment, business cycles and investment behaviour', in G. Dosi, C. Freeman, R. Nelson, G. Silverberg and Luc Soete (eds), *Technical Change and Economic Theory*, London, Pinter Publishers.

Freeman, C. and L. Soete (1997), *The Economics of Industrial Innovation*, London, Francis Pinter.

Freeman, R.E. (1984), *Strategic Management: A Stakeholder Approach*, Boston, Pitman.

Friedman, Joseph, Daniel Gerlowski and Johnathan Silberman (1989), 'The determinants of foreign plant location across States', mimeo, Temple University.

Fry, J. Maxwell (1996), 'How foreign direct investment in Pacific Asia improves the current account', *Journal of Asian Economies*, **7** (3), 459–85.

Gallie, D., R. Penn and M. Rose (1996), *Trade Unionism in Recession*, Oxford, Oxford University Press.

Garrett, Geoffrey (2001), 'Globalization and government spending around the world', *Studies in Comparative International Development*, **35** (4), 3–29.

Gedajlovic, E. (1993), 'Ownership, strategy and performance: Is the dichotomy sufficient?', *Organization Studies*, **15** (5), 731–52.

Gehani, R.R. (1999), 'Architectual concentration and the catastrophic financial crisis in the newly industrializing economies of East Asia', *Global Focus*, **11**, 121–37.

Geldner, Marian (1986), 'Integrating the theories of international trade and foreign direct investment', in H. Peter Gray (ed.), *Research in International Business and Finance*, Vol. 5, 95–107.

Gerlach, M.L. (1992), *Alliance Capitalism: The Social Organisation of Japanese Business*, Oxford, Oxford University Press.

Gersick, Connie (1991), 'Revolutionary change theories: A multilevel exploration of the punctuated equilibrium process', *Academy of Management Review*, **16** (1), 10–36.

Glickman, Norman J. and Douglas P. Woodward (1987), 'Regional pattern of foreign direct investment in the United States', final report prepared for the US Department of Commerce, Economic Development Administration, Research and Evaluation Division.

Glyn, Andrew, Alan Hughes, Alain Lipietz and Ajit Singh (1990), 'The rise and fall of the golden age', in Stephen Marglin and Juliet Schor (eds), *The Golden Age of Capitalism: Reinterpreting the Post-war Experience*, Oxford, Clarendon Press, 39–125.

Gomes, Lenn and Kannan Ramaswamy (1999), 'An empirical examination of the form of the relationship between multinationality and performance', *Journal of International Business Studies*, **30** (1), 173–88.

Gordon, Robert J. (2000), 'Does the 'New Economy' measure up to the great inventions of the past?', Oesterreichische Nationalbank 28th Economics Conference, 15–16 June, Vienna.

Granovetter, M. (1995), 'Coase revisited: Business groups in the modern economy', *Industrial and Corporate Change*, **4** (1), 93–130.

Gray, H. Peter (1996), 'The eclectic theory: The next generation', *Transnational Corporations*, **5** (2), 51–66.

Gray, H. Peter (1999), *Global Economic Involvement: A Synthesis of Modern International Economics*, Copenhagen, Copenhagen Business School Press.

Gray, H. Peter (2002a), 'International trade and economic development: A qualification', *Journal of World Investment*, **3** (1), February, 65–76.

Gray, H. Peter (2002b), 'The concept of globalization', *Global Economic Quarterly*, March.

Gray, H. Peter and John Dunning (2000), 'Towards a theory of regional policy', in John Dunning (ed.), *Regions, Globalization, and the Knowledge-based Economy*, Oxford, Oxford University Press, 409–34.

Gray, H. Peter and S. Lundan (1994), 'Nationhood, the GATT ideal and a workable international trading system', *Banca Nazionale del Lavoro Quarterly Review*, **188**, March, 99–114.

Gray, H. Peter and Lorna H. Wallace (1996), 'New Jersey in a globalizing economy', CIBER Working Paper Series no. 97.002, Newark, Rutgers University.

Grosse, Robert (1997), 'Foreign direct investment in Latin America', in *Generating Savings for Development in Latin America*, Coral Gables, North/South Center, November, 135–53.

Grosse, Robert and Len J. Trevino (1996), 'Foreign direct investment in the United States: An analysis by country of origin', *Journal of International Business Studies*, **27** (1): 139–55.

Guillén, M.F. (2000), 'Business groups in emerging economies: A resource-based view', *Academy of Management Journal*, **43** (3), 362–80.

Guisinger, S. (1985), *Investment Incentives and Performance Requirements*, New York, Praeger.

Hagedoorn, J. and S.M. Lundan (2001), 'Strategic technology alliances: Trends and patterns since the early eighties', in A. Plunket, C. Voisin and B. Bellon (eds), *The Dynamics of Industrial Collaboration*, Cheltenham, UK and Northampton, MA, Edward Elgar.

Halal, W.E. (1994), 'From hierarchy to enterprise: Internal markets are now the new foundation of management', *Academy of Management Executive*, **VIII** (4), 69–83.

Hämäläinen, Timo (2002), *National Competitiveness and Economic Growth: The Changing Determinants of Economic Performance in the World Economy*, Cheltenham, UK and Northampton, MA, Edward Elgar.

Hambrick, D.C. and S. Finkelstein (1987), 'Managerial discretion: A bridge between polar views of organizations', in L.L. Cummings and B.M. Staw (eds), *Research in Organizational Behavior*, Greenwich, CT, JAI Press, 369–406.

Harley, Knick C. (2000) 'A Review of O'Rourke and Williamson's globalization and history: The evolution of a nineteenth century atlantic economy?', *Journal of Economic Literature*, **38**, December, 926–35.

Harrison, Bennett (1994), *Lean and Mean: The Changing Landscape of Corporate Power in the Age of Flexibility*, New York, Basic Books.

Harrison, J.S. and C.H. St. John (1996), 'Managing and partnering with external stakeholders', *Academy of Management Executive*, **X** (2), 46–60.

Harrison, Lawrence E. and Samuel P. Huntington (2001), *Culture Matters: How Values Shape Human Progress*, New York, Basic Books.

Hart, S.L. and R.E. Quinn (1993), 'Roles executives play: CEOs, behavioral complexity, and firm performance', *Human Relations*, **46** (5), 543–74.

Hartung, William D. (1996), *Welfare for Weapons Dealers: The Hidden Costs of the Arms Trade*, New York, World Policy Institute, June.

Healey, Michael and Michael Rawlinson (1993), 'Interviewing business owners and managers: A review of methods and techniques.' *Geoforum*, **24** (3), 339–55.

Heilbroner, Robert and William Milberg (1997), *The Crisis of Vision in Modern Economic Thought*, New York, Cambridge University Press.

Helliar, C.V., A.A. Lonie, D.M. Power and C.D. Sinclair (1998), 'The risk of investing in emerging markets: An investor's perspective', mimeo, Department of Accountancy and Finance, University of Dundee, Scotland.

Helsingen Sanomat (2002), p. F1, 27 January.

Hennart, Jean-Francois (1991), 'The transaction cost theory of the multinational enterprise', in C.N. Pitelis and R. Sugden (eds), *The Nature of the Transnational Firm*, London, Routledge.

Hennart, Jean-Francois (1993), 'Explaining the swollen middle: Why most transactions are a mix of "market" and "hierarchy"', *Organization Science*, **4** (4), 529–47.

Hennart, Jean-Francois and Jorma Larimo (1998), 'The impact of culture on the strategy of multinational enterprises: Does national origin effect ownership decisions?', *Journal of International Business*, **29** (3), 515–38.

Henwood, Doug (1997), *Wall Street: How it Works and for Whom?*, London, Verso.

Hernandez, Leonardo and Heinz Rudolph, (1995), 'Sustainability of private capital flows to developing countries: Is a generalized reversal likely?', World Bank Policy Research Working Paper, no. 1518, Washington, DC.

Hill, C.W. and T.M. Jones (1992), 'Stakeholder-agency theory', *Journal of Management Studies*, **29** (2), 131–54.

Hillman, A. and G. Keim (1995), 'International variation in the business–government interface: Institutional and organizational considerations', *Academy of Management Review*, **20** (1), 193–214.

Hirsch, S. and I. Bijaoui (1985), 'R&D intensity and export performance: A micro view', *Weltwirtschaftliches Archiv*, **121**, 138–251.

Hitt, Michael, Robert E. Hoskisson and R. Duane Ireland (1994), 'A mid-range theory of the interactive effects of international and product diversification on innovation and performance', *Journal of Management*, **20** (2), 297–326.

Hitt, Michael, Robert E. Hoskisson and Hicheon Kim (1997), 'International diversification: Effects on innovation and firm performance in product-diversified firms', *Academy of Management Journal*, **40** (4), 767–98.

Hitt, Michael, B.W. Keats and S.M. DeMarie (1998), 'Navigating the new competitive landscape: Building strategic flexibility and competitive advantage in the 21st century', *Academy of Management Executive*, **12** (4), 22–42.

Holm, U. and T. Pedersen (eds) (2000), *The Emergence and Impact of MNC Centers of Excellence*, Basingstoke, Macmillan.

Hoojiberg, R., J.G. Hunt and G.E. Dodge (1997), 'Leadership complexity and development of the leaderplex model', *Journal of Management*, **23** (3), 375–408.

Hoojiberg, R. and R.E. Quinn (1992), 'Behavioral complexity and the development of effective managers', in R.L. Phillips and J.G. Hunt (eds), *Strategic Leadership: A mulitorganizational-level Perspective*, Westport, CT: Quorum Books, 161–76.

Hoojiberg, R. and M. Schneider (2001), 'Behavioral complexity and social intelligence: How executive leaders use stakeholders to form a systems perspective', in S.J. Zaccaro and R. Klimoski (eds), *The Nature of Organizational Leadership*, San Francisco, CA, Jossey-Bass-SIOP Frontier Series, 104–31.

Howell, C. (1998), 'The lost perspective? Trade unions between ideology and social action in the new Europe', *Industrial and Labor Relations Review*, **51** (3), 541–42.

HSE (Helsinki Stock Exchange) (2002), www.HEX.fi.

Hume, David (1754/1985), *Essays: Moral, Political and Literary*, edited by Eugene Miller, Indianapolis, Indiana, Liberty Fund.

Hume, S. (1993), *Managing the Multinational: Confronting the Global–Local Dilemma*, New York, Prentice Hall.

Huolman, M., P. Walden, M. Pulkkinen, J. Ali-Yrkkö, R. Tainio and P. Ylä-Anttila (2000), *Omistajien etu – Kaikkien etu?*, Helsinki, Taloustieto.

Hymer, Stephen H. (1960), 'The international operation of national firms: A study of direct investment,' *PhD dissertation*, MIT (Published by MIT Press in 1976).

Hymer, S. (1976), *The International Operations of National Firms: A Study of Direct Foreign Investment*, Cambridge, MA, MIT Press.

Institutional Investor (1996–1998), Country credit ratings, various issues.

International Monetary Fund (1998), 'Financial crises: causes and indicators, *World Economic Outlook*, May.

International Trade Administration (1990–1995), *Foreign Direct Investment in the United States – 1989 (through 1994) Transactions*, Washington, DC, US Department of Commerce.

Itaki, Masahiko (1991), 'A critical assessment of the eclectic theory of the MNE', *Journal of International Business Studies*, **22** (3), 445–60.

Jacobs, T.O. and P. Lewis (1992), 'Leadership requirements in stratified systems', in R.L. Phillips and J.G. Hunt (eds), *Strategic Leadership: A Multiorganizational-level Perspective*, Westport, CT, Quorum Books, 15–27.

Jacques, E. (1986), 'The development of intellectual capability: A discussion of stratified systems theory', *Journal of Applied Behavioral Science*, **22** (4), 361–83.

Jane's Defence Weekly (1996), 'Mergers becoming a business imperative,' 12 January, 23.

Jensen, M.C. and W.H. Meckling (1976), 'Theory of the firm: Managerial behavior, agency costs and ownership structure', *The Journal of Financial Economics*, **18** (10), 305–60.

Jones, Ronald W. (1956), 'Factor proportions and the Heckscher-Ohlin Theorem', *Review of Economic Studies*, 1–10.

Jorde, T.M. and D.J. Teece (1989), 'Competition and cooperation: Striking the right balance', *California Management Review*, **XXXI**, Spring, 25–37.

Kaminsky, Graciela L., R. Lyons and S. Schmukler (2001), 'Mutual fund investment in emerging markets: An overview', World Bank Working Paper, Washington, DC.

Kanter, R.M. (1990), 'When giants learn cooperative strategies', *Planning Review*, **18** (1), 15–22.

Kanter, R.M. (1994), 'Collaborative advantage: The art of alliances', *Harvard Business Review*, July–August, 96–108.

Karuppur, Devi Prasad and C.M. Sashi (1992), 'A transactions cost perspective on franchising in global markets', in Patrick J. Kaufmann (ed.), *Franchising: Passport for Growth and World of Opportunity*, Proceedings of the Society of Franchising Conference, Palm Springs, CA.

Katz, D. and R.L. Khan (1996), *The Social Psychology of Organizations*, New York, John Wiley and Sons.

Kets de Vries, M.F.R. and E. Florent-Treacy (1990), *The New Global Leaders*, San Francisco, Jossey-Bass.

Kim, Saeng Wi and Esmerald O. Lyn (1986), 'Excess market value, the multinational corporation, and Tobin's q-ratio', *Journal of International Business Studies*, **17** (1), 119–25.

Kim, Saeng Wi and Esmerald O. Lyn (1990), 'FDI theories and the performance of multinationals operating in the US', *Journal of International Business Studies*, 41–54.

Klein, Benjamin (1980), 'Transaction cost determinants of "unfair" contractual arrangements', *American Economic Review*, **70**, 356–62.

Kleinbaum, David G. (1994), *Logistic Regression: A Self-learning Text*, New York, Springer Verlag.

Knickerbocker, F.T. (1973), *Oligopolistic Reaction and the Multinational Enterprise*, Cambridge, MA, Harvard University Press.

Kobrin, S.J. (1979), 'Political risk: A review and reconsideration', *Journal of International Business Studies*, **10**, 67–80.

Kobrin, S.J. (1995), 'Regional integration in a globally networked economy', *Transnational Corporations*, **4** (2), 15–33.

Kogut, B. (1985), ' Designing global strategies: Comparative and competitive value-added chains', *Sloan Management Review*, Summer, 15–28.

Kogut, B. (1988), 'Joint venture: Theoretical and empirical perspectives', *Strategic Management Journal*, **9**, 319–32.

Kogut, B. (1989), 'Research notes and communications: A note on global strategies', *Strategic Management Journal*, **10** (4).

Kogut, B. (1999), 'What makes a company global?', *Harvard Business Review*, **77** (1), 165–70.

Kogut, B. and Nalin Kulatilaka (1995), 'Operating flexibility, global manufacturing, and the option value of a multinational network', *Management Science*, **40** (1), 123–39.

Kojima, K. (1958), 'Nihon Keizai no Gamkokeitaiteki Hatten to Boeki no Yakuwari [The flying-geese growth pattern of the Japanese economy and the role of trade], in K. Kojima (ed.), *Nihon Boeki no Kozo to Hatten [The Structure and Growth of Japan's Trade]*, Tokyo, Shiseido, 1–25.

Kojima, K. (1982), 'Macro economic versus international business approaches to foreign direct investment', *Hitotsubashi Journal of Economics*, **23**, 1–19.

Kojima, Kiyoshi (2000), 'The "flying geese" model of Asian economic development: Origin, theoretical extensions, and regional policy implications', *Journal of Asian Economics*, **11** (4), 375–401.

Kojima, K. and Terutomo Ozawa (1984), 'Micro and macro economic models of direct foreign investment,' *Hitotsubashi Journal of Economics*, **25** (1), 1–20.

Kojima, K. and Terutomo Ozawa (1985), 'Toward a theory of dynamic comparative advantage', *Hitotsubashi Journal of Economics*, **26** (2), 135–45.

Kostova, Tatiana and Srilata Zaheer (1999), 'Organizational legitimacy under conditions of complexity: The case of the multinational enterprise', *Academy of Management Review*, **24** (1), 64–81.

Kovacic, William and Dennis Smallwood (1994), 'Competition policy, rivalries, and defense industry consolidation', *Journal of Economic Perspectives*, **8** (4), 91–110.

Krugman, Paul (1991), *Geography and Trade*, Cambridge, MA, MIT Press.

Kuhn, Thomas (1970), *The Structure of Scientific Revolutions*, Chicago, IL, University of Chicago Press.

Kuhn, Thomas (1975), *The Structure of Scientific Revolutions*, Chicago, University of Chicago Press.

Lall, S. (1990), *Building Industrial Competitiveness in Developing Countries*, Paris, OECD.

Lall, S. (1992), 'Transnational corporations and economic development', *United Nations*.

Landes, David S. (1969), *The Unbound Prometheus*, Cambridge, Cambridge University Press.

Leamer, E. (1980), 'The Leontief paradox reconsidered', *Journal of Political Economy*, **88**.

Lei, D. and Hitt, M. (1995), 'Strategic restructuring and outsourcing: The effect of mergers and acquisitions and LBOs on building firm skills and capabilities', *Journal of Management*, **21** (5), 835–59.

Lewin, A.Y. (1999), 'Application of complexity theory to organization science', *Organization Science*, **10** (3).

Lewis, Cleona (1938), *America's Stake in International Investments*, Washington, DC, The Brookings Institution.

Liebeskind, Julia and Tim Opler (1994), 'Corporate diversification and agency costs: Evidence from privately held firms', Working Paper, Ohio State University.

Lipsey, Richard G. (1997), 'Globalization and national government policies: An economist's view', in J.H. Dunning (ed.), *Governments, Globalization, and International Business*, London, Oxford University Press.

Lovering, John (1990), 'Fordism's unknown successor: A comment on Scott's theory of flexible accumulation and the re-emergence of regional economies', *International Journal of Urban and Regional Research*, **14** (1), 159–74.

Lundan, S.M. and J. Hagedoorn (2001), 'Alliances, acquisitions and multinational advantage', *International Journal of the Economics of Business* **8** (2), 229–42.

Lundan, S.M. and G. Jones (2001), 'The "Commonwealth effect" and the process of internationalization', *The World Economy*, **24** (1), 99–118.

Lundquist, Jerold (1992), 'Shrinking fast and smart in the defense industry', *Harvard Business Review*, November–December.

Lundvall, Bengt-Ake (1999), 'Technology policy in the learning economy', in D. Aribuigi, J. Howells and J. Mitchie (eds), *Innovation Policy in a Global Economy*, Cambridge, Cambridge University Press.

Lundvall, Bengt-Ake (1992), *National Systems of Innovation: Towards a Theory of Innovation and Interactive Learning*, London, Pinter.

Lynk, M. (2000), 'Union democracy and the law in Canada', *Journal of Labor Research*, **XXI** (1), 37–63.

Mahoney, J.T. and J.R. Pandian (1992), 'The resource-based view within the conversation of strategic management', *Strategic Management Journal*, **13**, 363–80.

Markusen, Ann (1991), 'Government as market: Industrial location in the US defense industry', in Henry Herzog and Alan Schlottmann (eds), *Industrial Location and Public Policy*, Knoxville, University of Tennessee Press.

Markusen, Ann (1994), 'Studying regions by studying firms', *The Professional Geographer*, **46** (4), 477–90.

Markusen, Ann (1996), 'Sticky places in slippery space: A typology of industrial districts', *Economic Geography*, **72** (3), 293–313.

Markusen, Ann (1997), 'The economics of defence industry mergers and divestiture', *Economic Affairs*, **17** (4), 28–32.

Markusen, Ann (1998), 'America's military industrial makeover', in Clarence Lo and Michael Schwartz, *Social Policy and the Conservative Agenda*, Oxford, Basil Blackwell, 142–50.

Markusen, Ann (1999a), 'Fuzzy concepts, scanty evidence, policy distance: The case for rigor and policy relevance in critical regional studies', *Regional Studies*, **33** (9), 869–84.

Markusen, Ann (1999b), 'The Post Cold War persistence of defense specialized firms', in Gerald I. Susman and Sean O'Keefe (eds), *The Defense Industry in the Post-Cold War Era: Corporate Strategies and Public Policy Perspectives*, Oxford, Elsevier, 121–46.

Markusen, Ann (1999c), 'The rise of world weapons', *Foreign Policy*, **114**, 40–51.

Markusen, Ann, Peter Hall, Scott Campbell and Sabina Deitrick (1991), *The Rise of the Gunbelt*, New York, Oxford University Press.

Marshall, Alfred (1920), *Principles of Economics*, London, Macmillan.

Martin, Robert E. (1988), 'Franchising and risk management', *American Economic Review*, **78** (5), 954–68.

Mason, M. (1992), *American Multinationals and Japan: The Political Economy of Japanese Capital Controls, 1899–1980*, Cambridge, MA, Harvard University Press.

Massey, Doreen and Richard Meegan (1978), 'Industrial restructuring versus the cities', *Urban Studies*, **15** (3), 273–88.

Mathewson, G. Frank and Ralph A. Winter (1985), 'The economics of franchise contracts', *Journal of Law and Economics*, **28**, 503–26.

Matsusaka, John (1993), 'Takeover motives during the conglomerate merger wave', *Rand Journal of Economics*, **24**, 357–79.

McGrew, A.G. and P.G. Lewis (1992), *Global Politics: Globalization and the Nation-State*, Cambridge, MA, Blackwell.

McIntyre, Faye S. and Sandra M. Huszagh (1995), 'Internationalization of franchise systems', *Journal of International Marketing*, **3** (4), 39–56.

Mendenhall, William and Terry Sincich (1993), *A Second Course in Business Statistics: Regression Analysis*, 4th edn, London, Macmillan.

Michel, A. and I. Shaked (1986), 'Multinational corporations versus domestic corporations: Financial performance and characteristics. *Journal of International Business Studies*, **17** (3), 89–106.

Milberg, W.S. and H. Peter Gray (1992), 'International competitiveness and policy in dynamic industries', *Banca Nazionale del Lavoro Quarterly Review*, **180** (3), 59–80.

Miller, William (1991), 'After desert storm: What next for defense?', *Industry Week*, **240**, July, 48–53.

Minkler, Alason P. (1990), 'An empirical analysis of a firm's decision to franchise', *Economics Letters*, **34**, 77–82.

Mintz, John (1995), 'Going great guns', *The Washington Post*, 2 October.

Mintzberg, H. (1983), *Power in and around Organizations*, Englewood Cliffs, NJ, Prentice Hall.

Mishra, Chandra S. and David H. Gobeli (1998), 'Managerial incentives, internalization, and market valuation of multinational firms', *Journal of International Business Studies*, **29** (3), 583–98.

Mitchell, R.K., B.R. Agle and D.J. Wood [formerly D.J. Wiid) (1997), 'Toward a theory of stakeholder identification and salience: Defining the principle of who and what really counts', *Academy of Management Review*, **22** (4), 853–86.

Morck, R. and Yeung, B. (1991), 'Why investors value multinationality', *The Journal of Business*, **64** (2), 165–87.

Morrocco, John (1991), 'Uncertain U.S. military needs hamper industry restructuring', *Aviation Week and Space Technology*, **134**, 17 June, 62–3.

MTI (1996), *A New Outlook on Industrial Policies: From Global Economic Change to Sustainable Growth*, Finnish Ministry of Trade and Industry Publications, April.

Mudambi, R. (1995), 'The MNE investment location decision: Some empirical evidence', *Managerial and Decision Economics*, **16** (3), 249–57.

Mudambi, Ram (1998), 'The role of duration in multinational investment strategies', *Journal of International Business Studies*, 2nd quarter, **29** (2), 239.

Mudambi, Ram (1999), 'Multinational investment attraction: Principle-agent considerations', *International Journal of the Economics of Business*, **6**, 65–79.

Mukherjee, Sougata (1997), 'New survey ranks Pittsburgh a low-cost international center', *Pittsburgh Business Times*, **17** (5), 29 August.

Mundell, Robert A. (1961), 'A theory of optimum currency areas', *American Economic Review*, **53** (4), 657–65.

Nachum, Lilach (1999), *The Origins of the International Competitiveness of Firms*. Cheltenham, UK and Northampton, MA, Edward Elgar.

Nachum, Lilach (2000), 'Economic geography and the location of TNCs: Financial and professional service FDI to the USA', *Journal of International Business Studies*, **31** (3), 367–85.

Nachum, Lilach and J.D. Rolle (1999), 'Home country and firm-specific ownership advantages: A study of US, UK, and French advertising agencies' *International Business Review*, **8** (5–6), 633–60.

Nagelkerke, N.J.D. (1991), 'A note on general definition of the coefficient of determination', *Biometrika*, **78**, 691–2.

Narula, R. (1993), 'Technology, international business and Porter's "Diamond": Synthesising a dynamic competitive development model', *Management International Review*, **33**, 85–107.

Narula, R. (1996), *Multinational Investment and Economic Structure*, London, Routledge.

Narula, R. and J.H. Dunning (1998), 'Explaining international R&D alliances and the role of governments', *International Business Review*, **7**, 377–97.

Narula, R. and J.H. Dunning (2000), ' Industrial development, globalization and multinational enterprises: New realities for developing countries', *Oxford Development Studies*, **28** (2), 141–67.

Narula, R. and K. Wakelin (2001), 'The pattern and determinants of US foreign investment in industrialised countries', in R. Narula (ed.), *International Trade, Investment in a Globalising World*, New York and Kidlington, Pergamon.

Nelson, Richard and S. Winter (1982), *An Evolutionary Theory of Economic Change*, Cambridge, MA, Belknap Press.

Nelson, R.R. (ed.) (1993), *National Innovation Systems: A Comparative Analysis*, New York, Oxford University Press.

Nguyen, The-Hiep and Jean-Claude Cosset (1995), 'The measure of the degree of foreign involvement', *Applied Economics*, **27** (4), 343–51.

Norris, F. (1996), 'Those wild swings examined', *The New York Times*, 29 February.

North, D.C. (1981), *Structure and Change in Economic History*, New York, Norton.

North, D.C. (1991) 'Institutions', *Journal of Economic Perspectives*, **5**, Winter, 97–112.

Oden, Michael (1999a), 'Cashing-in, cashing-out and converting: Restructuring of the defense industrial base in the 1990s', in Ann Markusen and Sean Costigan (eds), *Arming the Future: A Defense Industry for the 21st Century*, New York, Council on Foreign Relations Press, 74–105.

Oden, Michael (1999b), 'Defense mega-mergers and alternative strategies: The hidden costs of Post-Cold War defense restructuring', in Gerald Susman (ed.), *The Defense Industry in the Post-Cold War Era: Corporate Strategies and Public Policy Perspectives*, Oxford, Elsevier Science.

Oden, Michael (2000), 'Federal defense industrial policy, firm strategy and regional conversion initiatives in four American aerospace regions', *International Regional Science Review*, **23**, (1), 25–47.

Oden, Michael, Elizabeth J. Mueller, and Judy Goldberg (1994), *Life after Defense: Conversion and Economic Adjustment on Long Island*, project on Regional and Industrial Economics, New Brunswick, NJ, Rutgers University.

Oden, Michael, Catherine Hill, Elizabeth J. Mueller, Jonathan Feldman and Ann Markusen (1993), *Changing the Future: Converting the St. Louis Economy*, project on Regional and Industrial Economics, New Brunswick, NJ, Rutgers University.

Oden, Michael, Ann Markusen, Dan Flaming, Jonathan Feldman, James Raffel and Catherine Hill (1996). *From Managing Growth to Reversing Decline: Aerospace and the Southern California Economy in the Post Cold War Era*, project on Regional and Industrial Economics, New Brunswick, NJ, Rutgers University, February.

Ohlin, Bertil (1933), *Interregional and International Trade*, Cambridge, MA, Harvard University Press.

Ohmae, Kenichi (1995), *The End of the Nation State: The Rise of Regional Economies*, New York, Free Press.

O'Rourke, Kevin H. and Jeffrey G. Williamson (1999), *Globalization and History: The Evolution of a Nineteenth-Century Atlantic Economy*, Cambridge, MA, MIT Press.

Ozawa, Terutomo (1992), 'Foreign direct investment and economic development', *Transnational Corporations*, **1**, February, 27–54.

Ozawa, Terutomo (1995), 'The flying-geese paradigm of tandem growth: TNC's involvement and agglomeration economies in Asia's industrial dynamism', paper presented at the 1995 AIB annual meeting in Seoul.

Ozawa, Terutomo (1996), 'Japan: The macro-IDP, meso-IDPs and the technology development path (TDP)', in John Dunning and Rajneesh Narula (eds), *Foreign Direct Investment and Governments*, London, Routledge, 142–73.

Ozawa, Terutomo (2000a), 'Small- and medium-sized MNCs, industrial clusters and globalization', in Neil Hood and Stephen Young (eds), *The Globalization of Multinational Enterprise Activity and Economic Development*, London, Macmillan, 225–48.

Ozawa, Terutomo (2000b), 'The "flying-geese" paradigm: Toward a co-evolutionary theory of MNC-assisted growth', in K. Fatemi (ed.), *The New World Order: Internationalism, Regionalism and the Multinational Corporations*, Amsterdam, Pergamon, 209–23.

Ozawa, Terutomo (2001a), 'Japan in the WTO', in A. Rugman and G. Boyd (eds), *The World Trade Organization in the New Global Economy*, Cheltenham, UK and Northampton, MA, Edward Elgar, 191–215.

Ozawa, Terutomo (2001b), 'The "hidden" side of the "flying-geese" catch-up model: Japan's *dirigiste* institutional setup and a deepening financial morass', *Journal of Asian Economics*, **12** (4), 471–91.

Pajarinen Mika, Petri Rouvinen and Pekka Ylä-Anttila (1998), *Small Country Strategies in Global Competition: Benchmarking the Finnish Case*, Helsinki, ETLA/SITRA.

Pak, Yong Suhk (2000), *Determinants of Foreign Market Entry Modes of International Franchisers: A Knowledge-based Framework*, Doctoral dissertation, Newark, NJ, Rutgers University.

Papanastassiou, M. and R. Pearce (1990), 'Host country characteristics and the sourcing behaviour of the UK manufacturing industry', University of Reading Discussion Papers in International Investment and Business Studies, series B, **2** (140).

Pasture, P., J. Verberckmoes and H. de Witte (eds) (1996), *The Lost*

Perspective? Trade Unions Between Ideology and Social Action in the New Europe, Aldershot, Avebury, Vol. 1, 284; Vol. 2, 409.

Pavitt, K. (1987), 'International patterns in technology accumulation', in N. Hood and E. Vahlne (eds), *Strategies of Global Competition*, London, Croom Helm.

Peck, F.W. (1996), 'Regional development and the production of space: The role of infrastructure in the attraction of new inward investment', *Environment and Planning A*, **28** (2), 327–39.

Pedersen, T. and S. Thomsen (1997), 'European patterns of corporate ownership: A twelve-country study', *Journal of International Business Studies*, **28** (4), 759–78.

Peres Nunez, W. (1993), 'The internationalization of Latin American industrial firms', *CEPAL Review*, **49**, 55–75.

Peres, Wilson (ed.) (1998), *Grandes Empresas y Grupos Industriales Latinoamericanos*. Santiago, Chile, CEPAL.

Perez, Carla (1985), 'Microeconomics, long waves, and world structure change', *World Development*, **13**, 441–63.

Perez, Carlota and Luc Soete (1988), 'Catching up in technology: Entry barriers and windows of opportunity', in Giovanni Dosi, Christopher Freeman, Richard Nelson, G. Silverberg and Luc Soete (eds), *Technical Change and Economic Theory*, London, Pinter Publishers.

Peteraf, M. (1993), 'The cornerstone of competitive advantage: A resource-based view', *Strategic Management Journal*, **14** (3), 179–91.

Peters, Tom J. and Robert H. Waterman (1982), *In Search of Excellence*, New York, Harper and Row.

Petrick, J.A., R.F. Scherer, J.D. Brodzinski, J.F. Quinn and M. Fall Ainina (1999), 'Global leadership skills and reputational capital: Intangible resources for sustainable competitive advantage', *Academy of Management Executive*, **13** (1), 58–69.

Phillips, Charles, F. Jr (1993), *The Regulation of Public Utilities*, Public Utilities Reports, Inc.

Piore, Michael and Charles Sabel (1984), *The Second Industrial Divide: Possibilities for Prosperity*, New York, Basic Books.

Pitelis, Christon N. and Roger Sugden (eds), *The Nature of the Transnational Firm*, London and New York, Routledge.

Pohjola, Matti (1996), *Tehoton Pääoma*, Helsinki, WSOY.

Pohjola, Matti (ed.) (2001), *Information Technology, Productivity, and Economic Growth: International Evidence and Implications for Economic Development*, Oxford, Oxford University Press.

Porter, M.E. (1985), *Competitive Advantage*, New York, The Free Press.

Porter, M.E. (1990), *The Competitive Advantage of Nations*, New York, The Free Press.

Porter, M.E. (1992), *Capital Choices: Changing the Way America Invests in Industry*, Washington, DC, Council on Competitiveness.

Porter, M.E. (1998), 'Clusters and the new economics of competition', *Harvard Business Review*, Nov–Dec, 77–90.

Poterba, Jamesa and Lawrence Summers (1991), 'Time horizons of American firms: New evidence from a survey of CEOs', Washington, DC, Council on Competitiveness and the Harvard Business School, October.

Powers, Laura and Ann Markusen (1998), *A Just Transition? Lessons from Defense Workers' Experience in the 1990s*, Washington, DC, Economic Policy Institute.

Prahalad, C.K. and Y.L. Doz (1987), *The Multinational Mission: Balancing Local Demands and Global Vision*, New York, The Free Press.

Prebisch, Raul (1950), *The Economic Development of Latin America and Its Principal Problems*, New York, United Nations [reproduced as 'The economic development of Latin America and its principal problems', *Economic Bulletin for Latin America*, 1962, **7** (1), 1–51].

Pred, Allan R. (1977), 'The location of economic activity since early nineteenth century: A city systems perspective', in B. Ohlin, B.O. Hellelborn and P.J. Wijkman (eds), *The International Allocation of Economic Activity*, London, Macmillan, 127–47.

Project on Demilitarization and Democracy (1995), *Hostile Takeover*, Washington, DC, November.

Przeworski, Adam (1995), *Sustainable Democracy*, New York, Cambridge University Press.

Quinn, J.B. and F.G. Hilmer (1994), 'Strategic outsourcing', *Sloan Management Review*, **35** (4), 43–55.

Rahman, M.Z. (1998), 'The role of accounting disclosure in the East Asian financial crisis: Lessons learned', *Transnational Corporations*, **8**, December.

Rajan, Ramkishen S. (2001), ' Economic globalization and Asia', *ASEAN Economic Bulletin*, **18** (1), 1–11.

Ramaswamy, Kannan, K. Galen Kroeck and William Renforth (1996), 'Measuring the degree of internationalization of a firm: A comment', *Journal of International Business Studies*, **27** (1), 167–77.

Riahi-Belkaoui, Ahmed (1998), 'The effects of the degree of internationalization on firm performance', *International Business Review*, **7**, 315–21.

Ricardo, D. (1817), *On the Principles of Political Economy and Taxation*, London, John Murray, Albemarle-Street.

Ring, P.S. and Van de Ven, A.H. (1994), 'Development processes of cooperative interorganizational relationships', *Academy of Management Review*, **19** (1), 90–118.

Robertson, Ross M. (1955), *History of the American Economy*, New York, Harcourt, Brace and World.

Romer, P. (1986), 'Increasing returns to scale and long-run growth', *Journal of Political Economy*, **94**, 1002–37.

Root, Franklin R. (1994), *Entry Strategies for International Markets*, New York, Lexington Books.

Rosenberg, Nathan and L.E. Birdzell, Jr (1986), *How the West Grew Rich: The Economic Transformation of the Industrial World*, New York, Basic Books.

Rostow, W.W. (1990a), *Theorists of Economic Growth from David Hume to the Present*, New York, Oxford University Press.

Rostow, W.W. (1990b), *The Stages of Economic Growth*, 3rd edn, Cambridge, Cambridge University Press.

Rubin, Paul H. (1978), 'The theory of the firm and the structure of the franche contract', *Journal of Law and Economics*, **21**, 223–32.

Rueyling Tzeng and Brian Uzzi (eds), *Embeddedness and Corporate Change in a Global Economy*, New York, Peter Lang, 283–300.

Rugman, Alan M. (1979), *International Diversification and the Multinational Enterprise*, Lexington, MA, Lexington Books.

Rugman, Alan M. (1980), 'Internalization as a general theory of foreign direct investment: A reappraisal of the literature', *Weltwirtschaftliches Archiv*. 365–79.

Rugman, Alan M. (1987), *Outward Bound Canadian Direct Investment in the United States*, Washington, DC, Howe Institute and National Planning Association.

Rugman, Alan M. (1997), *The Scientific Papers of Alan Rugman*, Cheltenham, UK and Lyme, US, Edward Elgar.

Rugman, Alan M. (2000), *The End of Globalization*, London, Random House.

Ruigrok, Walter and R. van Tulder (1995), *The Logic of International Restructuring*, London, Routledge.

Savage, G.T., T.W. Nix, C.J. Whitehead and J.D. Blair (1991), 'Strategies for assessing and managing organizational stakeholders', *Academy of Management Executive*, **5** (2), 61–75.

Saxenian, AnnLee (1994), *Regional Advantage: Culture and Competition in Silicon Valley and Route 128*, Cambridge, Harvard University Press.

Saxenian, AnnLee (2000), 'Transnational enterpreneurs and regional industrialization: The Silicon Valley–Hsinchu connection', in S. Schadler, C. Carcovic, A. Bennett and R. Khan (1993), 'Recent experience with surges in capital inflows', *IMF Occasional Paper*, **108**, Washington, DC, International Monetary Fund.

Schadler, S., C. Carcovic, A. Bennett and R. Kahn (1993), 'Recent experiences with surges in capital inflows', *IMF Occasional Paper*, **108**, Washington, DC, International Monetary Fund.

Schienstock, Gerd (1999), 'Transformation and learning: A new perspective on national innovation systems', in Gerd Schientock and Osmo Kuusi (eds), *The Challenge for the Finnish Innovation System: Transformation Towards a Learning Economy*, Helsinki, Sitra.

Schienstock, Gerd and Timo Hämäläinen (2001), 'Transformation of the Finnish Innovation System: A network approach', Sitra Report Series, no. 7, Helsinki.

Schine, Eric (1991), 'Defenseless against cutbacks', *Business Week*, 14 January, 69.

Schneider, M. (2002), 'A stakeholder model of organizational leadership', *Organization Science*, **13** (2), 209–20.

Schneiner, F. and B.S. Frey (1985), 'Economic and political determinants of foreign direct investment', *World Development*, **13**, 161–75.

Schoenberger, Erica (1991), 'The corporate interview as a research method in economic geography', *The Professional Geographer*, **44**, 180–9.

Schoenberger, Erica (1997), *The Cultural Crisis of the Firm*, Cambridge, Blackwell.

Schumpeter, Joseph A. (1934), *The Theory of Economic Development*, New York, Oxford University Press.

Schwartz, R.A. (1991), 'Institutionalization of the equity markets', *Journal of Portfolio Management*, **17** (4), 44–9.

Scott, Allen (1988), 'Flexible production systems and regional development: The rise of new industrial space in North America and Western Europe', *International Journal of Urban and Regional Research*, **12** (2), 171–86.

Scott, Allen (1996), 'Regional motors of the global economy', *Futures*, **28** (5), 391–411.

Scott, B.R. and G.C. Lodge (1985), *U.S. Competitiveness in the World economy*, Boston, MA, Harvard Business School Press.

Securities Industry Asociation (1999), *Securities Industry Association Fact Book*, New York, Securities Industry Association.

Selznick, P. (1957), *Leadership in Administration*, New York, Harper and Row.

Servaes, Henri (1996), 'The value of diversification during the conglomerate merger wave', *The Journal of Finance*, **51** (4), 1201–25.

Serwer, Andrew E. (1994), 'McDonald's conquers the world', *Fortune*, 17 October, 103–116.

Shane, Scott A. (1996), 'Hybrid organizational arrangements and their implications for firm growth and survival: A study of new franchisers', *Academy of Management Journal*, **39**, 216–34.

Shaver, Myles, J. (1998), 'Do foreign-owned and US-owned establishments exhibit the same location pattern in American manufacturing industries?', *Journal of International Business Studies*, **29** (3), 469–92.

Simard, F. (1999), 'Bargaining laws and union density in the civil service: The Japanese paradox', *Journal of Collective Negotiations in the Public Sector*, **28** (1), 17–28.

Simões, V.C., R. Biscaya and P. Nevado (2002), 'Subsidiary decision making autonomy: Competences, integration and local responsiveness' in Sarianna M. Lundan (ed.), *Network Knowledge in International Business*, Cheltenham, UK and Northampton, MA, Edward Elgar.

Simon, Herbert A. (1962), 'The architecture of complexity', *Proceedings of the American Philosophical Society*, **106** (6), 467–82.

Smith, Adam (1776), *An Inquiry into the Nature and Causes of the Wealth of Nations*, London, Routledge, reproduced, New York, E.P. Dutton (1908).

Smith, Ann (1993), 'A punctuated equilibrium model of organizational transformation: A case study of the Regional Bell Operating Companies and their international expansion 1984–1991, PhD dissertation, University of North Carolina, USA.

Sokoya, Sesan Kim and Kenneth R. Tillery (1992), 'Motives of foreign MNCs investing in the United States and the effect of company characteristics, *The International Executive*, **34** (1), 65–80.

Solinger, Dorothy J. (2001), 'Globalization and paradox of participation: The Chinese case', *Global Governance*, **7** (2), April–June, 173–96.

Spender, J.-C. (1979), 'Theory building and theory testing in strategic management', in Dan Schendel and Chuck Hofer (eds), *Strategic Management: A New View*, Boston, MA, Little, Brown and Co., 394–404.

Spender, J.-C. (1997), 'Publicly supported R&D projects: The US's advanced technology program', *Science and Public Policy*, **24** (1), 45–52.

Standard and Poor's, Sovereign Ratings (1996–1998) various issues.

Stiglitz, Joseph E. (1989), 'On the economic role of state', in Joseph E. Stiglitz (ed.), *The Economic Role of State*, Oxford, Basil Blackwell.

Stiroh, Kevin J. (2001), 'Information technology and the U.S. productivity revival: What do the industry data say?', Federal Reserve Bank of New York.

Stopford, John (1995), 'Competing globally for resources', *Transnational Corporations*, **4**, August, 34–7.

Stopford, John and L. Turner (1985), *Britain and the Multinationals*, Chichester, John Wiley.

Storper, Michael (1995), 'The resurgence of regional economies, ten years later: The region as a nexus of untraded dependencies', *European Urban and Regional Studies*, **2** (3), 191–221.

Sullivan, Daniel (1994), 'Measuring the degree of internationalization of a firm', *Journal of International Business Studies*, **25** (2), 325–42.

Sullivan, Daniel (1996), 'Measuring the degree of internationalization of a firm: A reply', *Journal of International Business Studies*, **27** (1), 179–92.

Sundaram, Anant and J. Stewart Black (1992), 'The environment and internal organization of multinational enterprises', *Academy of Management Review*, **17** (4), 729–57.

Tallman, Stephen and Jiatao Li (1996), 'Effects of international diversity and product diversity on the performance of multinational firms', *Academy of Management Journal*, **39** (1), 179–96.

Tan, K.Y. (1999), 'Financial crisis in Southeast Asia: Policy responses and lessons', *Global Focus*, **11** (2), 47–63.

Tassey, Gregory (1992), *Technology Infrastructure and Competitive Position*, Norwell, MA, Kluwer.

Taylor, M.P. and L. Sarno (1997), 'Capital flows to developing countries: Long- and short-term determinants', *The World Bank Economic Review*, **11** (3), 451–70.

Teece, David J., G. Pisano and J. Shuen (1997), 'Dynamic capabilities and strategic management', *Strategic Management Journal*, 18 (7), 509–33.

Thompson, D. (1967), *Organisations in Action*, New York, McGraw-Hill.

Thuermer, Karen E. (1998), 'The mid-Atlantic states', *World Trade*, **12**, January, 62.

Tipping, Emily (1999), 'Our resident international insiders', *Pittsburgh Business Times*, **19** (19), December, 1.

Tse, D.K., Y. Pan and K.Y. Au (1997), 'How MNCs choose entry modes and form alliances: The China experience', *Journal of International Business Studies*, **28** (4): 779–805.

Ulgado, Francis M. (1996), 'Location characteristics of manufacturing investments in the US: A comparison of American and foreign-based firms', *Management International Review*, **36** (1), 7–26.

UNCTAD (1991), *World Investment Report 1991: Trends and Determinants*, Geneva and New York, United Nations.

UNCTAD (1994), *World Investment Report 1994: Transnational Corporations, Employment and the Workplace*, Geneva and New York, United Nations.

UNCTAD (1995), *World Investment Report 1995: Transnational Corporations and Competitiveness*, Geneva and New York, United Nations.

UNCTAD (1996), 'Incentives and Foreign Direct Investment', Current Studies, Series A, No. 30, New York and Geneva, United Nations.

UNCTAD (1998), *World Investment Report 1998: Trends and Determinants*, Geneva and New York, United Nations.

UNCTAD (2000), *World Investment Report 2000: Cross-border Mergers and Acquisitions and Development*, New York and Geneva, United Nations.

UNCTAD (2001a), *World Investment Report: Foreign Direct Investment and Local Linkages*, Geneva, UNCTAD.

UNCTAD (2001b), *UNCTAD Handbook of Statistics*, New York and Geneva, United Nations.

US Department of Commerce (1988), *Franchising in the Economy 1986–1988*, Washington, DC, US Government Printing Office.

US General Accounting Office (1995), *Defense Downsizing: Selective Contractors Business Unit Reactions*, GAO/NSIAD-95-144, May, Washington, DC, US Government Printing Office.

Useem, M. (1996), *Investor Capitalism*, New York, Basic Books.

Useem, M., E.H. Bowman, J. Myatt and C.W. Irvine (1993), 'US institutional investors look at corporate governance in the 1990s', *European Management Journal*, **11** (2), 175–89.

Uzzi, B. (1997), 'Social structure and competition in interfirm networks: The paradox of embeddedness', *Administrative Science Quarterly*, **42** March, 35–67.

Valencia, M. (2000), 'Lean, mean, and European: A survey of European business', *The Economist*, **355**.

Velocci, Anthony (1991), 'Ill-defined U.S. defense priorities making industry a "gambler's paradise"', *Aviation Week and Space Technology*, **17** June, 141–2.

Velocci, Anthony (1997) 'Competitive advantages of scale could elude Aerospace giants', *Aviation Week and Space Technology*, 10 February, 99–89.

Verspagen, B. and K. Wakelin (1997), 'International competitiveness and its Determinants', *International Journal of Applied Economics*, **11** (2), 177–90.

Viner, Jacob (1950), *The Customs Union Issue*, New York, Carnegie Endowment for International Peace.

Vyas, Bindu J. (2000), 'Foreign direct investment from developing economies in the United States', dissertation, Rutgers University, NJ, USA.

Vyas, Bindu, J. and Margarita Rose (2000), 'Foreign direct investments in Pennsylvania', *Pennsylvania Economic Association Conference Proceedings*, Clarion, Clarion University.

Wakelin, K. (1997), *Trade and Innovation: Theory and Evidence*, Cheltenham, UK and Brookfield, US, Edward Elgar.

Wallace, L.H. (1998), 'Foreign direct investment into the state of New Jersey', PhD dissertation, Rutgers University, NJ.

Wallace, Lorna (2000), 'Foreign Direct Investment in the USA: A subnational investigation', in J.H. Dunning (ed.), *Regions, Globalization and the Knowledge-based Economy*, Oxford, Oxford University Press, 225–55.

Wernerfelt, B. (1984), 'A resource based view of the firm', *Strategic Management Journal*, **5**, 171–80.

Wesson, Thomas J. (1993), 'An alternative motivation for foreign direct investment', PhD dissertation, Cambridge, MA, Harvard University.

Wheeler, D. and A. Mody (1992), 'International investment location decisions: The case of U.S. firms, *Journal of International Economics*, **33** (1–2), 57–76.

Whitley, R. (1992a), *Business Systems in East Asia: Firms, Markets, and Societies*, London, Sage.

Whitley, R. (1992b), *European Business Systems: Firms and Markets in their National Contexts*, London, Sage.

Wilkins, Mira (1974), *The Maturing Multinational Enterprise: American Business Abroad from 1914 to 1970*, Cambridge, Harvard University Press.

Williamson, O.E. (1991), 'Comparative economic organization: The analysis of discrete structural alternatives', *Administration Science Quarterly*, **36**, 269–96.

Wolf, B.M. (1977), 'Industrial diversification and internationalization: Some empirical evidence', *Journal of Industrial Economics*, **26**, 177–91.

Womack, J., D. Jones and D. Roos (1990), *The Machine that Changed the World*, New York, Macmillan.

Wood, A. (1994), 'Give Heckscher and Ohlin a chance!', *Weltwirtschaftliches Archiv*, **130** (1).

Wood, S. (1998), 'Trade unionism in recession', *Industrial and Labor Relations Review*, **51** (4), 706–8.

Woods, J.O. (1996), 'Corporate governance – An international comparison', *Benefits and Compensation International*, **25** (9), 2–9.

Woodward, Douglas (1992), 'Local determinants of Japanese manufacturing start-ups in the US', *Southern Economic Journal*, **58**, 690–708.

World Bank (1989), *Foreign Direct Investment from the Newly Industrializing Economies*, Washington, DC, Industry-development Division, World Bank.

World Bank (1993), *The East Asian Miracle: Economic Growth and Public Policy*, New York, Oxford University Press.

World Bank (2001), *Global Development Finance*, Washington, DC, World Bank.

Wyatt, E. (1997), 'The not-so-invisible hand of the great Dow climb', *The New York Times*, 16 February.

Wymbs, Cliff (1999), 'Transnational investment in the competitive transition of regulated industries', PhD dissertation, Rutgers University, NJ, USA.

Ylä-Anttila (2000). *Omistajien etu – kaikkien etu?*, Helsinki, Taloustieto.

Young, S., N. Hood and E. Peters (1994), 'Multinational enterprises and regional economic development', *Regional Studies*, **28** (7), 657–77.

Zaccaro, S.J., R.J. Foti and D.A. Kenny (1991), 'Self-monitoring and trait-based variance in leadership: An investigation of leader flexibility across multiple group situations', *Journal of Applied Psychology*, **76** (2), 308–15.

Zaleznick, A. (1992), 'Managers and leaders: Are they different?', *Harvard Business Review*, **70** (2), 126–35.

Zietlow, Dixie S. and Jean-Francois Hennart (1996), 'The international distribution of franchises by US franchiser', paper presented at EIBA, Stockholm.

Zorn, P. (1997), 'Public pensions', *Public Administration Review*, **57** (4), 361–92.

Index